OFF THE BEATEN TRACK

OFF THE
BEATEN TRACK

women adventurers
and mountaineers
in western Canada

CYNDI SMITH

Coyote Books

Canadian Cataloguing in Publication Data

Smith, Cyndi, 1956 -
    Off the beaten track

    Bibliography: p.
    Includes index.
    ISBN 0-9692457-2-6

    1. Women mountaineers - Rocky Mountains, Canadian (B.C. and
Alta.) - Biography.   2. Women explorers - Rocky Mountains, Cana-
dian (B.C. and Alta.) - Biography. 3. Women mountaineers - British
Columbia - Biography. 4. Women explorers - British Columbia
-Biography. 5. Women - Canada, Western - Biography. I. Title.

GV199.9.S45 1989   796.5'22'0922   C89-091255-6

Care has been exercised to trace ownership of copyright material contained in this text. The publishers will gladly receive information that
will enable them to rectify any reference or credit in subsequent editions.

ISBN 0-9692457-2-6   First printing May 1989
                                      Fourth Printing May 1998

Published by: Coyote Books
                     7-801-6 St.,
                     Canmore, Alberta
                     T1W 2E1
                     Canada

Front cover: (l-r) Caroline Hinman, Lillian Gest, Mrs. George Vincent
                    Courtesy Whyte Museum of the Canadian Rockies
                    Hand-colored by James Daubney, Banff

Inside cover maps by Cyndi Smith
Printed In Canada

CONTENTS

*To three women who
encouraged my own ventures
off the beaten track—
my mother, Sharon and Merri-Ann.*

FOREWORD

Mark Twain wrote about someone, I'm not sure whom, and I'm paraphrasing him: "She is not quite what you would call an undignified woman; she is not quite what you would call a dignified woman. She is the sort of woman who keeps a parrot."

As you read Cyndi Smith's portraits of mountain women, I suspect you will find yourself wondering if all of them kept parrots, for they are people for whom dignity seems unimportant in the equations of their lives. Intelligent, energetic, active, occasionally flamboyant women, yes, but not people overly concerned about their dignity.

Mary Schäffer Warren's parrot – yes, inevitably, one of them had to have one – spoke a few words: "Here's the boss!" he screamed when Billy Warren arrived home; and he lapsed into a broken record's imperative when he recited "Where, o where has my little dog gone? Where, o where can he be? ... Go on! ... Go on!"

Writing history and biography requires more than a parrot's skill. Were our recording angels but parrots, the shape, texture and dimensions of our past would be lacking. Yet in Mary Warren's reiteration to her parrot – "Go on!" – we hear echos of an imploring audience insisting the tale be told.

The cougar's milk may have run out, the campfire need another log, the bedroll be warmer than September's chill air: but, till the tale find its proper end, we stay gathered in ember light to hear its end. Stories keep us listening keenly, keep us community.

Mountain people, like wilderness and frontier people everywhere, form in storytelling the color of the situations and times they have lived and, sensing the shape of saga, tell stories with the skills of scops and bards, making their subjects vital and shaping their themes.

Encounters with bears and mountain sheep, endurance on mountains, the humor in dangerous situations – these tales were the richer television of the childhood in which I grew up. Listening to flimsy substitutes for storytelling, American radio programs filtered to us on

Canadian commercial radio in the 1940s, was far less important than hearing real stories from the people who had lived – and shaped – them. Heroic tales in mythic times – all epics tell tales which occurred before we were born – answered to an obvious and real landscape around me, peopling it as the Grimm Brothers' forests did not. Some tales had cautionary relevance: teaching us how to fell a log to cross a stream or to respond to enraged grizzlies. More often the joy of telling was their impetus. We listened in revelry.

Decades passed before I realized how mountain landscape tests the mettle of people who love it most, and how they magnify its difficulties. Reared amid mountains, I took years to appreciate the rare richness fortune brought me when most people were growing up in the Earth's burgeoning cities. Unpeopled desert, forest, tundra and polar regions challenge mountains for the difficulties they present, but mountains more diversely reveal and conceal their maziness; in them what is usually thought to be background, the world's beauty, becomes foreground.

I hope all of Cyndi Smith's readers will read her portraits of western Canada's mountain women in the spirit of the lavishing love her subjects gave our Rocky, Selkirk, Bugaboo and Coast mountains. All of us can learn something of the enigma of the human spirit, particularly when it meets the world of peaks where that most mystifying human endeavor, climbing mountains for the risk and joy of the act, is played out.

How significant is it that Cyndi Smith's subjects are women? Any historian bears the responsibility to make visible what has been hitherto neglected. The women of the western mountains,particularly the climbing women, have not been invisible, for accounts of their experiences and accomplishments have been published from the earliest years of the *Canadian Alpine Journal* and Mary Schäffer Warren's *Old Indian Trails.* Cyndi has not discovered these women, as she would say herself, but, for a broader public than those sometimes difficult to find texts can aid, she repeoples our landscape and kindles our community with numerous women who deserve as much consideration as the men more frequently written about. (After Mary Warren, for example, the reader will find few references to women in, say, Esther Fraser's *The Canadian Rockies: Early Travels and Explorations.)*

Several years ago in my weekly column in the *Crag and Canyon* (at the time called "Where Man and Mountain Meet," a quotation from

William Blake; when Georgia Engelhard Cromwell died I renamed it "When Peaks and People Meet") I wrote that Dorothy Gow blasted me from time to time for writing about men all the time, the Simpsons, Peytos and Wilsons, and her father Nell "Tex" Vernon-Wood, rarely mentioning women. "Dorothy," I said, "do your part: get yourself to the Archives of the Whyte Museum of the Canadian Rockies, record a tape about your mother, talk about how she held the family together while Tex had all the fun; tell us how it was to be a warden's wife, and tell us about yourself too, a mountain guide. If you don't put it into the place where stories are recorded, you can't blame those of us who most frequently tell stories we've heard and read there." (In the spring of '88 I saw Dorothy pushing two shopping carts full of groceries down the street. She hollered out, "This is my pack string.")

Cyndi's book is not the encyclopedia of Canada's mountain women. Three of my now-deceased Banff neighbors deserve the respect, attention and love that Cyndi brings to her adventurers, alpinists and working women: my aunt Catharine Whyte, one of the finest of Rockies landscape painters; Williamina Simpson, who trained her daughters to be the finest figure skaters in the world in the 1930s while she wrestled with keeping solvent her guide-outfitter husband's lodge business; Alma LaPalme Mills, a world-class cellist whose wavering path led her from a recital in the White House in Washington to gathering eggs in a chicken coop on Bear Street in Banff. They are but three; with a minute's recollection a dozen more could crowd my mind. This is just to say there are other books out there waiting to be written about other mountain women.

Cyndi knows yet other women worthy of record, but she has wisely limited the richness of her topic, and chosen her subjects for the extent of their contributions and their diversity. These are clearly the mountain aspects of her subjects' lives. Several of them, I know, deserve rounder treatment. What books did they read, what composer moved them to tears, how did they respond to the world's other faces? Did they love passionately, weep for lost opportunities, live in the wildness of cities as well as they did in the civilization of mountains?

The urbane Elizabeth Parker, for example, declared a conservation and outdoors ethic in ringing words, its value coming from both her genuine love of landscape and her lettered and sophisticated irony. It needs more fanfare than Cyndi gives it; her lapse gives me the privelege of emphasizing Mrs. Parker's vitality and vigor in praising, earlier and better than any Canadian man, the reward of Canadian wilderness experience, and arguing for, in the long-ago Edwardian age, the importance of preserving expanses of wildlands when only a most discerning mind could have seen how rare they could become in two generations. She wrote, in the first issue of the *Canadian Alpine Journal* (1907),

> The vulgar reach the mountain summits by a way in which the Alpine Club of Canada will set a face of flint. We know what way that is: the way of the monster, Mammon. By virtue of its constitution, the Alpine Club is a national trust for the defence of our mountain solitudes against the intrusion of steam and electricity and all the vandalisms of this luxurious, utilitarian age; for the keeping free from the grind of commerce, the wooded passes and valleys and alplands of the wilderness. It is the people's right to have primitive access to the remote places of safest retreat from the fever and the fret of the market place and the beaten tracts of life.

One object of the club, she continued, is "to promote the too much neglected exercise of walking. Your true lover of Nature is also a man of the unfamiliar roads and forest trails. It would be a great thing for young Canadians if all the automobiles vanished into space and walking for pleasure became the fashion." Age has not staled nor custom withered Elizabeth Parker's fine sentiments.

Cyndi's text witholds from you what I believe is integral to the stories she presents: she succeeds these women in her vocations. You should know that a mountain woman wrote these excellent contributions to the history and the mythology of us all. Cyndi is a working mountain woman. A warden in Jasper National Park, she can throw a diamond hitch, jingle horses in dew-laden dawns, shoot an injured animal, observe the health of the wilderness and explore both the minuscule and the immense universes of the highland meadows and the mountain wildlands. She too is a climber, and an explorer, though she wouldn't want me to say too much. Like Mary Schäffer Warren, she is definitely a mountain writer. I found myself saying when I read her text, "Go on! ... Go on!"

Jon Whyte
Banff, Alberta
March, 1989

PREFACE

Mountain literature is replete with stories of and by the men who penetrated the Rocky Mountain barrier and explored the vast valleys and stupendous peaks of the mountain ranges of western Canada. But the stories of women adventurers and mountaineers have largely been overlooked and their contributions underrealized. To date very little has been written about this aspect of our mountain history.

Living as I do in Jasper National Park, my attention was drawn to Mary Schäffer Warren[1]. She explored the Maligne Lake area and her name has since become almost synonymous with it. As I read more about Mary and the history of the Rockies, the names of other women came to light, usually with few details. I felt sure that there were many women whose adventures and stories deserved to be told.

I began my research by sifting through various published works, mountaineering club journals and the archives of the Whyte Museum of the Canadian Rockies in Banff, Alberta. As I compiled a list of names I realized two things: first, I could not do justice to all of them in one book, and second, with few exceptions, there was scanty information available.

Fortunately, the women's stories began to sort themselves out. The fourteen women whose lives are recalled in this book fit together in two ways. With one exception they were all active in the outdoors—they explored, took packtrips or climbed mountains.

---

1. For convention's sake I refer to my subjects by their maiden and final names. Mary Schäffer Warren, for example, was Mary Townsend Sharples when she first came to the Rockies in 1889, Mary Schäffer from 1890 until 1915 and Mary Schäffer Warren until her death in 1939. In this case I have retained the Schäffer, rather than Sharples, as she was so well known by that name.

And they fell into the same historical period, between the completion of the Canadian Pacific Railway in 1885 and the Second World War. It was a half-century of feverish exploration in the Rocky and Selkirk mountains and the excitement of first ascents of massive peaks. During the depressed years of the 1930s and the years of the Second World War many roads were built in the mountain parks. This, and the widespread use of the internal-combustion engine, made the mountains more accessible to everyone. Gone forever were the weeks-long packtrain trips. Also gone were many of the first ascents. What were left were first ascents of smaller peaks and ascents by new and harder routes.

In time the second of my problems—the lack of information—began to sort itself out also. I gleaned what information I could from the mountaineering journals and began to haunt the archives of the Whyte Museum. Then I reached out to other archives and institutions, and descendants and friends of my subjects. Some leads were dead ends, but gradually the material began to come together.

However, as a fellow writer said, there comes a point at which one has to pay attention to the law of diminishing returns. How much more time and energy can be spent to ferret out one more piece of information? For me, that time has come. But I can't help feeling that if I wrote just one more letter . . .

Throughout the book I have quoted the women's own words as much as possible. Rather than encumber the text by footnoting every quote, I have included a detailed list of sources by chapter, starting on page 268. On page 277 is a selected list of references on the history of the region, including other books about women in the western mountains. All of these publications are currently available.

By no means is this book intended to be a definitive one on the history of women in the mountains of western Canada. It barely scratches the surface with the history of a few select individuals. Doubtless many readers will know or remember other women who are also part of the fabric of the mountains. Their books remain to be written.

ACKNOWLEDGEMENTS

Over the course of the several years that I have spent researching and writing this book I have incurred debts to many people.

My greatest debt of gratitude is to the archives and library staff of the Whyte Museum of the Canadian Rockies, in Banff, Alberta: Margery Hadley, Don Bourdon, Alex Huculak, Mary Andrews and Lena Goon. Without their dedicated assistance in locating material, and their unfailing encouragement, I could never have completed this project. Craig Richard's excellent copy work on the photographs and maps adds greatly to the many illustrations. Jon Whyte and Ted Hart, both authors and historians, helped to steer me in the right direction, and their comments on my manuscript were welcome.

The long-distance nature of much of my research was frustrating at times. But the staffs of many institutions and organizations did their best to ferret out information for me: Patricia Fletcher, American Alpine Club, New York; Barbara Mathé and Nina Root, American Museum of Natural History, New York; Patricia Willis, The Beinecke Rare Book and Manuscript Library, Yale University, Connecticut; Sue Baptie, City of Vancouver Archives, Vancouver, British Columbia; Edwin B. Bronner and Eva Walker Myer of The Quaker Collection, Haverford College, Haverford, Pennsylvania; Beverley Booth, The Hocken Library, University of Otago, Dunedin, New Zealand; Helen Loftus, Alexander Turnbull Library, National Library of New Zealand, Wellington; Indiana Matters, Provincial Archives, Victoria, British Columbia; Jane

Mason, Research Toponymist, Surveys and Resource Mapping Branch, Victoria, British Columbia; Helen Schroyer, Purdue University Libraries, West Lafayette, Indiana; Maida Goodwin, Smith College Archives, Northampton, Massachusetts; William Massa, Jr., Susan Glenn and Bill Cox, Smithsonian Institution, Washington, D.C.; Jane Price, United States Naval Academy, Annapolis, Maryland; Carol Kimball, Mystic River Historical Society, Mystic, Connecticut; Susan Olmsted, Thames Science Center, New London, Connecticut; Leigh Ann Miller, Alumnae Association of Vassar College, Poughkeepsie, New York; Vicki Wallace, Jasper-Yellowhead Historical Society, Jasper, Alberta.

The personal anecdotes and reminiscences told to me by relatives and friends of my subjects were very important. I would like to thank the following for their assistance and encouragement: George Vaux, Henry Vaux, Pete Cromwell, Edith Wickham, John Tuzo Wilson, Eunice Rodman Packer, Sue Davidson Lowe, Flora Straus, Margaret Fleming, Frank Alack, Maura Benham, Eve Turner, Junee Ashurst and Gertie Marrs.

Two other women working on mountaineering histories shared their frustrations and achievements with me. Sallie Greenwood, of Arlington, Virginia, is writing a history of women in mountaineering. Pip Lynch, of Dunedin, New Zealand, is researching the history of women mountaineers in her country. Author and mountaineer, Bill Putman, was very encouraging. He also allowed me access to his extensive library.

I would like to acknowledge the financial assistance of Alberta Culture and the Alberta Foundation for the Literary Arts.

A special thanks is due to Ben Gadd, for his skilful and painless editing of my manuscript, and for constant encouragement during the production process.

Postscript
It is with sadness that I write of the passing of Jon Whyte on January 6, 1992. He was a mentor to many amateur historians and aspiring writers — he is missed.

INTRODUCTION

It wasn't until the completion of the Canadian Pacific Railway (CPR) in 1885 that the Rocky Mountains and the Selkirk Mountains became accessible to travelers. Prior to that time the only people interested in them were native Indians, fur traders and railway surveyors. Access was by canoe, horseback or on foot.

The coming of the railway opened up a vast new area. The first hotels were built by the railway to save the great expense of hauling heavy dining cars over the extreme grades of the line. To help pay for these hotels the company decided to promote the mountains as a scenic playground worldwide.

Even though the mountains were only a few days' train journey away from major Canadian cities, Canadians were not the ones who flocked to them to explore and climb—rather, Europeans and Americans were the takers. Thus it is that only five of the fourteen women in this book are Canadian. Like the men, these women came primarily to enjoy the grandeur of the peaks and to study the natural wonders of the mountains; later they developed an interest in exploration and climbing for their own sakes.

The early women visitors were merely tourists traveling with husbands, brothers or family friends. They observed the mountains from the comfortable security of a railway observation car, a carriage, or the verandah of a CPR hotel. But gradually their interest was drawn farther into the mountain fastness. Outfitters arranged day rides and short overnight excursions.

Most of the early tourists, men and women, were by-and-large well off; otherwise they couldn't have afforded to travel to the mountains by train and to stay in expensive hotels. This financial independence enabled women to pursue their interests and inclinations by hiring outfitters and guides independently.

Some of the women yearned for greater social freedom than was usual at the time. Mary Schäffer Warren wrote that in exasperation she finally said, "Why not?" to joining the heretofore all-male summer pilgrimages into the remote valleys. "We can starve as well as they; the muskeg will be no softer for us than for them; the ground will be no harder to sleep upon; the waters no deeper to swim, nor the bath colder if we fall in."

And muskeg and deep water there were. Much of the wilderness was still trackless, and the outfitters spent hours blazing and clearing trail. Frequent forest fires resulted in criss-crossed jumbles of blackened timber. There were no bridges across swollen glacial rivers. In some areas there was little feed for the horses. And everywhere hordes of mosquitoes and blackflies harassed beast and human alike.

It is no coincidence that two of the early women explorers in the region, Mary Vaux Walcott and Mary Schäffer Warren, were Quakers. The Quaker philosophy stressed the equality of the sexes and encouraged the practical pursuits of science, engineering, medicine and law. Both women were well educated and independent thinkers. Their Quaker upbringing was very important to them and influenced them throughout their lives.

In the late 1800s photography and the new Earth sciences were just emerging. Here was virgin and fertile ground for amateurs. The Vaux family had an abiding interest in the natural sciences, an avocation which Mary Vaux Walcott shared. They were forerunners in the study of glaciers and in mountain photography. Mary's scientific interests continued when she assisted her husband, Dr. Charles Walcott, with his geological work.

The two Quaker Marys were both accomplished watercolor artists. Mary Schäffer Warren assisted her husband with his botanical studies; she developed a technique for photographing plants to scale, and she also painted them in detail. After his death she finished his book and, shrugging off the yoke of conventionality, arranged months-long expeditions into her beloved wilderness. Mary Walcott prepared a five-volume set of lithographs from her watercolor paintings of North American wildflowers.

Although Mary Jobe Akeley and Caroline Hinman shared Mary Warren's deep-rooted love of exploring, their philosophies were slightly different. Mary Akeley wanted very much to be recognized as an ''explorer'' and a ''climber''—to make some notable achievements. Her exploration of the Mount Sir Alexander region in the northern Rockies earned her much-deserved recognition, although she wasn't beyond embellishing the facts a little to make a good story better. On the other hand, Caroline Hinman had a quiet, very personal commitment to the wilderness. Caroline and Mary did share a belief in introducing young women to the outdoors; Caroline with her ''Off the Beaten Track'' tours in the Canadian Rockies and Mary with Camp Mystic in Connecticut.

Elizabeth Parker had a very romantic vision of mountains and their role in the spiritual uplift of mankind. A lover of literature and nature, she wrote flowing prose about the mountains. She promoted the benefits of mountaineering for building character in individuals and in the young country of Canada. Her patriotic zeal was instrumental in the formation of the Alpine Club of Canada.

Seven of the women in this book were mountaineers. Even though mountain climbing had become a respectable and fashionable sport in Europe by the 1860s, it wasn't until 1888 that the first experienced climbers arrived at Glacier House—

the CPR hotel in Rogers Pass. It took another decade before climbing began in earnest in Canada. In 1899 the Canadian Pacific Railway finally listened to the oft-repeated suggestions that Swiss guides be hired. With their help, both the amateur climber and the tourist were able to scale the heights more extensively. Women were soon drawn to the freedom of mountaineering, using it as an opportunity to throw off Victorian conventions.

One of the misconceptions of early Rockies' history is that there were few women mountaineers. True, only a handful of women climbed in the first few years of the 20th century, but with the formation of the Alpine Club of Canada (ACC) in 1906 the numbers of women climbers rose dramatically. The ACC was one of the first of the mountaineering clubs to allow women to join. In 1907, a year after its inception, a third of its 250 members were women and within a decade that total had risen to nearly half.

At the first alpine club camp many of the women wore elaborate dresses, as was the custom of the day. These proved impractical, as progress was slowed by frequent stops to disentangle a skirt from tree or bush, and on steep sections the trailing material had to be kicked out of the way at each step. The Swiss guides soon persuaded them to tuck their petticoats into their bloomers or, better yet, to exchange the long skirts for knickers, which became the order of the day for women as well as men.

Ed Feuz, Jr., one of the CPR's elite Swiss guides, recalled that almost a quarter of the "exploratory mountaineers" were women.

> The women climbed as well as the men. ... Most ladies were not quite so strong, pound for pound, especially in the arms and shoulders; and most could not handle heavy loads. ... But women have better balance than men and, on delicate rock, better ability with their fingers. The real strength of women climbers is in their morale. Men can panic when things go wrong, but women rarely do. I think they have greater survivability. I know they have greater enthusiasm.

It was the famous 19th century alpinist and author, Leslie Stephen, who made the declaration that every mountain goes through three stages—an inaccessible peak, the most difficult climb, and an easy day for a lady. In the same vein some people have attempted to denigrate the accomplishments of the early women mountaineers by dwelling on their reliance on the Swiss guides. But during the first four decades of this century all mountaineers, men and women, hired the Swiss guides for their climbing expeditions. The women, unlike some of the men, though, gave full credit for the success of their climbs to their guides.

In their book *The Guiding Spirit,* Andrew Kauffman and William Putnam tabulate the records of first ascents in the Swiss guides' territory from 1885 until 1950. While there is understandably room for errors in such a massive compilation, the statistics are nonetheless very revealing. On 159 of the 638 first ascents which they record, there were women in the climbing party, and 76 different women made first ascents. Not surprisingly, the percentage of serious mountaineers making first ascents was the same among women as among men: roughly five percent. Of the twenty-three amateurs making more than ten first ascents, four were women, but two of them were in the top five, and the other two women were in the top eleven. Katie Gardiner made 33 first ascents, Georgia Engelhard Cromwell made 32, Bess MacCarthy made 26 and Margaret Stone made 23.

The first serious woman climber to come to Canada was an Englishwoman, Gertrude Benham. Although she was a prolific climber in the Alps, having made well over 100 ascents, she climbed for only one season in Canada. She did not retire though; instead, she went on to travel around the world eight times!

Henrietta Tuzo Wilson was the first Canadian-born woman climber. At the time of her climbs in Canada she was a resident of England, but she moved back to Ottawa in 1907.

Bess MacCarthy was a shy woman whose mountaineering accomplishments have frequently been overlooked because of her husband's: Albert MacCarthy made two very dramatic first ascents, Mount Robson in 1913 and Mount Logan in 1925. But it was Bess who discovered the joys of mountain climbing first and introduced Albert to it. They climbed together throughout the Rockies, Purcells and Bugaboos.

The two most prolific woman mountaineers were an American, Georgia Engelhard Cromwell, and an Englishwoman, Katie Gardiner. Georgia was a young, competitive woman who enjoyed the physical challenge of climbing, be it first ascents or new routes. She gained quite a reputation for running the guides ragged. In the late 1930s she and her husband-to-be, Eaton Cromwell, were among the first amateurs to begin climbing without guides in the Rockies and Selkirks. Katie, on the other hand, didn't begin climbing in Canada until she was 42 years old. She alternated climbing seasons between Canada and New Zealand, where she also made many first ascents. Although the two women were climbing during the same years they never climbed together, and in fact there was considerable rivalry between them.

Lillian Gest was a young American to whom the Canadian Rockies became a consuming passion. Her first visits were with Caroline Hinman's packtrips, but she soon caught the mountaineering bug. She frequently arranged trips with Katie Gardiner, and climbed at the annual Alpine Club of Canada camps. She achieved few first ascents, but she did a lot of guideless climbing with two other women, Polly Prescott and Marguerite Schnellbacher.

And then there is Phyllis Munday. Of all the woman mountaineers she is the one who may have loved the mountain wilderness the most. Hers is a story of exploration as much as it is of climbing. With her husband, Don, she opened up the little-known Coast Range mountains north of Vancouver. Frequently freighting 30-kg loads through the barely penetrable coastal rain forest, Phyl showed a strength and endurance seldom seen in men, let alone women. Although most of her exploits were outside of the geographic range of this book, Phyl's story belongs here.

Last in the book are the stories of Mona Harragin Matheson and Agnes Harragin Truxler. These sisters were the first licensed women trail guides in the national parks, in Jasper in the late 1920s. They both married men of the mountains—a park warden and a packer—and worked alongside them in the outdoors. They were at the forefront of the third wave of women (the first being women who followed their husbands to the mountains), those who chose to work in the outdoors.

Today women have joined the once-closed ranks of trappers, mountain guides, ski instructors, park wardens and rangers, biologists and outfitters, in numbers unimagined a few decades ago. Women are enjoying unprecedented success in making the mountain wilderness both their avocation and their vocation.

It is in my own outdoor work and explorations that I feel a kinship with the women whose stories I tell. As a park warden I have patrolled the backcountry on horseback and looked down on the valleys from the mountain peaks. And although the modern world presses ever upon the wilderness it is still possible, and to me necessary, to seek out the silent places.

All of the women in this book had many qualities in common. They were well-educated, had a lively curiosity and courage, were independent and showed good judgement, keeping calm when others weren't. Their activities and exploits were very personal and gave them immense satisfaction. Although most of their activities were firsts for women, their feats are memorable in their own right.

Can we hope that the day is not far off when our achievements will be judged on their own merits, rather than over-praised because we are women?

—Mrs. Dawson
Ladies' Alpine Club Journal, 1931

Mary Vaux Walcott
(1860-1940)

The climbing party left the hotel at Field, British Columbia in the early morning hours. In the group were Mary Vaux,[1] her brother George Vaux, Jr., and guides Christian Hasler, Sr., and Edward Feuz, Sr. Their route took them up the steep timber-covered lower slopes of Mount Stephen (3199 m). After many hours of toil, threading their way carefully up rock ribs and snow gullies, they reached the summit of the mountain. With vistas of snow-capped and glacier-clad peaks in all directions, Mary felt euphoric and "the view repaid us for all the exertion."

This was the first major ascent of a mountain over 3050m, by a woman, in Canada. It was July 21, 1900.

Although bound by the day's social attitudes toward dress, Mary had traveled in the mountains long enough to know that comfort was more important than style. She wore "high boots to the knees with heavy soles fortified with plenty of hobs, and a good coating of Swiss grease, worn over woolen stockings, a scant gymnasium suit of woolen material, felt hat, heavy gloves and snow glasses" and carried a Swiss ice axe.

Now, nearly a century later, this does not seem like such a monumental event. But at that time adventurous and independent women were still a rarity. And mountaineering itself was in its infancy in Canada. Mary was the forerunner of women who sought excitement and fulfillment in exploration of the outdoors.

---

1. Vaux is, contrary to its Norman-English roots, pronounced "Vawks."

National Archives of Canada/PA99822

Mary Vaux with guides Christian Häsler, Sr. (left) and Edward Feuz, Sr. on Mount Stephen, July 21, 1900.

The Vauxes—Mary, George and their brother William—first visited the Canadian mountains in 1887. A decade later their name was synonymous with pioneering work in photography and glacial studies.

The Vauxes were a renowned Quaker family from Philadelphia. At that time the city had a reputation as a centre of learning and culture through institutions such as the American Philosophical Society, the Franklin Institute and the Academy of Natural Sciences. Photography and the new Earth sciences were being eagerly pursued by amateurs. Although affluent, well-educated and active citizens, the Vauxes were aloof from many social aspects of Victorian society because they were Quakers.

The Quakers had started arriving in America in the late 17th century. Their doctrine was to demonstrate pacifism, simplicity, community and equality. Simplicity in dress, lifestyle and speech were part of their "Rules of Discipline." The Quaker order is formally known as the Religious Society of Friends. "Meetings for Worship" are held in place of church services. A "guarded" education stresses their social philosophy and the "Rules of Discipline," and the practical pursuits of science, engineering, medicine and law.

They still consider dancing, music, theatre and gambling as vain sports and intemperate use of alcohol as an unnatural activity. Histories, biographies and travel accounts were preferred to pure literature. The Friends have a long tradition of humanitarian activities.

By the nineteenth century the Quakers had become almost indistinguishable from the rest of American society in creature comforts and possessions. They tended to prosper due to their hard work and sound business practices. The testimony regarding simple dress was relaxed, and there were other liberalizing influences. Through it all, though, traditional Quaker values were maintained.

It was into this combination of liberal and traditional Quaker values that Mary was born on July 31, 1860. She was the eldest child of George Vaux, Sr., and Sarah Morris Vaux.

Mary, George and William Vaux.

Her brothers George and William were born December 18, 1863 and April 1, 1872, respectively.

George Vaux, Sr. (1832-1915) was considered an authority on Quaker history. His children received the standard Quaker education and were deeply committed to the Society of Friends. Their scientific and photographic interests and activities, however, placed them among the more liberal elements of the society. The Quakers, especially the Vauxes, believed in improving life experiences through travel and the study of nature.

Mary's uncle, William Sansom Vaux, Sr. (1811-1882), was a businessman, avid collector of almost anything, and a dedicated mineralogist. He was prominent in scientific communities, serving as curator of the Academy of Natural Sciences of Philadelphia from 1838 to 1860. His collection of minerals from America and Europe, bequeathed to the Academy, was considered the largest of its kind in America. His influence on the Vaux children was immense.

Mary attended the Friends' Select School in Philadelphia from 1869 until her graduation in 1879 with a standard Quaker education. This was a private secondary school, with tuition fees, but the enrollment included non-Quakers. Care was taken to provide proper influences for children, with a lack of exaggeration and the avoidance of trivial things in life. Although the Quakers were quite progressive about women's rights, and Mary was interested in attending Bryn Mawr College, she was bound by the social limitations of the Victorian era, and received no further education.

Mary's mother was interested in botany and painting, and she gave her daughter a watercolor paint box at the age of ten. Mary's obvious abilities prompted her mother to arrange for weekly lessons in drawing and painting from a private tutor. Art lessons were a common practice for young ladies of the time. Her brother, George, also took lessons but showed less aptitude than Mary. Mary took lessons for some four years. She always painted directly from her subject, without pencil-sketching first.

William was educated in private schools in Philadelphia; he graduated from Haverford College in 1893 with an engineering degree and worked as an architect. George was a very busy attorney specializing in humanitarian reform. He was active in a number of Philadelphia societies and, like his uncle William Vaux, had a life-long interest in mineralogy.

On December 14, 1880, Mary's mother died and she was left in the woman's traditional role of keeping house for her father and brothers, both at their home in Philadelphia and at a country place at nearby Bryn Mawr.

Their Bryn Mawr home was called Llysfran, which is Welsh for "nest of crows." They would move out to Bryn Mawr in May and stay until October, with only brief forays into the city for business and social functions. While Mary was still in school this meant that she missed almost two months of classes during the spring and fall.

The Vauxes owned nearby Harriton Farm, which Mary operated in a very efficient manner. She employed a farm manager who did the day-to-day work. They bred fine Guernsey cows for a milk route, raised pigs and chickens, and experimented in horticulture. One day she felt "quite high minded" as she had sold 15 head of animals at a good profit. William lost interest in the farm in 1907, and in 1915 Mary bought out George's remaining share of the stock. They sold the farm in 1922.

Mary once wrote despondently that "what with my regular work, and the farm, and the demands that father makes on my time, I find the days all too short to accomplish many things." It was the cry of a spirited woman to whom "escape from brick walls and city streets is the most desirable thing to do in the world."

European travel was very fashionable, and even expected, for well-to-do Americans. George Vaux forbade his children to go overseas as he considered ocean travel very dangerous, based on a belief that he had almost been lost at sea many years earlier when returning from Europe. Instead, he took them to Canada and to the American West.

In 1879 George took the children to Vermont and Maine, and in the fall of 1880, to Montreal and Quebec. The following year was their first visit to the American West. They visited Colorado and explored Pike's Peak and Rickett's Cove. They walked a lot, although Mary took every opportunity to ride horses, which she thoroughly enjoyed. On a ride to the summit of Grey's Peak their faces were "powdered a ghastly white, blue-lined bathing hats tied over our ears, necessary precautions to prevent soreness from sunburn." Mary painted and pressed flowers during their journey.

The Vauxes journeyed west again in 1883, through Colorado, Utah, Nevada and California. They visited Yosemite by stagecoach. Even on this early trip they took numerous photographs, already a consuming hobby. Mary's diary and sketchbooks showed attention to detail and a growing knowledge of nature. She was 23.

Mary and George were forerunners in scenic photography, considering it a pleasing art form. But their Quaker traditions always kept the Vauxes on the periphery of the artistic side of photography. As late as 1882 the official Quaker doctrine was that the "appreciation of art led to unholy thought." Art as illustration, though, was entirely acceptable, and even encouraged—thus their landscape photographs, and later their glacier photographs, were creative outlets. The official doctrine was liberalized towards the end of the 19th centruy.

In 1885 the Vaux family journeyed to Yellowstone National Park. After returning from the trip William wrote, printed and illustrated with his own photos a miniature descriptive book of the trip. (As a boy of 11 or 12 William had made his first pictures with a camera that he had constructed himself, using a pin-hole for a lens.) He made 27 copies of his book and sold them to relatives and family friends.

George and William were founding members of the Photographic Society of Philadelphia, a respected photographic organization in the United States. Their landscape views were first exhibited in 1887 at a Society-sponsored exhibit, and they were well-received. They presented their mountain photographs as views of a landscape integral to their lives.

The technical work on the negatives and the printing were Mary's responsibility. She learned the process of making platinum prints from William Rau, a professional photographer and master printer from Philadelphia. The photos were displayed in the style of the European salons, mounted on complementary dark-colored paper, in large frames and signed with a simple monogram. The Vauxes may have adopted the use of a monogram as the only way by which Mary's work could be included, because the Society didn't permit women members until 1895. At that time Mary was among the first to join.

Mary and George later became associate members of the photo-secession movement and their work was included in the members' show, which opened at the Little Galleries of the Photo-Secession in New York in 1905. The great photographer Alfred Stieglitz was instrumental in establishing this group and gallery. He defined the aims of the movement as being "to hold together those Americans devoted to pictorial photography in their endeavor to compel its recognition, not as the handmaiden of art, but as a distinctive medium of individual expression."

In 1887 the Vauxes again traveled west, this time through California and Oregon, north to Vancouver, and then east on the newly completed Canadian Pacific Railway (CPR) to Glacier House, in the Selkirk Mountains of British Columbia. This hotel was built to avoid the necessity of hauling heavy dining cars over the steep mountain grades. But within a few short years it became much more—the climbing mecca of North America—surrounded as it was by unclimbed peaks and scenic glaciers. They were the closest glaciers to public transportation in the world.

This was the first season that the hotel was open. The Vauxes were delighted with Glacier House and the Rockies at Banff, beginning a life-long family commitment to Canada's mountains. Mary spoke for them all when she wrote:

> But I really think we are spoiled for travel elsewhere ... for no where else is there such a wealth of beauty and interest, and I conclude that the haunts so attractive to the world have no attraction for me. Of course golf is a fine game, but can it compare with a day on the trail,

or a scramble over the glacier, or even with a quiet day in camp to get things in order for the morrow's conquests? Somehow when once this wild spirit enters the blood, golf courses & hotel piazzas, be they ever so brilliant, have no claim, and I can hardly wait to be off again.

The Vauxes' next visit to Glacier House wasn't until 1894, when George and William returned with their father. On their return to Philadelphia William began working full-time for an architectural firm, which would limit his holiday time in the future.

In 1895 the Vauxes set the pattern for many annual visits; George Vaux, Sr. and Mary would come to the Rockies for the whole summer, while William and George came for varying lengths of time. As he grew older, their father required more looking after, so they took turns spelling each other off. In letters Mary wrote of her longing for the freedom of the western mountains:

Sometimes I feel that I can hardly wait till the time comes to escape from city life, to the free air of the everlasting hills. I sometimes wonder how it is that those who love the out of doors so much, seem always to have their lots cast in the man made town, while the country folk travel to the cities as fast as possible.

The interests and specialties of the three Vauxes complemented each other. William was the scientific diarist, keeping track of measurements and observations of glaciers, and recording straightforward accounts of their mountain travels. He was not a climber per se. George, on the other hand, was an active mountaineer and more reflective about the mountains. Mary, like George, felt a keen kinship with the wilderness and was an active explorer, always interested in seeking new vistas. She was an accomplished watercolor artist, scenic photographer (an avid interest which George shared), writer and lecturer. The Vauxes maintained close family ties through their religion, the mountains and their love of wilderness.

The Vauxes had taken photographs of the Great (now Illecillewaet) Glacier in the Selkirk Mountains on July 17, 1887. William noticed unexpected changes in the glacier when he compared the old photographs to new ones taken in 1894. This sparked his interest and he became fascinated with glaciers. This, combined with his drive and technical ability (he specialized in structural engineering) caused the family to begin the first glacial studies in Canada, starting with the Illecillewaet. Two years later William started making accurate surveys. He would set iron plates in the ice and triangulate them with nearby mountain peaks, with a survey line set up across the plates. Thus, the following year they could measure any movement of the ice. William drew detailed maps from their measurements. Glaciology as a discipline was but 40 years old at this time.

In subsequent years the family also made observations of the Asulkan, Yoho, Victoria and Wenkchemna glaciers. Their data were frequently used by other scientists and authors and their photographs of glaciers illustrated many publications about the mountains. When her brothers became more involved with their professions, Mary went from assisting with the measuring and photographing to assuming responsibility for them. William's 1907 pamphlet on their glacier work was reprinted by the International Commission on Glaciers, the first time that organization published research not commissioned by them.

The Vauxes were fortunate in that they had a good relationship with the CPR. The latter supported their work through free rail passes to and from Montreal and free guide service on the ice. They, in turn, wrote and illustrated a pamphlet for the CPR entitled *The Glaciers of the Canadian Rockies & Selkirks.* The pamphlet was updated numerous times, the last being by Mary in 1922.

The Vauxes' surveying and photographic equipment—the transit, tripods, rod for glacier measurements, large view cameras and plate-holding boxes—weighed nearly 50 kg. Two packhorses were used to transport the equipment, and where trails for horses did not exist it was carried on men's backs. The work was extremely time-consuming, for a dozen transit observations or the shooting of a dozen glass negatives could take a full day. Their studies demanded hard work from their guides, but the latter entered with spirit into the Vauxes' glacial studies.

Smithsonian Institution/88-7390

Mary Vaux with climbing guide Edward Feuz, Jr.

Their standard camera for glacier photography was the four-inch by five-inch view camera, but they also used a full plate (6-½'' x 8-½'') view camera in the mountains. By the early 1880s dry plate and flexible negative material had been invented, which freed photographers from the wet plate process, but the equipment was still cumbersome. The Vauxes had to go into a tent after dark, covering themselves further with blankets, and load or unload the plate-holders from the boxes which they came in. Development was done at home after their return.

In their glacial studies they recognized that photographs were a superb documentary tool. Panoramas were produced by leveling the camera and then pivoting it, being very careful to match the negatives accurately.

George and William shot most of the pictures during their early years in the mountains, particularly with the large view cameras, but Mary gradually became more involved in that aspect.

Each winter in Philadelphia the Vauxes gave lantern-slide lectures to various organizations and spoke of their glacial studies to scientific groups. Less formally, this was quiet, polite parlor entertainment; educated Philadelphians would invite some friends and arrange for the Vauxes to show their mountain photographs. Through these lectures the Vauxes inadvertently advertised the Canadian mountains at great length, and many of their friends and acquaintances became attracted to the area. Some joined them there each summer. The artistic coloring of the slides was done by Mary; it was very detailed, demanding and time-consuming work.

Mary elaborated on the vagaries of photography in the mountains in an article in the *Canadian Alpine Journal*:

> A kodak, if no larger instrument can be managed, yields most satisfactory results, although the better records from a larger sized camera are an increased delight, when one has the patience and skill to obtain them. For changing plates in camp, an improvised teepee can be made of the blankets, and, if this is done after sundown, is quite satisfactory. We have never known plates to be fogged by the operation. Cut films are more convenient than glass plates, as they are so much lighter and not subject to breakage, although not so easily handled. The actinic properties of the light are very great and care must be used to avoid overexposure.

Mary's involvement in scientific pursuits was a milestone at a time when women were usually discouraged from such activities and often weren't even allowed to attend meetings and lectures of scientific societies.

Mary's mountaineering accomplishments were few. On July 25, 1897, George and Mary climbed Mount Abbot (2466 m), her first climb. On August 15, 1899, she ascended Avalanche Mountain (2864 m) with her brothers, guided by Dan Frazier and accompanied by Albert Duchesney. Then, on July 21, 1900, Mary made her historic climb of Mount Stephen. From its summit she had a tantalizing glimpse of the "Wapta Fall" (now Takakkaw Falls) in the Yoho Valley.

The Vauxes had been instrumental in encouraging the Canadian Pacific Railway to hire Swiss guides for the professional and amateur mountaineers who were already flocking to the mountains. They saw the potential of the Selkirk and Rocky mountains for recreation and they also realized the necessity of the guides for their glacier work.

William was a founding member and treasurer of the American Alpine Club. In June, 1906, all three Vauxes applied for active membership in the fledgling Alpine Club of Canada (ACC). Mary's qualification for membership was her ascent of Mount Stephen. She was made an Honorary Member in 1914.

In his notebook George once recorded a short climber's prayer:

Lord, thro this hour
Be Thou our guide
So by Thy power
No foot shall slide.

On August 26, 1900, the entire Vaux family traveled from Emerald Lake to Takakkaw Falls, via Yoho Pass. They were but the second party to explore the Yoho Valley since Jean Habel's original exploration in 1896.

Four years later George and William again visited the Yoho, this time with George's future wife, Mary James, along. Meanwhile Mary had to stay with their ailing father at Emerald Lake. Strong-willed and keen as she was, and enamored of the Yoho Valley, this must have sorely tried her patience and sense of duty. A few days later the two Marys and George went into a camp up the Ice River Valley for a week. Although Mary James was not an avid camper, the three also traveled by packtrain into Mount Assiniboine in 1907.

In 1905 Mary Vaux and her friend Mary Schäffer were the first women to explore the subsequently famous "Deutschman" (now Nakimu) cave near Glacier House. They were guided by Charles Deutschman, the former trapper who had discovered the cave.

> When we began the descent we were a trifle timid, because we were not at all sure what the cavernous unknown held in store for us. What we saw well repaid us for the chances we took. We lighted our way with large candles.
>
> The gloom was great when we entered, and before going many steps a huge vaulted gallery appeared as if by magic. At our feet coursed a stream of water that looked blood-red. Further along we saw a great volume of water dashed over a cliff, and the spray was literally dripping blood, the well was a deep crimson, and one involuntarily felt such a small, helpless bit in nature's plan.
>
> We found a creepy-looking gallery, and followed it. It grew smaller and smaller every step. Finally we came to a place where, after squeezing through, we found ourselves in a beautiful gallery, the ceiling containing hundreds of finely colored stalactites. We christened this gallery "Fat Man's Misery." A stout man never would have got through.
>
> As our candles were burning low we went only a short distance further, following an arched gallery, at the end of which was a deep hole. We could not see the bottom. We christened this "Big Hole." We returned by the same route, squeezing through "Fat Man's Misery" in a hurry, as one candle was out. The other went out before we reached the mouth of the cavern, and we climbed the steep incline to the entrance in the dark.

Mary Sharples Schäffer was also a Quaker from Philadelphia and the two Marys had met while studying art there. They were of similar age and similar interests, and both became highly skilled wildflower artists. The friendly rivalry between the two was intense. It seems quite likely that Mary Schäffer learned her photographic skills from Mary Vaux. The Vauxes and Schäffers visited frequently in Philadelphia, and both Marys lectured for various societies. A few years later, in 1908, Mary Schäffer named a prominent peak at Maligne Lake in Jasper National Park, for her friend: Mount Mary Vaux (3201 m).[2]

William died of tuberculosis in 1908, at the age of only 36. Although William was the driving force behind the glacial studies, Mary and George competently took over the observations after his death. They were assisted by Arthur O. Wheeler, surveyor and president of the Alpine Club of Canada. Mary added the measurements of the Victoria and Yoho glaciers in 1910. After that season George didn't return to the mountains (he had married in 1907). Mary kept the studies going for another two years, when due to marriage and other interests her involvement lapsed. She maintained sporadic interest until 1922. Wheeler, under the auspices of the ACC, continued the research for many years.

In 1909 the ACC held their annual camp in the Yoho Valley. When the packtrain, with participants on foot and horse, left the Laggan (now Lake Louise) railway station, the transcontinental passengers gaped at this version of the wild west. Mary, dressed in buckskin shirt and knickers, was "snap-shotted without mercy" as she went to post a letter at the office. Later, in camp, Mary conjured up two fat and tender turkeys for the evening's sumptuous feast! Before leaving Lake Louise she had likely cajoled the proprietor of the lodge there, Miss Mollison, into giving her entry to the chalet's larder. But whether it was by "sorcery, blandishment or barter," the crew was far too hungry to inquire.

After the official camp a group of 32 people spent six days completing a high circuit of the valley from Sherbrooke Lake to the Little Yoho Valley, and then to Emerald Lake. They journeyed over snowfields and glaciers. According to one participant, Mary's "cheerfulness in putting up with the little inconveniences of camp life and readiness to give a hand wherever needed, charmed all, and contributed much to the pleasure of the trip." Besides camping and exploring, Mary

2. Mount Vaux near Field, British Columbia, was named by Dr. James Hector for William Sandys Wright Vaux, a distant British relative of the family. There is a small glacier on Mount Sir Donald named for George Vaux, Jr.

conducted measurements of the Yoho Glacier. She also entered the valley from Bow Lake via Vulture Col, crossing the Waputik Icefield and the Great Divide to the Balfour and Yoho glaciers,

Whyte Museum of the Canadian Rockies

Mary Vaux's glacier notes.

in 1910. It was a small group that got together after the ACC Consolation Valley camp, and included A. O. Wheeler, Byron Harmon and F. V. Longstaff.

Mary held a special reverence for the Yoho Valley:

> Thee knows I feel a sense of ownership in it, being the first white woman that visited it. ... It is to me the loveliest spot to be found, and it always quickens my blood when I hear and speak of it. I can imagine no greater delight than camping there away from the tourist, and the noise of the iron horse.

On another outing Mary camped for a few days at Lake O'Hara after making the traverse over Abbot Pass from Lake Louise, guided by Christian Hasler, Sr. They carried dried foods, which could be prepared such that "with hunger sauce" their appetites were fully satisfied. They had many nocturnal visitors at Lake O'Hara:

> Our camp had one disadvantage—the porcupines. They seemed so pleased to have us & visited us at all hours; tried the flavor of our bacon, & the softness of the guides' bed in their tent. When they found we did not encourage greater intimacy they climbed the large tree immediately back of the tent, & watched us from this point of vantage all day. Then at night they would scratch on the canvas just by our heads & grunt in the most impudent manner. Christian killed one with his ice axe, as he filled the guides [sic] blankets with quills & would not come out of their tent. We would have eaten him but Dan did not understand how to prepare him for the table, & he looked so formidable in his spiny coat.

In 1914, at the age of 54, Mary Vaux married Dr. Charles Doolittle Walcott. Walcott was the former director of the U.S. Geological Survey and was then the secretary of the Smithsonian Institution in Washington, D.C.—a powerful scientific administrator. He was a paleontologist and leading authority on Cambrian geology and fossils, well known for his studies of trilobites. A colleague said that he could "smell a fossil." Mary first met Dr. Walcott in 1907, and the Vauxes often visited Walcott's camp near Field.

Walcott never earned an academic degree, but during his distinguished career he was showered with honorary degrees from learned institutions throughout the world.

In the Rockies, Walcott's most important discovery was a large deposit of unique invertebrate fossils on Mount Wapta, near Field, in August, 1909. Their party, including his wife Helena and their three children, were camped near Burgess Pass while searching for fossils on the ridge above. One popular story of the discovery is that Mrs. Walcott's horse stumbled on the trail on the way to the railroad on the last day of the season. When Walcott dismounted to study the offending slab of rock, he discovered a magnificent fossil trilobite.[3] The significance

---

3. There is a possibility that Walcott may have been led to the Burgess Shale site: unknown to the scientific community at the time, a sensational horde of fossils had been discovered in the area in the 1870s by a railway surveyor/engineer named

of this fossil site, now known as the Burgess Shale, has since been recognized in its declaration as a World Heritage Site by the United Nations.

Walcott had two sons and a daughter from previous marriages (Mary Vaux was his third wife). Tragedy seemed to dog his life. His first wife, Lura Rust Walcott, died of natural causes, and in 1911 his second wife, Helena Breese Walcott, was killed in a railroad accident between Washington and Boston. In that same year his oldest son, Charles, died while a student at Yale University. His youngest son, Stuart, was shot down in 1917 while serving in the elite Lafayette Escadrille, an American-manned flying unit of the French army.

Walcott was doing field work in Yoho at the time of his second wife's tragic death. Mary went up to his camp at the fossil beds to give condolences. She later wrote to him of her own grief after William's death: "As we work here in the mountains, where we have passed so many happy days together, my brother Will seems with me all the time, and I do it [glacial studies] for him, and as carrying on his work."

During a frequent correspondence before their marriage, Mary and Charles exchanged scientific articles on glaciers and fossils, and photographs of their work in the Canadian mountains. They had mutual interests in the outdoors and the sciences.

Mary and Charles were married at her brother George's house on June 30, 1914, in a Friends ceremony. The same day, they left for Montreal and the Rockies on their first annual geological expedition. Theirs was a marriage of congeniality, and it brought together two people with a singleness of purpose—an understanding of natural mysteries. Back in Washington in the fall, Mary was immediately thrown into rounds of socializing, dining out and giving elaborate dinner parties—a far cry from the campfires of the Rockies and her

Otto Klotz. Although there is no doubt about the significance of Walcott's trilobite discovery there is some dispute in scientific circles as to just what day he made the discovery and doubt about the fairytale-like story of finding it on the last day of the field season.

quiet Quaker life in Philadelphia.

Mary provided invaluable assistance to Charles in his geological expeditions, from driving the buckboard and collecting fossils to sketching geological sections and developing their photographic plates. When Charles collected mammal

Smithsonian Institution/88-7392

Mary Vaux Walcott.

specimens for the Smithsonian, Mary assisted the guides in preparing the skulls and skins for transport, and in drying the meat for food.

Mary's own scientific interest was deep and sincere:

> I don't know why it is. Women have time for bridge parties and dances, yet they miss so much by not turning their attention to scientific studies and using their eyes. There is a thrill one receives from breaking a rock and finding a fresh fossil that nothing else can give. There is the romance of not knowing what one will find.

During their first trip to the Rockies together, Charles helped Mary with her measurements of the Great and Asulkan glaciers. His assistance was mostly encouragement, as when Mary and the guides went up on the glacier he only "went along to look on." On their way back from the British Columbia coast they stopped for a number of weeks in Montana to collect fossils.

On April 20, 1915, George Vaux, Sr. died. In Quaker fashion Mary observed a year of mourning after her father's death, and did not socialize or entertain. The Walcotts did not visit the Canadian Rockies but spent three months in Yellowstone National Park and the Grand Canyon. Charles's daughter, Helen, accompanied them. She and Mary got along splendidly.

In 1916 the Walcotts were back in Canada for four months. In what became a familiar pattern, they arrived by train and went immediatly to their camp near the Buffalo Paddock outside Banff townsite. Their camp was already set up by Arthur, a black employee of the Smithsonian who worked for Walcott year-round. He would arrive in Banff before them to get the outfit ready. He was with Walcott for over 25 years, and the outfitters rated him as an "unbelievable" cook.

They would spend a few days socializing in Banff, with old friends such as Mary Schäffer (now married to outfitter Billy Warren) and then hit the trail. Although out for weeks at a time, their outfitter would return to Banff or Lake Louise to resupply, and Mary would ride in for the mail if they weren't too far away. She would leave Charles alone for a few days while she returned to Glacier House, Yoho and Lake Louise to make her annual glacier measurements, and to visit old haunts. She also attended the annual Alpine Club of Canada camps.

Charles loved going to the Rockies, where there was "a wide interest, health, and almost absolute freedom from contact with fellow humans!"

The Dominion Park Service (as the Canadian Parks Service was known then) assigned one of their wardens, Nello Vernon-Wood, usually called Tex Wood, to assist the Walcotts in 1917. After he quit the government and acquired his own pack outfit in 1919 Tex continued to escort them on their summer expeditions from Lake Louise. The Walcotts often brought their own ex-army packer with them. Prior to outfitting with Tex the army packer would take their horses to Montana to winter. Later, Tex wintered them with his.

They would hire other packers locally, but it "wasn't everybody got along with them." Mary was a very determined woman and the first time Tex outfitted for them he told her in no uncertain terms that "I was quite open to suggestions, but I was running the pack outfit," after which she left him alone. Walcott himself was easygoing. Another summer, they hired two local packers, only to have one quit and the other one dismissed. The former was the most "inefficient, useless man" Charles had ever seen. Another packer, William Shea, left camp "mad because he could not use cowboy camp manners at dinner table. A capable packer but heedless, egotistic and unreliable," according to Charles. At trying times, when packers refused to work, or had quit, Arthur also filled in as the wrangler.

The Walcotts' equipment was United States Army issue. The tents were made of sail silk, also known as Egyptian cotton. They had a collapsible wood stove with an oven that allowed Arthur to make raised bread—quite a luxury. Camp cots were another luxury. Their camp was certainly more elaborate than the average one of the day. They required ten or twelve horses for the yearly three- or four-month excursion—it took one horse to carry the panorama camera alone.

When outfitting for the Walcotts, Tex would often hunt large mammals for the Smithsonian collections, Walcott would be geologizing, and Mary would be painting flowers. Helen sometimes joined them on the trail. Tex said of Walcott's daughter that she was as "good as any man I ever knew when it came to scrambling around in the hills."

The baggageman at the railway station at Lake Louise didn't appreciate Walcott's collections of rocks. He once told an outfitter to tell his brother, who was a priest, to "say a prayer for this guy that's shipping this box of rocks, because I'm going to kill him off!" It's doubtful that the outfitters and packers appreciated the loads either.

In Washington the Walcotts led a frenetic public life, entertaining frequently. They were both very involved with organizations and causes in the capital. Mary assisted Charles in the formation of the Freer Gallery of Oriental Art at the Smithsonian, as well as the Carnegie Institute of Washington and the National Advisory Committee for Aeronautics. Taking full advantage of her position as the wife of the Smithsonian's secretary, Mary promoted public understanding of scientific research, particularly in her own field of interest, botany.

They established the Charles D. and Mary V. Walcott Research Fund "for the development of geological and paleontological studies and publishing results thereof," which is still in existence. When Mary died, nearly $400,000 from her estate was added to the fund.

In the spring of 1921 the parks service officials asked outfitter Cecil Smith to guide the Walcotts for the summer. They went from Banff to Lake Louise, then north through the Ptarmigan and Skoki valleys to the Red Deer River, where they camped for a while. Walcott wanted to go to the Columbia Icefield, even though the guide hadn't been there before. They traveled over Pipestone Pass to the Siffleur River, then up the North Saskatchewan River to the Alexandra, and thence to Castleguard Meadows. While tracking the horses one morning Cecil discovered the entrance to Castleguard Cave, now the longest known in Canada (20 km of explored passages). The Walcotts visited the cave several times.

Mary had shown considerable artistic ability since her childhood. Her interests seem to have been mainly in landscape painting until one summer at Glacier House, when a botanist friend asked her to paint a rare alpine arnica. Thereafter she concentrated on wildflowers, which were a "joy and inspiration" to paint. Wherever she traveled her watercolor kit was always with her. All told, she painted well over a thousand watercolors of wildflowers.

When traveling by horseback Mary carried her paint box and pads on the back of her saddle, and her camera boxes over the pommel. Sometimes she would paint by a fire to keep her stiffened fingers warm. At other times she would bring the flowers back to camp, where she would re-arrange them in water and paint them in better light.

Mary Vaux Walcott sketching in her tent, ca. 1925.

In the early 1920s Mary's watercolor paintings of wildflowers began to attract national attention. Her work was exhibited in various galleries and museums in Washington, New York and Chicago. With this recognition came urgings from botanists and art critics for a publication.

Mary's crowning artistic achievement came in 1925, when the Smithsonian Institution published her watercolor drawings in a five-volume set, *North American Wildflowers.* The set was described as "the Audubon of Botany" and hailed by botanical experts as being both scientifically accurate and artistically pleasing. It contained reproductions of 400 watercolors with her own brief one-page descriptions of each, which included the necessary scientific data, but also interesting facts about the plant, such as medicinal uses, occasional poetic references and even the circumstances of painting them. The plants were from all over the continent, including lawns and gardens. Some of the plants were collected or contributed by friends.

Mary's paintings were excellent reproductions of form and coloring of wildflowers. The painting of the flowers not only required artistic skill, but abundant enthusiasm and an ability to withstand the rigors of travel in rough country.

The cost of publishing the paintings looked almost insurmountable, but Mary spent years soliciting subscriptions from leading horticultural societies of the world, people who saw her exhibits and read reviews of them, libraries, universities, museums, as well as wealthy flower-loving individuals. Subscribers were found ahead of time for the deluxe edition of 500 books, each of which sold for $500. The publishing costs were some $236,000. Its success later enabled the Smithsonian to offer a library edition of 2500 copies at $100 each.

The publication of the series was not only a triumph for Mary personally, but also for the artisans of papermaking and color printing. Mary was very particular about the quality of the reproductions, and she searched for a long time to find a printer who could do them justice. The reproduction process used was a new one, invented by William Edwin Rudge of New York City, a craftsman in the vanguard of new methods of color printing. He perfected a process that would faithfully reproduce the original colors. In what became known as the "Smithsonian process," the paper passed through a battery of four-color presses and was then thrown into a tub of water, which fixed the colors. Pure rag paper was used to assure faithful color retention as well as durability. The prints were laboriously dried by hand on bath towels.

The accumulated income from her published works was used to establish the Mary Walcott Fund for Publications in Botany, at the Smithsonian.

In 1923 the Walcotts were back in new mountain territory, near Radium Hot Springs, British Columbia, and west to the Lake of the Hanging Glaciers and Horsethief Creek. In 1924 they visited the Burgess Pass area again, and spent most of their summer along the headwaters of the Red Deer River.

Mary was an original council member of the Trail Riders of the Canadian Rockies, whose main objective was the encouragement of travel by horseback through the Rockies. At the first annual ride in the Yoho Valley, on July 17, 1924, she read a speech of welcome to special guest Tom Wilson, one of the Rockies' pioneer outfitters. The annual trail ride became

Smithsonian Institution/88-3135

Mary and Charles Walcott in the Yoho Valley, 1924.

the focal point for the organization.

The couple's last year in the Rockies together was 1925. They arrived from the west this time, via San Diego, Portland, Seattle and Vancouver, and they spent three months north of Lake Louise in the Ptarmigan, Skoki and Red Deer River areas. Charles was beginning to feel the effects of his age, and for the first time was glad to leave camp for home.

Dr. Walcott died on February 9, 1927. After his death Mary continued to live in Washington. Charles's passing seemed to stimulate rather than diminish her interest in the institution which was so dear to him. She was particularly concerned about the plight of the Smithsonian in light of shrinking endowments, which resulted in her making a very generous bequest. In turn she was made an Honorary Collaborator, and in 1929 she carried out unspecified field work for the institution in the Rockies.

On October 28, 1927, Mary was appointed by President Coolidge to succeed her brother George on the Board of Indian Commissioners, a $1/year post which she held until its dissolution in 1933. The board members were from around the country; they traveled on inspection tours to reservations and later advised the Department of the Interior and Congress on Indian affairs. In this post she visited over 100 Indian Reservations to study their situation and conditions. She had a compassionate concern for native Americans. Her home in Washington housed a vast collection of native artifacts.

Mary took to driving to the Canadian Rockies in a chauffeured car every year. She would usually travel across the United States to the west coast, visiting many national parks and Indian reservations on the way. Then it was north to her beloved Selkirk and Rocky mountains. After spending a number of weeks there she would motor across Canada to visit friends in New Brunswick and then complete the circle home. In this way she amassed some 20,000 km or more every summer. Occasionally one of her nephews would join her. She also took one overseas trip, to Japan in 1936, to visit a childhood friend. To Mary, age was "an emancipation" and trivial things no longer worried her.

On her last trip to the Yoho Valley in 1939 Mary wrote that "there are many tourists in the mountains this year, and they are not at all a help as so few of them care for scenery or anything worth while. Most of them come just to say they have been."

She continued to frequent the annual ACC camps and the annual rides of the Trail Riders of the Canadian Rockies. She was often referred to as the "Grand Dame" of the mountains, or simply as "The Artist." Mary calculated that she had traveled more than 8000 km on horseback, and reportedly she celebrated her 77th birthday with a 30-km ride in the mountains.

Throughout her life Mary had maintained good health. She stood tall and erect, and walked gracefully, but with a firm step. Bright, merry blue eyes were set in a clear unlined face. Being strong-willed and self-reliant, she had a commanding presence, which was tempered with ready sympathy. She attributed her health and longevity to abstinence from alcohol and tobacco, and to the months spent each year in the outdoors.

Through the years Mary was an active member of many organizations: Alpine Club of Canada, American Alpine Club, American Association for the Advancement of Science, the Colonial Dames of Philadelphia, the Photographic Society of Philadelphia and the Trail Riders of the Canadian Rockies. Mary's scientific contributions were recognized by her election to the prestigious Academy of Natural Sciences of Philadelphia in 1892, one of the few women to be so honored at that time. She joined the Society of Woman Geographers in 1926, the year following its founding. In 1933 she became its second national president, a post which she held for two terms. She lectured on her beloved Rockies and wildflowers before many noteworthy groups, including the Royal Canadian Institute in Toronto. Numerous charities received Mary's attention, both as director and as benefactor.

Mary was very active in the Society of Friends. While still living in Philadelphia she served for years as the clerk of the Twelfth Street Meeting. She always adhered to her Quaker beliefs of restraint and strict attention to the truth. She never hesitated to state her opinion about anything, whether she agreed or disagreed with the speaker.

The need for a suitable structure for a Meeting for Worship in Washington arose following the election of Herbert Hoover, a Quaker, to the presidency in 1928. Mary personally raised some $45,000 to purchase the land. Lucy M. Wilbur Foster of Rhode Island pledged money for the building, which was designed by architect Walter Price. The meeting house was built in 1930. Mary also landscaped the site. On the 25th anniversary of the Friends Meeting of Washington the Mary Walcott-Lucy Foster Fund was established in their memory to provide loans and grants for educational purposes.

In 1935 Mary contributed 15 paintings to a book on pitcher plants, also published by the Smithsonian Institution.

Mary Vaux Walcott died of a heart attack on August 22, 1940, at the home of friends in St. Andrews, New Brunswick, just past her 80th birthday. When she died, Mary was readying two volumes of recent watercolors for publication.

Mary's name will always stand in the annals of scientific, photographic and artistic achievements in the mountains of western Canada.

Mary Schäffer Warren
(1861-1939)

> Bowing as though in a drawing-room and doffing his spotless hat, he said, "I hope I don't intrude?" Not wishing to be outdone in politeness even under such limited circumstances, I struggled up as far as the confines of the sleeping-bag would permit, ducked as gracefully as possible, and murmured "Certainly not."

Such was the way in which Mary Schäffer described her unexpected meeting with L. Q. Coleman, brother and companion of famed alpinist-explorer Dr. A. P. Coleman, of Toronto. The Colemans must have been slightly surprised by the encounter, for in 1907 women simply were not found camping 150 km from the nearest railroad in the wilds of the Canadian Rockies.

Mary, though, was no ordinary woman. At a time when others were delicately curtseying in eastern society, she was tramping through mud, muskeg and downed timber in the western wilderness. She was the first non-native woman to travel in much of what is now Banff and Jasper national parks. She was also an accomplished writer and photographer.

She was born Mary Townsend Sharples, to Alfred Sharples[1] and Elizabeth Cope, a wealthy Quaker family in West Chester, Pennsylvania, just outside of Philadelphia, in 1861. She was

---

1. Various family members spelt their name with one or two s's. Mary always spelt her name Sharples, although her father used the Sharpless form.

the third of five children: Henry Lewis, Joseph Townsend, Mary Townsend, Frederic Fraley and Herman Hoopes. Henry and Joseph died very young. Her father's family had emigrated from England in 1644, and they retained a great attachment and sentiment for the mother country. Their English-style home was full of British furnishings. Even in later years, Mary balked at being called an American.

Alfred Sharpless was the former superintendent of the Schuylkill Navigation Company, but he became a gentleman farmer in 1870, also serving as a bank director and a member of the local borough council. He and Mary's mother were both wealthy, and Mary wanted for nothing as a child. The household was well staffed with maids and servants.

A well-educated child, Mary received schooling in mathematics, languages, Latin and other subjects. But it was obvious that she excelled in art. She learned to paint flowers under the direction of George Lambden, a renowned flower artist of the time. She also enjoyed traditional embroidery and needlework.

Her father had an avid interest in the natural sciences, particularly mineralogy, and he spurred Mary's own life-long interest in natural history. Many of Alfred's friends and frequent guests were scientists. From the early age of six Mary would accompany her father on drives in the country with his friend the great Swiss geologist, Dr. Joseph Leidy, a member of the Academy of Natural Sciences of Philadelphia. From them she absorbed a good deal of "the story of stones, grasses and the small things people attach no importance to."

There was also a strong literary tradition in her family, with numerous relatives having written both fiction and journalism. Her father was a well-known contributor to newspapers on agricultural and other events of the day, under the pseudonym "John Plowshare."

Mary's Quaker upbringing was not just a ritual; it was a philosophy and an attitude of mind. It was evident in her attitude toward the country she traveled through and the people that she met. In the unspoiled wilderness she felt that she was close to the Creator's handiwork.

She was a precocious child and said that she never liked West Chester, having "always had a sense of stepping out beyond what was expected or tolerated by my very prim relatives." When she was a child she liked to act, and she wrote that she was on a "private stage" until she was 18.

As a child, Mary heard stories of the Indians from Cousin Jim, who served in the United States Army out west. Once, as she hid undetected in a corner, he told of rescuing an Indian baby from its dead mother's arms. She sobbed in horror, was discovered, and never did hear the baby's fate. But the images remained with her forever and governed many of her compassionate acts as she grew older. She tramped the Pennsylvania hills looking for arrowheads, and she dreamed about the Indian people.

Mary's first sight of "real" Indians came on a trip to the west coast as a teenager, when the train stopped in the Mojave Desert. At the various towns her fellow passengers treated the Indians they met like beggars and second-class citizens—she was disgusted at how supposedly educated people could treat other human beings with such contempt. Her Quaker upbringing led her to treat all people with common dignity and respect. But in her naiveté, and with images from childhood stories, she carried a little revolver on this first trip because she was sure she would need it for protection from Indians.

A second visit to the west included a voyage on a freight steamer up the west coast of Canada to Alaska. It penetrated many bays and inlets, where Mary had ample opportunity to observe Indians in a more natural setting. She made a fine collection of native baskets.

These trips in her late teens and early twenties awoke in Mary a love for travel, which led her to the Canadian Rockies in 1889. While traveling to Vancouver on the Canadian Pacific Railway, her party of nine stopped at Banff. From there to Lake Louise they traveled on the top of a boxcar, inhaling ample amounts of smoke and cinders. Finally they stopped at Glacier House, the new railway hotel in Rogers Pass.

During her brief visit at Glacier House Mary met Dr. Charles Schäffer, a medical doctor whose abiding interest was botany. Dr. Schäffer, a member of the Academy of Natural Sciences in Philadelphia, had been intrigued by the Vaux family's description of the flora of these mountains. He had come there to study the area firsthand. Their friendship grew upon their return to Philadelphia, and Charles and Mary were soon married.

Although she had supervised her younger brothers, Fred and Herman, from the age of nine, Mary had never learned domestic chores such as housekeeping or cooking until she married Dr. Schäffer. He wanted her to make a pie—the chickens got the first one! She did learn to manage the household under the guidance of Schäffer's maid, Serena Potts, but she certainly did not excel at domestic tasks. Potts, herself a painter of flowers, used to pinch the young bride to get her to "behave."

In 1891 the Schäffers returned to Canada to continue Charles's botanical studies, and for over a decade they made annual excursions to the environs of Glacier, Field, Lake Louise and Banff. Most of the Schäffers' rambles were confined to within easy access of the railroad because he suffered from heart disease.

Dr. Schäffer had no idea of Mary's knowledge of art until she sprang it on him. He wanted very scientific, detailed paintings showing every petal and stamen perfectly, while her artistic bent was to attractive groupings. She destroyed many a sketch until one passed his judgement and then he "began to appreciate his much younger wife." (Charles was some 25 years older than Mary.) Mary's help was indispensable to her husband's studies over the next decade. She dried and pressed the specimens which he collected, reproduced them in detailed watercolors and developed a technique for photographing them to complete the scientific record. Mary held no pretentions of being a botanist, considering herself rather a trained painter, photographer and collector.

Mary was elected a member of the Academy of Natural Sciences of Philadelphia in 1896. She was also a member of the Geographical Society of America. Her photographs of botanical subjects received considerable scientific and artistic attention. In 1900 eight of her silver prints appeared in a salon exhibit in Paris, titled "American Woman Photographer," assembled by Frances Benjamin Johnston. All of the photographs were of flowers, with the exception of one print of Mount Sir Donald.

Mary and Charles first visited Lake Louise in 1893. Tom Wilson, pioneer outfitter and guide, provided the horses and appointed two Stoney Indian guides, William and Joshua Twin, to assist them. The Indians, accompanied by their families, had brought the horses the 130 km from Morley to take the Schäffer party a few kilometres from the train station to the lake! The entourage set up camp by the shore of the lake. (The small log chalet, built in 1890, had burned down before their arrival.)

> We had to sleep in tents, with boards put on the ground for mattress and horse blankets for covering. I remember at the end of the first day I crawled under the blankets in my clothes, and then nearly froze to death. Mrs. Allan, one of our party, whose son, Sam Allan, was the first explorer on Lake Louise, brought me a hot stove lid and stayed beside me to put me to sleep.

From the tent door she "looked out upon that magnificent scene with chattering teeth and shivering bodies and vowed never again to camp in the Canadian Rockies." Fortunately it was a vow which she did not keep.

Wilson continued to haul "a poor little delicate tourist to points she would not have reached" over the next few years. In 1898 she took a long carriage ride and hike from Revelstoke to the magnificent canyon at the Big Bend of the Columbia River.

But her idyllic world of leisure ended in November, 1903, when Dr. Schäffer died, succumbing to his chronic heart problems. At about the same time Mary was also hit with the death of both her parents: her mother two months before, and her father less that a month later.

Charles had little business acumen, and would simply give her anything money could buy. He had suffered substantial losses in the stock market. Mary's father was very impractical with money, spending it especially on poor relations and "gay horses." Being very shrewd herself, Mary was disgusted that both men gave money to almost any "inconsequential" who could talk a good cause. She was actually left with very little. But with good advice she was able to pull together her financial affairs.

With her financial house in order, and to soothe her sorrows, she returned to the Rockies to complete her husband's work. Mary wrote that "work, and hard work at that, is a great panacea for broken threads in life." Mary enlisted the aid of Stewardson Brown, a well-respected botanist and curator of the herbarium of the Academy of Natural Sciences of Philadelphia, to finish her husband's project, promising him full credit for the task. Over the next three years he worked on their existing collection and expanded it.

Its completion, though, required exploration in more remote areas. Previously, her husband's illness had required that they travel near the railway, returning every night to one of the comfortable railway hotels. But now she needed to go further afield. Because of her deathly fear of horses—to her they all looked "tricky and vicious"—and bears, Mary asked Tom Wilson, who by now had become a treasured friend, to find someone to take charge of her longer wilderness outings. In 1904 Wilson assigned a young guide, William "Billy" Warren, to take charge.

Warren was born in Essex County, England, in 1880 and graduated from St. Mary's College, where he had studied accounting. He enlisted in the Imperial Yeomanry and served in the Boer War in South Africa. But, discontent with his clerk's job in London after the war, he came to Canada. He had quite a battle to find work because many Canadians were tired of the English "remittance men" who were unreliable workers, quitting their jobs as soon as money arrived from home. Warren showed up in Banff in 1902, and Tom Wilson immediately saw his potential, giving him a job as a packer. Mary's respect and admiration for him grew rapidly as "there are older ones, there are better hunters perhaps, with wider experience in forest lore,

Mary Schäffer at Kootenay Plains, 1906.

more knowledge of the country, but for kindness, good-nature (such a necessary adjunct), good judgment under unexpected stress, he had no superior."

During the 1904 season they made short forays to the Yoho and Ptarmigan valleys, which were rich in new botanical specimens. In 1905 she traveled further afield, to the North Saskatchewan River. While preparing for the pack trip north of Lake Louise, Mary agreed to take one companion, and then three others begged to join them. Within a few days into the trip Mary said that three of the women were already pining for a bath and a bar of soap. But the fourth was a kindred spirit, Mary "Mollie" Adams, a teacher of geology at Columbia College in New York. Thereafter Mary never journeyed with more than one companion, and "we never had a riffle of disagreement in the thousands of miles we meandered."

Another quiet, capable Quaker, Mollie spent many hours of their trips collecting fossils and other geological specimens. While Mary's diary flows with descriptive phrases, Mollie's reflects the practicality of her scientific training, giving more thought to exact localities. Mollie probably had more in common with botanist Brown, who was "pickling a few toads and such in whiskey" on one trip.

After returning from the North Saskatchewan trip, Mary joined her friend Mary Vaux on a tour of Deutschman Cave (see chapter on Mary Vaux Walcott, page 35). When they left the cave she was "glad to slip back into daylight."

With their collecting finished in 1905 Brown worked on the analysis and writing. Two years later, in 1907, G. P. Putnam's Sons published *Alpine Flora of the Canadian Rocky Mountains*. It sold for $3.00. Mary's exacting watercolor drawings (30 full-page plates) and photographs (98) proved an essential component of the book. The book was dedicated to the memory of Dr. Schäffer "who early recognized this region as a new and interesting field for study."

To Mary's everlasting disappointment their book was eclipsed by the work of Julia Henshaw, who published her *Mountain Wildflowers of Canada* the previous year. It was a

Whyte Museum of the Canadian Rockies — Vaux collection

Julia Henshaw and Mary Schäffer, 1910.

bitter blow. When Dr. Schäffer was botanizing at Field, Julia had asked many questions about his work and Mary's painting and photography of plants. Mary frequently ranted about "a certain party getting the F.R.G.S. [Fellow of the Royal Geographical Society] by showing MY slides at the Royal Geo. Society."

But with her late husband's work completed, what was she to do now with her life? A chance meeting in 1903 with geologist-explorer Sir James Hector, who had gained fame with the Palliser Expedition,[2] had planted seeds of unrest in her heart and fired her imagination. With her new-found confidence she realized that her true desire was to travel deep into the wilderness and view those wild regions.

The mountain trails, though, were considered the domain of men only. For some time she acquiesced to tradition, sat quietly and watched enviously as trappers, hunters, explorers and mountain climbers rode off into the wilderness, returning with exciting stories of wild animals and untrod valleys. Her

---

2. Hector was one of four scientists who traveled under the auspices of Captain John Palliser from 1857 to 1859. The expedition members gathered information about the suitability of the Northwest Territories (then including Alberta and Saskatchewan) for cultivation, and the potential for railways and roads to surmount the mountain barrier.

Quaker upbringing, which had stressed the equality of the sexes, finally won through, though. In exasperation she and Mollie finally said, "Why not?" to joining the summer pilgrimage. "We can starve as well as they; the muskeg will be no softer for us than for them; the ground will be no harder to sleep upon; the waters no deeper to swim, nor the bath colder if we fall in." So they planned an expedition. Mary was 46 years old.

It was a major decision, for in 1907 it was against Victorian mores for women to go camping in the mountains, far from civilization, with two unrelated male guides. To the nay-sayers, Mary replied: "Why must they settle so absolutely upon the fact, that the lover of the hills and the wilderness drops the dainty ways and habits with the conventional garments and becomes something of coarser mould? Can the free air sully, can the birds teach us words we should not hear, can it be possible to see in such a summer's outing, one sight as painful as the daily ones of poverty, degradation, and depravity of a great city?"

So they set out on a four-month packtrip. Ostensibly their aim was to explore the headwaters of the Athabasca and North Saskatchewan rivers, but more simply they wanted to "delve into the heart of an untouched land, to tread where no human foot had trod before, to turn the unthumbed pages of an unread book, and to learn daily those secrets which dear Mother Nature is so willing to tell to those who seek."

They were guided again by Billy Warren, whom Mary referred to as "Chief," assisted by Sid Unwin. Like Warren, Sidney J. Unwin was born in England and also served in the Boer War, where he was decorated for bravery in battle. He worked as a clerk in London after the war and emigrated to Banff in 1904. He was soon unsurpassed in woodcraft, resourcefulness and determination on the trail and was to earn the title "Prince of Guides" from his satisfied customers. This man who threw diamond hitches on the packhorses and cooked the bannock, was also capable of making jokes in Latin.

In her gear Mary packed two thick woolen skirts, a kerchief, a pair of stout serge riding breeches, a short riding skirt, sturdy hob-nailed shoes, low rubber-soled canvas shoes, an Indian buckskin jacket, and a duffel bag into which to stuff it all. She also carried photographic gear and a plant press, and Mollie carried a geologist's hammer.

Mary and Mollie were quite willing to be tourists, letting Warren and Unwin take complete control of the horses and the camp. After a few disastrous culinary attempts over the open fire they left that chore alone too, to the relief to the guides! Whenever they offered to help, the suggestion was invariably that "you two go off and play now." The one exception was whenever the men were off hunting, scouting or clearing the trail. Then out would come the collapsible hand basin, soap and water, and their clothes and blankets would receive a thorough cleaning.

After their first major expedition Mary bought air mattresses to save the needless chore of making bough beds at the end of a wearisome day and to provide the ultimate in comfort, although she never quite got over the feeling that it was a little "dudish" to use them. "Doubtless to those who took us on the long trails, we were dudes in a sense, but they never used the word or I think I would have immediately taken the back trail."

In 1907 they traveled north from Lake Louise until they crossed the North Saskatchewan River, which they followed farther north. Eventually they left it behind and crossed Sunwapta and Wilcox passes. From the latter they could look down upon the Athabasca Glacier, which is a tongue of the vast Columbia Icefield.[3]

It was here that Mary realized she would not make a mountaineer, being "scared stiff at rocks and precipices" when the guides took them up Mount Wilcox (2884 m). Near the summit, unroped, she had to jump a crack between two rock ledges, with the valley far below: "What we do not do for fear of being laughed at." Thereafter, she vowed only to look at

3. The route Mary traveled was similar to the present route of the Icefields Parkway, the renowned scenic highway between Lake Louise and Jasper. At the time there were few blazed trails through the area.

Whyte Museum of the Canadian Rockies

Mollie Adams, Mary Schäffer, Billy Warren and Joe Barker in camp.

mountains from a lower level. The charm of exploring to her was "to keep from the beaten path and go where no one has ever gone before." She did join the Alpine Club of Canada, to whose journal she became a frequent contributor about her explorations and on botanical subjects.

Mary's observations of life on the trail were full of the minute detail of the day's events, particularly those of the horses, which were so vital to the success of a trip. They all had their own quirks and their names—such as Buck, Pinto, Nibs, Fox, Pinky, Brownie, Bugler, Dandy and the Heavenly Twins—crop up time and again in her stories.

> Every horse moved along in good order excepting Buck, who fairly sought trouble. Like many a human being he was entirely too inclined to "know it all" in those school-days of his, consequently he plunged in where wiser feet feared to tread. To cross a torrent he persisted in taking the narrowest part instead of following the leader, with the consequence that several times he and his bacon were submerged, which made him very cross and was certainly of no benefit to the bacon.

They then followed Dr. Coleman's 1898 route to Fortress Lake via the Sunwapta, Athabasca and Chaba Rivers. To Mary a "delicious uncertainty enveloped the day's work" even though they had a vague knowledge of the area from reading the articles by Jean Habel and the book by A. P. Coleman. The Athabasca was traced to its headwaters at the base of Mount Columbia. After backtracking to the North Saskatchewan River they followed its north fork (now called the Alexandra River) to its headwaters at Thompson Pass.

As they still had a few weeks before the autumn storms normally started they went in search of a hidden lake that Jimmy Simpson said the Stoney Indians called "Chaba Imne" (Beaver Lake). So they trailed north again, but this time they climbed east over Nigel Pass and on to Brazeau Lake. The mystery lake lay somewhere further to the north, but their progress was halted by an impenetrable headwall and deep snow. They realized that Chaba Imne would have to wait until next season, and headed back to Lake Louise.

On the return trip they crossed Cataract Pass to Pinto Lake and then continued down the Cline River to the Kootenay Plains on the North Saskatchewan River. In that protected valley it was if they had suddenly dropped back into summer. A band of Stoney Indians was camped there, to whom Mary was known as "Yahe-Weha" or "Mountain Woman," from her visits with them the previous year. One of their members, Sampson Beaver, had visited Chaba Imne as a child twenty years before, and he sketched a map of the approach for Mary.

Many explorers tend to forget the travels of the Indian when they state that they were the first to see a certain place or travel a certain valley. But Mary always humbly referred to the prior presence of Indians in the places she went.

In late September Mary's group arrived back at Lake Louise. The author and poet Rudyard Kipling wrote a wonderful description of meeting them on the return trail:

> As we drove along the narrow hill-road a piebald pack-pony with a china-blue eye came round a bend, followed by two women, black-haired, bare-headed, wearing beadwork squaw-jackets, and riding straddle. A string of pack-ponies trotted through the pines behind

them.

"Indians on the move?" said I. "How characteristic!"

As the women jolted by, one of them very slightly turned her eyes, and they were, past any doubt, the comprehending equal eyes of the civilised white woman which moved in that berry-brown face.

"Yes," said our driver, when the cavalcade had navigated the next curve, "that'll be Mrs. So-and-So and Miss So-and-So. They mostly camp hereabout for three months every year. I reckon they're coming in to the railroad before the snow falls." ...

The same evening, at an hotel of all the luxuries, a slight woman in a very pretty evening frock was turning over photographs, and the eyes beneath the strictly-arranged hair were the eyes of the woman in the beadwork jacket who had quirted the piebald pack-pony past our buggy.

Praised be Allah for the diversity of His creatures!

With Sampson Beaver's map clutched tightly in her hand, Mary returned to Philadelphia. The following winter was spent in dreaming of Chaba Imne, and on making plans to search for it the next summer. The search for the elusive lake was "a good excuse to be in the open, to follow the trail for the simple love of following it, and explore places of which we knew nothing."

Each winter Mary returned to Philadelphia where her vivid stories, always accompanied by her hand-colored lantern slides, were sought after entertainment.

In spite of the fact that I had entree to art circles, musical circles—all that goes to make a city life adored by those who are willing to endure the black dust of rail-roads, clanging of cars twenty-four hours of the day, puddles of mud on rainy days, broiling heat of summer, etc., my heart turned ever to my memory of pictures of the Rockies and open spaces.

By June of 1908 plans were set for another expedition in search of Chaba Imne. Warren and Unwin were assisted by Reggie Holmes, and the group was accompanied once again by Stewardson Brown. After difficulties with late season snow, and a detour up the wrong valley, they found the lake, which is now known as Maligne—one of the jewels of the Rockies.[4]

---

4. Mary never made any claims that they were the first people to visit Maligne Lake. Besides the Stoney Indians and Metis hunters, railway surveyor Henry McLeod had visited it in 1875 and called it "Sorefoot Lake."

The men quickly built a raft, which was christened the "H.M.S. Chaba." With this unlikely-looking craft they rowed and sailed down the lake, naming mounts Unwin, Charlton, Warren and Mary Vaux, and Sampson Peak as they went. Nearing what they supposed to be the end of the lake, they found instead a narrows, which, upon passing through, opened up a vista that "all in our little company agreed, was the finest view any of us had ever beheld in the Rockies. ... There it lay, for the time being all ours,—those miles and miles of lake, the unnamed peaks rising above us, one following the other, each more beautiful than the last."

They spent a number of blissful days on the shore of the lake before starting out for their next objective, Mount Robson, far to the west. But five hard days of trail-clearing by the men along the valley of the Maligne River gave no progress against the thick, downed timber and they had little recourse but to return the way they had come, over Maligne Pass to the Sunwapta River, before heading north to the Athabasca River. At the Sunwapta, Brown and Holmes left them to return to Lake Louise.

The packtrain crossing Poboktan Pass, 1908.

Whyte Museum of the Canadian Rockies

Eventually the others reached the mouths of both the Maligne and Miette Rivers—a 150-km detour to cover a straightline distance of about 30 km! The Miette River started them on their journey toward Mount Robson, again following in Coleman's footsteps. Finally, after battling numerous stretches of muskeg, Mount Robson "loomed refreshingly up from behind a hill, cold, icy, cleancut, in a sky unclouded and of intensest blue."

They camped at Tête Jaune Cache where they met some prospectors. The meeting was later reported with excitement in the *Edmonton Bulletin*:

> The women had no husbands, brothers or other encumbrances, along with them, and needed none. They are described as anything but masculine in appearance, but nature to them is an open book, and the warders of the wilderness are to them a plain tale of the hills. Incidentally, they are botanists, geologists and entomologists, and the packs they took out carry many interesting specimens which will undoubtedly find lodgment in some eastern university or museum.

After a few days the party set its sights once again on Lake Louise, many days' travel away. As they journeyed, Mary bemoaned the realization that "the hideous march of progress, so awful to those who love the real wilderness, was sweeping rapidly over the land and would wipe out all trail troubles."

After the 1908 trip, Mary and Mollie traveled to Japan. There they joined Dr. I. Nitobe, a Japanese scientist and worker for peace who had married a friend of Mary's family, a woman interpreter who was a graduate of Bryn Mawr College. One of the highlights for Mary was traveling to see the aboriginal Ainus on the island of Hokkaido. They traveled for a few months before the trip ended disastrously: Mollie contracted an unknown illness and died. Mary buried her friend in Kobe.

Once more Mary returned to her dear Rockies to soothe an aching heart. In 1911 she made a return trip to Maligne Lake to survey and map it for the Dominion Government. This was at the request of D. B. Dowling of the Geological Survey of Canada, who felt that the information would be valuable and that her fame would help to advertise the beauties of the area.

Mary was accompanied by her sister-in-law Caroline Sharpless and her nephew Paul. They traveled via the new Grand Trunk Pacific (GTP) Railway to the end of the line at Hinton, then by horseback. She viewed the new railway as the beginning of the end, as there would soon be no true wilderness left.

On her trip to Maligne Lake, the government provided ten men to cut a trail out over Shovel Pass. She named Mount Charlton for H. R. Charlton of the GTP Railway. He had realized that the lake could become one of the area's most scenic attractions and materially aided Mary's survey of the lake. After the trip Mary applied to the government to have a steam launch put in operation on the lake. She was indignant that Maligne, as well as other areas, had recently been excluded from park status. Her outcry may have helped to have some of these areas reinstated.

With her rediscovery of Maligne Lake, and her subsequent exploration and mapping there, Mary's name became synonymous with the lake. It was to be the last of her long trips in the wilderness, although she continued to undertake shorter journeys.

Earlier in the same year Mary had gained fame as an author, with the publication of her book *Old Indian Trails in the Canadian Rockies*.[5] She had had her first article published in 1904 and since then had written for numerous newspapers, magazines, scientific and mountaineering journals. Her stories were based on material gathered from her experiences on the trail.

Old Indian Trails received favorable reviews in newspapers across the continent. One reviewer wrote that Mary's life "would have little appeal to the average woman whose time is divided between her dressmaker's, her clubs and the management of her maids." Mary's descriptions of the mountains, camplife and the packstring are as much a delight to read today as they were at the time of their publication. She conveyed a sense of excitement and risk, as well as the details of a careful observer and lover of nature.

Mary was once sent a copy of *Trails* to inscribe that seemed

---

5. In 1980 the Whyte Foundation reissued the book under the title *A Hunter of Peace*. It includes the previously unpublished account of her 1911 expedition.

to have a dead fly smacked into it every few leaves—a "long and lonely game." With a wry sense of humor she inscribed the owner's name and added "it's the most perfect fly-catcher I have ever seen, all but the flies on the Athabaska."

She frequently expressed indignation at the "rot" written by others who traveled only briefly through country she knew so well. She especially detested eastern writers who spruced up their stories by stretching the truth about local color and sketching the people of the west according to their own preconceived notions.

Mary spent the winter of 1912 in her beloved Banff as a test, with the idea of moving there permanently. Upon Mary's request, Billy Warren bought a house for her in 1913, which she called Tarry-a-while. She retreated to Banff to be peaceful and alone—all of her previous homes were tainted by death.

In 1915, at the age of 54, she married Billy Warren, who was devoted to her despite their considerable difference in age (she was 20 years older). The relationship was based on mutual respect and admiration. After marrying, Warren still did some trapping, and Mary occasionally accompanied him on scouting forays. But Warren sensed the coming changes in the outfitting business, and with Mary's financial assistance he expanded his operations into local business enterprises. He was a good businessman, having learned much from his father about bookkeeping. This enabled them to live comfortably. Mary quite enjoyed having money, for the freedom it gave her to travel and to live in her chosen home.

Mary spent her remaining years taking short trail trips when healthy (she was plagued all her life by neuritis), and entertaining friends and acquaintances from far and wide with stories of her travels. People always wanted to meet the famous author, and to buy her books.

Her door was aways open to friends, relatives and acquaintances. In later years Mary surrounded herself with young people, organizing many activities for them, such as Sunday evening bridge at her place—win, lose or draw, each participant was awarded a prize. It was unfortunate that she never had children of her own, for she loved them, saying that "there are so many mothers God never gave a child and here is one." Mary's pet monkey and parrot were a real attraction to neighborhood children.

In July, 1924, the Trail Riders of the Canadian Rockies mistakenly awarded Mary the badge for having ridden only 200 miles (320 km). She was indignant, of course, for "I know I have at least 8000 [miles] to my credit!" This was later corrected, and she was given the badge for over 2500 miles (4000 km).

While touring in California Mary was quite taken with a talking parrot, and she wanted to buy it. The man said that Charlie Chaplin had offered $5000, inferring that she couldn't come close to that. After all, she was wearing "last year's" clothes. So she offered another thousand on top of anything Charlie would offer. "I was not scared that I might have to face several thousand for a bird, but I did think he thought me rather shabby." Mary seemed to take pleasure in dressing in nondescript clothes and being "looked down upon" by snobbish women whose attitudes changed once they knew her status in life.

Mary's health began to deteriorate in the early 1930s, after a series of falls and an automobile accident, and about this time Billy also began to experience heart trouble. Mary died on January 23, 1939, and Billy Warren died four years later.

A city-bred woman of many talents—artist, photographer, journalist, writer, lecturer—Mary will be best remembered for her encompassing and contagious love of the mountain wilderness. With the railways and roads entering her beloved valleys, Mary bemoaned the changes she saw:

> We went; we went year by year; we watched the little chalets grow, watched our secret haunts laid bare to all who came ... point by point, we fled to them all, as the dawn of the knowledge of the hills grew, each one a stronghold on civilization's limits. In them we learned the secret of comfort, content and peace on very little of the world's material goods, learned to value at its true worth the great unlonely silences of the wilderness.

She once wrote to a friend that "they like to say 'explorer' of me; no, only a hunter of peace. I found it."

Elizabeth Parker
(1856-1944)

Arthur O. Wheeler was a Canadian surveyor who had made extensive use of photo-topographical surveying techniques. With this need to get to the tops of mountains he mastered the art of climbing under the tutelage of the guides at Glacier House. With new-found enthusiasm for the sport he wrote an article entitled "Canadians as Mountaineers," but to his disappointment, it drew slight response. After continued "scepticism and indifference" from Canadians, Wheeler accepted the idea of forming a Canadian branch of a proposed North American Alpine Club. The idea was suggested by Charles Fay, president of the Appalachian Mountain Club (formed in 1876). The other major American mountaineering organization, the American Alpine Club, had been more recently formed in 1901. In 1905 Wheeler wrote letters to many leading newspapers in an effort to gain support for this idea.

Shortly thereafter Wheeler received a copy of the *Manitoba Free Press*, with a review of his just-published book *The Selkirk Range.* The reviewer chastised him for being unpatriotic in even suggesting the idea of joining an American club, writing that:

I, myself, am ashamed to record that when I have made the mountaineering appeal these fifteen years to healthy, vigorous prosperous and even intellectual compatriots of my own, I have usually received one response "What's the good of that hard work, and risking your life? The Americans are welcome to get to the summits of the Rocky mountains first. They have plenty of money and leisure." ... It knocks me speechless and fills me with shame for young Canada. I understand there is a movement on foot for the formation of a Canadian Alpine club in affiliation with the American club. I ... would protest against Alpine organization on any such basis. We are, and always shall be, profoundly grateful, as we ought to be, to the American club for its strenuous and splendid gratuitous service to Canada and her mountains. And we shall give it the praise and welcome it to further mountain tours. But we owe it to our own young nationhood in simple self-respect, to begin an organized system of mountaineering on an independent basis. Surely, between Halifax and Victoria, there can be found at least a dozen persons who are made of the stuff, and care enough about our mountain heritage to redeem Canadian apathy and indifference. It is simply amazing that for so long we have cared so little.

The gauntlet had been thrown! The article, signed simply "M.T.," took Wheeler roundly to task: "declaimed my action as unpatriotic, chided my lack of imperialism and generally gave me a pen-lashing in words sharper than a sword." Such an accusation aroused his interest and his ire, and he wrote to "M.T.", and was surprised to dicover that his "Dear Sir" was a woman columnist for the paper, Mrs. Elizabeth Parker of Winnipeg.

Elizabeth berated readers of her columns for leaving "the hardships and the triumphs of first ascents to foreigners." She wrote: "Is the mountaineering prestige gained by climbing our high mountains to be held by Americans and Englishmen?" She advocated that a strong alpine club could help improve the moral fabric of the nation.

Wheeler was still dubious about the success of organizing a strictly Canadian club, but Elizabeth was adamant that patriotism would take root. He continued his correspondence with Fay, who reminded him that the term America stood for the entire continent, a statement which Elizabeth scoffed at— to her it had "a national not geographical significance." She was also worried about the eagle, an obviously American symbol, on the club's crest. Elizabeth soon convinced Wheeler of the necessity for a truly Canadian club.

Elizabeth also convinced her editor, J. W. Dafoe, to open the newspaper's columns for the promotion of the club. He, too, became a very strong supporter. Elizabeth's propaganda campaign, along with similar views aired by Rev. Dr. Herdman in the *Calgary Herald,* and letters by Wheeler, made other papers take notice. In this way the ground was prepared for the organization of a Canadian alpine club.

The advocates were soon busy answering inquiries and accepting names for membership. Wheeler approached William Whyte, second vice-president of the Canadian Pacific Railway, for their sponsorship, securing 20 railway passes to bring selected delegates together for a meeting. The meeting was held on March 27-28, 1906, at Winnipeg. Elizabeth had tirelessly arranged accommodation, meeting places and luncheon engagements. At the first meeting Wheeler was elected president, Elizabeth secretary, and her daughter Jean became the librarian. The temporary headquarters were to be at the Parker home. Thus began Elizabeth's life-long involvement with the Alpine Club of Canada (ACC).

Although a driving force behind the formation of the ACC, and a lover of the mountains, Elizabeth was not a mountaineer herself, having climbed no higher than treeline on Cascade Mountain. Rather, she was one of the "unknown company which scales the rock and cuts the ice-stairway in imagination only."

Elizabeth Parker was born in Colchester County, Nova Scotia, on December 19, 1856, to George Fulton and Mary Tupper Fulton. Her mother died when she was only two years old; her father remarried. She always credited her stepmother with directing and developing her interests and tastes in literature: as her ill stepmother lay in bed, Elizabeth would read to her. Elizabeth received a good education in the public schools and then attended normal school at Truro, where she obtained her teaching certificate. She taught school for only one year before marrying Henry John Parker at the age of 18.

The founding members of the Alpine Club of Canada: Elizabeth Parker is in the front row, and Jean Parker behind her. Arthur O. Wheeler is on Elizabeth's right.

The newlyweds moved to Halifax, where they lived for a number of years. In Halifax, Elizabeth immersed herself in literary clubs and organizations and attended lectures at Dalhousie University. The Parkers had three children: sons Henry and James Glen, and daughter Jean. In 1892 the family moved to Winnipeg. In Winnipeg, Elizabeth also kept up her literary interests, as well as joining a number of church and charitable organizations.

It was attendance at a recital of the works of the poet Robert Browning, of whom Elizabeth was a great admirer, that sparked her career as a literary critic. Enthusiastic about the readings, Elizabeth complained to an editor at the *Manitoba Free Press* that the paper was not giving sufficient appreciation to the series of recitals. The fellow told her to "write one yourself, but don't make it too long!" Her first report appeared on January 13, 1904. Thus began a series of weekly, and later daily, "causeries" on books and authors that continued with few interruptions for nearly four decades. She believed in touching even unworthy or mediocre books "as gently as possible," often finding something to praise in any literary work. In no way did she consider her critical reviews as "highbrow." Over the years the name of her columns varied: The Free Press Causeries, Literary News of the Day, and A Reader's Notes. Hers was the only daily literary column in the country. Occasionally her articles appeared on the editorial page. She used three pennames in her columns: "M.T." (the initials of her mother's maiden name), "A.L.O.W." (for A Lady of Winnipeg) or simply "The Bookman." She received hundreds of letters of support and appreciation over the years, which sparked a voluminous correspondence with readers, authors and publishers the world over.

A decade after moving to Winnipeg, though, Elizabeth's never-robust health deteriorated. In the summer of 1904 she moved to Banff for the rejuvenating mountain air and to "take the waters," as it was called then, at the Banff hot springs. Elizabeth and the children lived there for 18 months before rejoining Mr. Parker in Winnipeg. It was during this time that she gained her appreciation of the mountains, and she became one of the first people in Canada to write regularly about them in newspapers and magazines.

While living in Banff, Elizabeth visited Lake Louise, Field and Glacier House. From Field she took the coach to Emerald Lake, stopping on the way to visit the natural bridge over the Kicking Horse River. She stayed at the Emerald Lake chalet which "opened homely friendly doors to us as the old Lake Louise chalet used to do before compelled to hotel fashions by the invading tourist horde." From Emerald Lake she took a horseback trip to Yoho Pass, to a point overlooking Takakkaw Falls. She was a bit disappointed with the overall view of the valley, having expected it to be flanked by soaring mountains overhung with glaciers and snow cornices. The falls, though, fulfilled her expectations, with the cascades shattering into "millions of feathery crystals" before reaching the base of the mountain. Rather than returning to Emerald Lake, the party followed the new trail over Burgess Pass and down to Field.

Elizabeth also spent a few days at Lake Louise. One afternoon she made the short excursion to the Saddleback, with its views of Mount Temple and Paradise Valley. She was startled by the shrill human-like whistle of the marmot. Another day she rode to Moraine Lake and the Valley of the Ten Peaks. She found the trail a series of delights, from the mushrooms on the edges to the sweet trailside strawberries and the glistening glaciers. She wrote glowing articles for the *Free Press* about these grand holiday spots, encouraging readers to go there for "inspiration and refreshment."

After the formation of the ACC Elizabeth regularly attended the annual camps—until 1913, when deteriorating health prevented her from traveling that far from Winnipeg. The annual camp was extremely important as it was frequently the only function the far-off members could attend. Although the ACC hadn't intended to be exclusive, it was initially the reserve of middle- and upper-class professionals. They were the only ones that could afford to attend the camp, around which the mountaineering program was centred. But, in later decades many ordinary Canadians were introduced to the sport. In its earliest years the ACC was very influential in the mountain parks. It was to play an active part in promoting recreation, particularly climbing and mountaineering, and in lobbying the parks to improve trails, campsites and roads.

In her writings Elizabeth also espoused a conservation ethic. In the first issue of the *Canadian Alpine Journal,* in 1907, she wrote that

> the Alpine Club is a national trust for the defence of our mountain solitudes against the intrusion of steam and electricity and all the vandalisms of this luxurious, utilitarian age for the keeping free from the grind of commerce, the wooded passes and valleys and alplands of the wilderness. It is the people's right to have primitive access to the remote places of safest retreat from the fever and the fret of the market place and the beaten tracts of life. ... It is the Club's business to support the picturesque and wholly enjoyable transit to the mountain-places by pack-horse and saddle, and to promote the too much neglected exercise of walking. ... It would be a great thing for young Canadians if all the automobiles vanished into space and walking for pleasure became the fashion.

Jean Parker, Elizabeth's daughter, also attended the camps. She was a small person and Ed Feuz, Jr., described her as being "the neatest little climber I ever had in my young days." She had three climbing seasons between 1906 and 1909. During that time she climbed the Vice President (3066 m), mounts Wapta (2778 m), Temple (3543 m), Whyte (2983 m), Tupper (2816 m), Sir Donald (3297 m), Victoria (3464 m), The Mitre (2889 m) and the Wiwaxy Peaks (2703 m). Mount Tupper and The Mitre were second ascents. They climbed Mount Tupper from the Rogers Hut (now called the Hermit Hut). Jean did not enjoy the trail:

> Nothing is too bad to say about that trail. It is very steep, very stony, and, on this occasion, very wet and slippery and altogether stupid. I found it necessary to stop often, and my stalwart companion felt anxious, as he afterwards confessed, about my staying powers for the real climb. However, we reached the hut at six o'clock. Once arrived, it is a favourable place for a bivouac, for the view is well worth a longer and more tedious climb.

Jean became a member of the Ladies' Alpine Club of

Whyte Museum of the Canadian Rockies

Jean Parker with guide Edward Feuz, Jr., on the left, and a Mr. Watson, 1906.

England[1] in 1911 and served as its Canadian vice-president from 1922 until 1967. She also joined the Ladies' Scottish Climbing Club (founded in 1907) in 1911. Her last ACC camp was also at Mount Robson in 1913. At their comfortable home in Winnipeg, Elizabeth and Jean extended their hospitality to local club members and visiting mountaineers alike.

One of Elizabeth's favorite areas was the Selkirk Mountains.

1. The Ladies' Alpine Club was formed in 1907, as the prestigious Alpine Club, also of England, did not allow women to join. In 1975 the two clubs amalgamated under the name of the latter.

"No man (and the word includes woman) can climb above these forests and over these glaciers, measuring these peaks with their own footsteps, without becoming thrall to the snowy Selkirks." In 1911 she and Wheeler co-authored *The Selkirk Mountains— A Guide for Mountain Pilgrims and Climbers.* Elizabeth wrote the text based upon Wheeler's explorations in 1901, 1902 and 1905, aided by information from other contributors. (The "Miss Canada" climber in the book is Jean Parker.)

Elizabeth contributed frequently to many Canadian, American and British magazines and journals. In Canada her articles appeared in *The Dalhousie Review* and *Scribner's.* And the *Canadian Alpine Journal* was rarely without her articles and book reviews.

Elizabeth viewed the mountains in a very romatic way, influenced no doubt by Victorian writers such as Ruskin. In her writings there is a loyalty to Romantic thought: the mountains represented spiritual, moral and political freedom. There is also a tone of high moral purpose that seems essentially Victorian.

> Our interest in Nature is rooted deep in human emotion. The relation may be closer, but that is beyond my comprehension. That there is mystery in the influence of Nature over those who meet her half way is beyond dispute, but I think the mystery is not in Nature herself, but in the methods employed by her Maker and ours, Him who moves in a mysterious way.

There is also a faint tone of colonial defensiveness, where the establishment of a Canadian climbing club had to be justified and explained.

Through her columns Elizabeth educated Canadians about their mountains. She reviewed current mountaineering and exploration books, such as *The Rockies of Canada* by Walter Wilcox, *Climbs and Explorations in the Rockies* by Collie and Stutfield, and *The Heart of the Canadian Rockies* by James Outram. Although she was a kind critic, she could also be caustic: "I have read accounts of distinguished mountaineers of exploring and climbing in the Canadian Alps, which had no more of the breath of nature in them than there is in a hardware invoice."

One of her favorite correspondents was Tom Wilson, from whom she collected stories and historical facts for a book that she was planning on the Canadian Rockies. "The early history of the Mt. places is very important if we are to have a complete alpine literature. And the *beginnings* of anything become more important as the years go on." She was always searching for "authentic facts." She contributed historical articles to the *Canadian Alpine Journal* but unfortunately never finished her proposed book.

In 1931 Elizabeth was honored by having the ACC hut at Lake O'Hara in Yoho National Park named for her. In that year the ACC exchanged its original lease on the shore of the lake for a lease in a nearby meadow. Two cabins on the site, owned by the Canadian Pacific Railway and operated as a bungalow camp, were donated to the club. The main cabin (built in 1919) was renovated and furnished by the Winnipeg section of the ACC. She humbly felt that it should be called the "Winnipeg Hut," but it was named the Elizabeth Parker Hut. The second building, called the Annex, is the original Wiwaxy Lodge. It was built for the Parks department in 1911 by the Swiss guides, and had served as a shelter for climbing parties.

Elizabeth was well-known as a stickler for accuracy, but she also had a quiet sense of humor. In an article in the *Canadian Alpine Journal* Wheeler told this apocryphal story:

> At our Mt. Robson camp in 1913, the first one, the distance from the railway station to the camp, nineteen miles, was too far for her to walk, so she was provided with a pony, which followed along behind the pack train, led by Jack Otto, an old time outfitter and trail guide. Jack had a yell of his own to keep the ponies on the move. It sounded like "Yo! upp!" "Yo! upp!" and was frequently applied. Presently, a voice came faintly from the rear "Jack, how do you spell that?" At that moment a commotion occurred among the ponies in front, commonly called a "jackpot," when the leading pony turns off the trail to snatch a bite of grass and breaks back into the following line. All was confusion. I saw Jack take a reef in his belt, but he refrained from using the only language thoroughly understood by pack ponies, in respect for the lady with the party. The same faint voice again came up from the rear "Jack! say damn." Jack took another reef in his belt and turning to me said, "Wouldn't that knock you."

Elizabeth Parker died on October 26, 1944. She was predeceased by her husband in 1920, and by her sons. Her daughter Jean died in October, 1967, in Winnipeg.

Elizabeth Parker was gifted with a ready pen, and had immense enthusiasm for the Canadian mountains. Through her articles in the newspaper and magazines, personal correspondence with prominent Canadians, and interviews, she was a moving force in the formation and success of a national mountaineering club.

Mary Jobe Akeley
(1878-1966)

Mary Jobe was a young American schoolteacher who yearned to be an explorer. As the 20th century dawned she was looking for a frontier to explore, and in doing so she discovered the mountains of western Canada. Her first interest was in native peoples, but she soon turned her attention to mountaineering and searching out the little-traveled areas of the northern Rockies. Her desire to achieve recognition as a bona fide explorer had a somewhat desperate quality, and at times her efforts and expeditions seemed almost contrived, with that end in mind. Nevertheless, she did bring attention to a new area north of Jasper National Park. Later she became known for her support of African parks.

Mary Lenore (Lee) Jobe,[1] was born on January 29, 1878, in Tappan, Ohio, to Richard Watson Jobe and Sarah Jane Pittis. She had one sister. Mary's early childhood, growing up in the hills of eastern Ohio, undoubtedly influenced her lifelong outdoor activities. She tramped 5 km a day to school, where she excelled in geography, English and history. Her parents were both college educated, and they encouraged Mary to seek higher education, providing a private tutor to prepare her for college. Mary was an athletic person, described by friends as a "plucky young brunette."

---

1. The "e" is silent, thus Jobe rhymes with "lobe".

In 1897 Mary graduated from Scio College (now Mount Union College) in Alliance, Ohio, with a Bachelor of Arts in Philosophy. She then did postgraduate work from 1901 to 1903 at Bryn Mawr College. During this time she taught night classes at Temple University in nearby Philadelphia. From 1903 until 1906 she taught history at a state college in Cortland, New York. Mary then moved to New York City, where she taught history at the normal college (now Hunter) from 1906 until 1916. During this time she completed courses to earn a master's degree in English and American history from Columbia University in 1909. She later attended graduate courses towards a doctorate, but she discontinued her studies, only four points short of a degree, for financial reasons.

Mary's first visit to the Canadian west was on a three-month trip in 1905 when she joined college friends in the Selkirk Mountains of British Columbia. She traveled up the west coast of the United States to Spokane, Washington, and then took a train north to Nelson and Rossland. The train stopped at the international border long enough for the passengers to enjoy the Dominion Day celebrations. With her interest in native people, she was enthralled.

> Riding races, polo, sack races, hurdle races, etc., were on the programme. Beyond the track on a slight elevation, a sort of natural terrace, a strange-looking crowd was gathered. ... Men in white and in yellow khaki suits and shiny boots; wagons of all sorts, horses, dogs and children lined the sides of the track and stretched up the rising ground. At the rear, thirty lodges of Indians (Kootenai) had stationed themselves, the young braves lounging up and down in shirts and blankets that dazzled the eyesight when the sun struck them ... while the chiefs leaned over the wooden barrier, surveying the scene, and the squaws crowded at their feet.

By a combination of railway and stern-wheeler, Mary continued to Revelstoke, the centre of a thriving lumber and mining industry. Being a day early her friends were not there to meet her, so she hired a buggy to reach their camp on the banks of the Columbia River only five kilometres out of town. The group was under the leadership of botanist Dr. Charles H. Shaw, of the University of Pennsylvania. In a spirit of adventure they dubbed themselves the "Selkirk Pathfinders."

From the base camp members of the group took expeditions to gold mines, lumber camps and fruit orchards throughout the Columbia River Valley. At one gold mine they spent three hours inside searching for gold, which was "deadening to enthusiasm as well as to jack-knives," and did not even catch a gleam of the precious metal.

The foreman of one lumber company gave them a tour of towns and camps 25 km inland from the Arrow Lakes. Her diary was filled with notations on the lumbering work and life. She noted that the lumberjacks were paid from $2.50 to $3.00 per day and then had to pay $1.00 per day for their room and board. She also measured 37 trees to obtain an average diameter from which to calculate the number of board feet obtainable.

They also made excursions by packtrain and foot further to the north. On one three-day trip Mary was one of only four women, three of whom were schoolteachers, in a party of eight people. They went on a ten-day trip later, in an unsuccessful attempt to penetrate the mountain barrier on the east side of the valley. Mary found Shaw's belief in the ability and efficiency of women as explorers greatly encouraging. He felt that it was only a matter of time before women would equal men in such pursuits.[2]

Mary then headed east, stopping at Glacier House, Banff and places across the Canadian prairies.

In 1909 Ben S. Comstock, an American Alpine Club member from New York, invited Mary to join an expedition to the headwaters of the Gold River in the Selkirks. To encourage her he said that another woman, Bess MacCarthy, would also be along, and that he felt the two of them would get along splendidly. Professor Hershel C. Parker (head of the physics department at Columbia University in New York) and Howard Palmer (a lawyer from Connecticut) were heading the expedition for the Dominion Topographical Survey. They wanted to climb the "White Elephant," more properly known

---

2. Tragically, Shaw drowned in 1910 while alone in a canoe on Kinbasket Lake during yet another botanical excursion in the Selkirks.

as Mount Sir Sandford (3530 m).

The group left Golden on June 14th. The five expedition members were being guided by Emanuel Dainard of Golden and they hired four woodsmen as packers and trailmakers. The women were in a wooden canoe and the three men in a new canvas canoe. Bess paid for the employ of two of the men and rent of the extra canoe. From Beavermouth, on the Canadian Pacific Railway (CPR) line west of Golden, they traveled by canoe down the flooding Columbia River and then west up the Gold River.

After negotiating some rapids on the Gold River the second day, they repacked and took to the woods. A food cache had been established at a hunter's cabin beforehand. Their food supplies included bacon, sausage, beans, beef, flour, potatoes, onions, butter, malted milk, chocolate, raisins, figs, prunes, pickles, sugar, maple syrup, tea, jam, marmalade, rice, oatmeal, cheese, and bread made in a Dutch oven.

Each day the men would cut trail; when a suitable location was reached they would move the camp there and proceed to cut more trail. The trail-clearing in the valley was horrendous: narrow canyons were choked with downed timber, alder thickets, muskeg and the ever-present devil's-club (a tall plant that has spines on the stem and underside of the leaves). And over all was the torment of hordes of mosquitoes. The Gold River area was referred to by early explorers as the "Mosquito Captial of the World." Occasional avalanche paths added the tangled chaos of old tree trunks to their troubles. Mary felt that they were spending too much time camping and could have proceeded without clearing the trail so well. Her opinion was that the guides were slowing things down to get more pay for a longer trip. A few days into their expedition they realized that because of the slow progress they would soon run low on provisions, so two of the guides were sent back to Golden to get more. This, of course, delayed their progress even further.

Mary carried a large knife, for which she drew comments such as: "Aren't you afraid to carry it?" and "A bear would run from that." While alone at camp one day she carried her ice axe with her when she went to fetch water, for fear of bears.

On a couple of occasions Palmer and Parker scrambled above treeline to judge their progress. One day Bess accompanied them up the slopes of Mount Taurus for a view to the headwaters of the Gold River. They finally reached the head of the valley on June 22 and set up their base camp below the tongue of the Sir Sandford Glacier. It had taken them eight days to travel the 40 km from Beavermouth. Upon first sighting the glacier Mary pronouced it "almost terrifying in its stupendous proportions," extending down from far above. They spent days reconnoitering nearby ridges and snowfields. A trip up the main glacier was cut short by a snowstorm. Mary was overawed by the mountain, and she "felt the sheer folly of attempting it with our present equipment."

Their days at the base camp were ones of rain and snow. Delayed by the slow trail-clearing and poor weather, Comstock had to return to business engagements in New York. Mary and Bess left with him, while Palmer and Parker stayed longer. They did not succeed in scaling the mountain, either.

Mary and Bess stayed to explore the Columbia Valley for a number of weeks and then proceeded to the 1909 Alpine Club of Canada (ACC) camp at Lake O'Hara. As they embarked from the CPR train a man circumspectly studied the label on Mary's trunk and then just as keenly studied her. "Obviously, such bronzed, trail-tattered feminine wanderers were as much of a rarity at the Annual Camp of the Canadian Alpine Club as would be a coyote in the streets of New York." While at the camp Mary climbed Mount Schaffer (2692 m) and explored the myriads of trails in the area.

Then they were invited on a two-day circle trip traversing five of the high passes: Opabin, Wenkchemna, Wastach, Mitre Col and Abbot. Their equipment consisted of "the simplest and most practical of climbing costumes—sweaters, knickerbockers, heavy hob-nailed boots, and soft felt hats, while we carried only necessities—ruck-sacks, ice-axes, snow glasses, mittens, extra coats, and the most sustaining of all foods, chocolate." Leaving Lake O'Hara they climbed quickly over the

Mary Jobe and Bess MacCarthy, at Lake O'Hara, 1909.

glacier-bound Opabin Pass and then labored over Wenkchemna Pass to the Valley of the Ten Peaks. They traversed high above Moraine Lake and then climbed over their third pass, Wastach, which dropped them into Paradise Valley, where a prepared camp awaited them. It was a mountaineers' scramble of slightly over six hours, and they arrived in "spif" condition. The men went short on blankets that night so that the ladies could sleep warmly.

In the morning they breakfasted on toast, porridge, tea and coffee before scrambling up to Mitre Col. The descent from it was hampered by blowing snow, which rapidly filled in the steps that the guide cut. The piercing sleet cut their faces. The storm was soon over, but with the sunshine and fresh snow came the ominous roar of avalanches from all sides. Rightfully fearing to attempt the couloir to Abbot Pass (named the "Death Trap") in such conditions, they unanimously agreed to retreat to the Chateau Lake Louise for the night. At the Chateau they encountered tourists of the "swell-loafer" variety, who wanted to know if they were Indians, if they used their ice axes to chop down trees, and why the women were wearing knickers!

The following morning they were on the trail in the weak dawn light, so that they could climb up to Abbot Pass before the summer sun sent avalanches down the chute. On the Victoria Glacier they jumped numerous crevasses. It was Mary's first experience among crevasses and she was fearful.

> "Can you make that?" asked the Guide, as he lightly leaped over a crevasse five feet wide. Could I? For once in my life I would have exchanged places gladly with one of my simian ancestors. A little tightening of the rope ahead—I had the feeling of being coaxed as an obstreperous monkey is wheedled by the hand-organ man, a desperate resolve, a mighty upheaval of hobnailed boots, and I struck the other side, shaking and terrorized.

They traveled as swiftly as possible through the Death Trap and duly arrived on the "high tower of the world." They enjoyed the encompassing views of ranges of mountain peaks while eating lunch in the sunshine. Then it was down the scree, a glissade to the lake and back to camp. The trip was their first exposure to the splendor of the mountains and the feeling of accomplishment that comes from such a challenging activity.

The following summer, 1910, Mary was back in the Rockies. In August she took a packtrip to Mount Assiniboine via Healy Creek. From camp, she was enthralled as Assiniboine shone against "a background of black changing to deep blue, deep amethyst and then lavender before it merged with the blue grayness of the early light." After returning from Assiniboine she joined a packtrip going north of Banff to Baker Lake and the headwaters of the Red Deer River. As they hit the trail they stopped at the mining town of Bankhead to buy tobacco and peaches.[3]

In 1912 Mary spent a few days climbing around Lake Louise, where she ascended Mount Temple (3543 m). She then joined Jack Brewster's packtrip from Lake Louise to Jasper along the valleys paralleling the Great Divide. They traveled along the Bow, the North Saskatchewan and the Sunwapta rivers. From the Sunwapta they headed east over Maligne Pass to Maligne Lake and then to Jasper via Shovel Pass, the route pioneered by Mary Schäffer in 1908 and 1911.

During the New York City winters Mary lectured about her Canadian adventures to schools, resorts and institutions. Her lantern-slide shows were well received. She also began writing articles for magazines. She exhorted the reader to go to the mountains.

> But you are not a mountain climber, you say? Well, if you do not clamber, go into the mountains on the back of a cayuse and if you cannot or will not ride ... then see the mountains from the window of an observation train and from the piazza of the luxurious mountain hotels ... but go, at any cost, and live among the mountains, forgetting that there is anything else in life, save freedom, jubilant activity and the sweet sleep of night time.

Mary's interest in aboriginal people came to the forefront in 1913 when she journeyed to northern British Columbia and Alaska to gather information on the language, customs and history of the Indian tribes there, particularly the Gitksan

---

3. The coal-mining town of Bankhead existed in Banff National Park, along the road to Lake Minnewanka, from 1905 until just after the First World War. Its coal was used in large quantities during the war to fuel troop-ships.

Indians. She visited Skeena River, Kitwanga and Hazelton. At Hazelton she hired a saddle horse to go to Babine Fort for four days at $3 per day. She recorded that the locals referred, tongue-in-cheek, to the Hudson's Bay Company as "Here Before Christ." She hired two Indian guides for a further ten weeks travel. Her notebook is filled with notes on Indian ways, ceremonies, food, language, marriage customs and so on. Her solo adventure received wide publicity in New York. She was touted as the first white woman to explore the region, but one woman wrote the *New York Times*, rightfully chiding it for such an elitist statement, mentioning the numerous wives and daughters of missionaries and fur traders who had been there many years before.

She ended her ethnographic expedition at Tête Jaune Cache where she joined the Alpine Club for its annual camp being held at Robson Pass. While at the camp Mary was intrigued about stories of a magnificent peak to the north being sighted from the high summits by climbers. It had been noted the previous year by Samuel Prescott Fay, of Boston, who had seen it from the north. That same fall Curly Phillips had also seen it while hunting on the Smoky River. During the following winter Mary made plans for an expedition to search for it. It was her opportunity to do some real exploring and perhaps achieve a first ascent.

Curly Phillips, the Jasper guide who had outfitted for the ACC camp, was duly hired for the summer of 1914 at a cost of $16.50 per day. Her companion was Margaret Springate of Winnipeg, who had also been at the 1913 camp.

They left Grant Brook, a railway station west of Jasper, on July 30. After three days traveling through the muskeg and burnt timber along the Moose River they reached the lovely alpine slopes of Moose Pass. From nearby Mount Pamm [4] (2829 m) they saw "a great pyramid of snow and rock" far to the north which towered above its neighbors. It was Mary's first view of

---

4. Mount Pamm was named by Caroline Hinman in 1913 and is not officially recognized by the Geographical Names Board of Canada.

what she named "Mount Kitchi," after a Cree word meaning "mighty."

They camped at Berg Lake for a few days while Curly returned to Jasper for more supplies and the rifle that he had forgotten. He brought news back that war had just erupted between France and Germany. On August 7th, Bert Wilkins, Curly's brother-in-law and assistant, joined them with more horses. They immediately set out down the Smoky River then

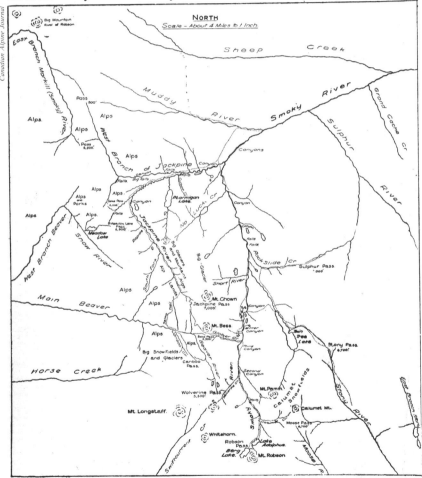

Curly Phillips's sketch of the Mount Robson region.

up Chown Creek and over the shoulder of Mount Bess to Jackpine Pass. In Bess Pass they found well-used bear trails, where the animals had all stepped in the same track, wearing a deep path.

Traveling northward along the valley of the Jackpine River, they saw many game trails of goat, moose and caribou. Curly shot a goat and they lunched on fried goat, rice and gravy washed down with the ever-present tea. From a couple of Curly's winter caches and cabins they obtained more provisions. Leaving the Jackpine behind they took to the ridges of the Great Divide, which was good traveling but frequently interrupted by valleys and passes running east-and-west across their path. They had to cut trails through these thickly forested low points; on one hill the men cut 28 switchbacks for the trail. Mary was exasperated by the shintangle of downed logs and "rhodies," or Rocky Mountain rhododendron growth. Graze was not always plentiful and more than once the horses were "feeding on a stonepile."

At the end of three weeks travel from the railway the party was within striking distance of Mount Kitchi. On August 19th, taking only four days worth of provisions, they started off on foot for the mountain. The women's packs weighed only about 7 kg and the men carried the rest. The women each carried an eiderdown quilt, personal belongings and their heavy cameras, while the men carried the small tent, one frying pan, two small pails, four cups and spoons, and the food. The men had a small canvas bed-cover in lieu of a blanket. As a precaution they left a blaze on a tree, with a description of their route and destination. When Curly gallantly offered to carry them across a stream Margaret replied that "if one can't wade a stream, how could one expect to climb a mountain?"

On the first day of the hike Curly and Mary were unexpectedly charged by a black bear which stopped only two metres away. Bert rushed up with the rifle, and Curly shot and wounded it. Fortunately the bear turned and ran. Their travel calculations were slightly off and it took them two whole days to reach the mountain, rather than one. They had short rations of bannock, coffee and rice for breakfast, with a bit of chocolate.

On August 22 Curly, Bert and Mary attempted to climb the mountain but were turned back by crevasses at about 2100 m. While returning to camp Curly killed six ptarmigan, which enabled them to make a mulligan stew for supper. It also served them as breakfast. Desperately low on provisions they headed back for their base camp.

On their return Curly was fortunate enough to shoot a caribou cow and calf. With this stroke of fortune Curly and Mary decided to return immediately to the mountain for another attempt to ascend it. Bert was complaining of rheumatism in his shoulder and continued back to base camp, accompanied by Margaret.

A day later, on August 25, Mary and Curly were again on the mountain. After climbing for hours up the glacier, carefully crossing many crevasses, Curly called back to Mary, asking what she thought of the peak now. "When I stopped and looked up, instead of the long snow slope we anticipated, there shooting up in the sky was a sharp pinnacle of ice and rock like an elongated church steeple. Surely only a steeple jack with his proper paraphernalia could climb it." When they gained the ridge, they took photographs and built a cairn in which they left the date and their names, and the legend "mountain too sporty for our blood." The attempt exhausted Mary and she was very weakened when they finally returned to their base camp. Only sheer willpower enabled her to make it back.

When the party was together once more they lost no time in starting out on the return trip to the railway. With their lighter loads, and blazed trails, it took them only half as long.

Recovered from her previous experience, Mary still wished to make a first ascent, and in an unexplored area to boot. She got her chance in 1915.

This time she was accompanied by Caroline Hinman, whom she had met at the 1913 Robson camp, and who also felt the urge of exploration. As they arrived in Jasper the mountains gleamed in the moonlight, looking "wild and different, romantic & western" in Caroline's eyes.

Once again outfitted by Curly Phillips, they left Robson Station a month earlier than before, on the first of July. Caroline described Curly's assistants—Frank Doucette, "the whirlwind of a packer"; Joe Soper, "the peach of a cook"; and the "three ever cheerful Tyler boys," Arnold, David and John. The Tylers were from New York and had come at Caroline's request as packers. Besides their eight saddle horses, they had fifteen packhorses. The staple items in their provisions were flour, cornmeal, whole wheat, oatmeal, cream-of-wheat, bacon, ham, prunes, raisins, peaches, canned pineapple, apples, chocolates, sardines, tomatoes, peas, corn, rice, beans, onions, dessicated potatoes and jam.

While camped at Mount Robson Curly built a small raft and he and Caroline poled and rowed out on Berg Lake amidst some icebergs. Near Tumbling Glacier they beached and walked up the moraine, tumbling huge rocks off it into the lake. On the way back some ice calved off the glacier front, sending waves across the surface of the lake.

Ten days into their trip they were delayed by a heavy snowfall. But the fresh snowfall did allow for good tracking and Curly spent four hours trailing a caribou before getting close enough to shoot it. After skinning it he headed back to camp carrying 20 kg of the meat. But when he neared camp he saw a moose, and as it was closer than the caribou meat, he shot it. They had fresh caribou steak for breakfast and spent much of the next day preserving the meat. They cut it in strips, covered them with salt and let them stand for three hours, and then dried them on a rack over a slow fire. They frequently found old abandoned hunting camps of Indians from the Grande Cache area; they noted the tepee poles and drying racks.

Slowly the women picked up the picturesque talk of the country, some of which were from the Chinook dialect. "Skookum" meant powerful and "jake" meant all right. After one especially fine day of mountain scrambling they returned to camp to one of Joe's "skookum" meals: "caribou mulligan, broiled moose tender as a sirloin, Johnny cake, tea, potatoes, cornstarch with apricots & cream & wonder of wonders, a chocolate cake!''

Heading to Forget-me-not Pass on a misty day, Mary and Caroline went ahead of the outfit, but at a crucial place they turned in the wrong direction. A while later they saw two of the men silhouetted on the skyline and halloed to them. The men waved back, but obviously did not see them. Unknown to the women, the packtrain was actually ahead of the men and had already turned off the ridge into the other valley. So, thinking they were on the right track, they continued down the valley. After some time they decided to wait for the packtrain. Mary had four matches and used three of them before getting a fire to light. They ate some lunch, dried out a little, and ''halloed ourselves hoarse all to no avail.''

After an hour of waiting Mary suggested proceeding futher down the valley and up to the alpine to look for the horses. Caroline doubted this course of action but agreed to go. They had hard traveling through thick timber and muskeg in the pouring rain and finally decided to stop under a large spruce tree to wait either for the packtrain or for a rescue party. Twenty minutes later the latter arrived in the form of Curly, who had tracked them when he realized they'd gone astray. They were very glad to see him, and when Caroline asked him where the pack train was he said ''where it ought to be over the pass at the end of the next valley!'' Curly led them to camp by a shortcut, but they still arrived at dark, weary and hungry. Over supper everyone had stories to tell. The route over the ridge had been steep and Arnold quipped, ''I had to make Blackie curl up his tail to keep the saddle on coming up the hill.'' Coming down the other side, one pack had slipped over a horse's neck and another had slipped under a belly.

The weather improved as they reached the Great Divide. Forget-me-not Pass was an alpland filled to overflowing with colorful flower displays: red Indian paintbrush, purple asters, yellow buttercups, and, of course, myriads of blue forget-me-nots.

Caroline felt ''far away & remote in these silent woods with no sound but the waving pine boughs & the swish of the river below." It was a relaxed group and everyone got along well. There were many layover days in camp. There were the routine chores to be done, such as washing, sewing and oiling of boots. There was time for writing up a diary or going hiking, climbing, hunting or fishing. The Tyler boys and Frank would frequently show off, doing stunts on the horses, rope-throwing, or swinging from trees. Caroline and Mary developed their films at night. A pack mantle fixed over two logs in the stream was used as a basin for washing the film. The evenings were spent around a campfire in the forest glade or inside one of the tents if it was raining. Card games were popular: Hearts, Pedro, Hangman, Stop Jack and Animals. They played guessing games or read out loud; Robert Service's poems and Dickens's *Pickwick Papers* were popular. Many hours were spent singing songs or simply talking. Caroline's diary is filled with the evident joy of being in the woods, a feeling of great personal well-being, away from the troubles of the outside world.

A camp highlight was a quick bath and swim in some cold lake on a sunny day. Caroline "got into bathing suit w. stockings & raincoat & ran around lake to point where my entrance was hidden from camp" and splashed and swam in the water, feeling much refreshed afterwards.

They only saw one bear, a huge grizzly on an avalanche slope. "When he ran his coat moved in the sunshine like a field of waving, gold-brown grain."

They arrived at the base of Mount Kitchi on July 21. They had taken a slightly different approach than the year before and were camped on the notheast side. Curly, Caroline and David went for a jaunt up the glacier across from camp. Coming back, Curly had cut steps down to the moraine, but Caroline slipped, dragging David feet first after her. Luckily no one was hurt. The next day, from another ridge, Caroline's inspection of the mountain's steep slopes and corniced summit "took away much of the desire I had had to climb it."

Still, four days later they made a strong attempt. As they traveled up the glacier on the 25th, the fresh tracks of a grizzly

Mount Sir Alexander.

Mystic River Historical Society

ran parallel to their route. Caroline noted three or four small birds frozen in the ice, probably having been caught in a snowstorm. The women stopped at a higher point than Mary and Curly had attained the previous year but Curly, Frank and John continued. Caroline and Mary waited anxiously, trying to keep them in view as long as possible. Having not seen the men for some time, and with daylight waning, Caroline had started gathering up stones to form a shelter, when the men again came into sight. Well up on the summit ridge a threatening storm had caused them to turn back without reaching the summit (3270 m). During a later thunderstorm, the glacier looked to Mary like "an abode of black death." It was nearly dark when they glissaded down the snowfield, then crossed a rockslide and waded the stream back to camp.

As the days wore by it became obvious that there was a trail romance in the offing. Caroline noted that "Curlie and Jobie" frequently went off by themselves to take readings with the transit, to take the horses out to graze or to explore the next day's route. Curly would wait for Mary on outings and turn back to camp with her if she tired. Mary's back frequently bothered her and she felt "very disconsolate at not being able to do things well." Sometimes they had their own campfire and once "Mary slept in Curly's lean-to." Curly gave Mary the endearing nickname "Nitchie."

Mary herself wrote about sitting around the campfire with Curly, talking late into the night. Mary was thinking about what she was trying to accomplish on the trip and in her life, and the part Curly was playing in both. "Wild thoughts came to me that night."

It was an idyllic summer spent in the fresh air and splendor of the wilderness.

Curly, accompanied by John and Arnold, left on a backpacking trip to explore the country to the north. Phillips always loved to explore new country, for its own sake as well as for hunting or trapping possibilities. While they were gone the others idled the time away. "Still another day of bridge, solitaire & Pickwick—still steaming hot & plenty of mosquitoes,

Mary Jobe, ca. 1917.

Bull dogs & black flies—managed to find <u>something</u> to do all day & time passed more quickly than seemed possible," wrote Caroline, "but I <u>long</u> for a trip of some sort—a week of doing nothing gets on my nerves." Four days later the men returned, happy with having filled in a few more blank spaces on the map. Arnold had lashed the sole of one boot on with rope.

Caroline gave the horses some salt. Thereafter they had a devil of a time keeping them away fron the grub pile in camp. One horse stole Caroline's silk handkerchief and ran away from her reach, then calmly devoured it!

A few days after Curly returned, the men made another attempt to climb Mount Kitchi. Mary and Caroline watched them from Thunder Ridge behind camp, from where they looked like "flies sticking to a wall." The men were once again turned back, but only 30 m or so from the top this time. Once they had a close look at the dreadful cornices on the summit they all agreed that "there is more in life than being cached in a big ice grotto for all eternity."[5]

On the sixth anniversary of Curly's climb of Mount Robson they had a party.[6] Caroline made up poems and put together special bouquets for everyone. They all dressed up a little, such as they could, and had a nice meal.

On August 4 they made ready to leave their base camp for the long journey home. The horses were quite rambunctious after their layoff. One of them had a "better take care" look on his face when he was brought in. There were a number of small "rodeos" before the outfit was straightened out on the trail.

From their base camp the party headed north through Jarvis Pass and five days later they were down on the Smoky River

5. The long-sought first ascent was made in 1929 by A.J. Gilmour, N.D. Waffl and Helen Buck. They were outfitted by Curly, which was only fitting.

6. In 1909 Curly supported Rev. George Kinney in four attempts to scale Mount Robson, at 3954 m the highest peak in the Canadian Rockies. Kinney claimed to have made the first ascent but Curly later admitted thay they turned back near the summit. The first ascent was made in 1913.

near Grande Cache. They found Ewan Moberly's[7] canoe, about ten metres long and dug out of a single cottonwood tree. It was chained and padlocked to a tree with a notice in English on one side and Cree on the other, saying that anyone using the canoe owed him $10, and $50 if they lost it! So Curly and the men cut 14 logs for a raft, which they lashed together with cinch ropes. It measured seven-by-five-metres and had a seven-metre sweep on the stern. After chasing the horses into the river they placed all of their duffel on the raft and went across in one trip. With Curly manning the sweep and Frank and Arnold manning the two big oars, sitting in the water to their waists, it only took them four minutes to go across the river, landing about a kilometre downstream. They were in good hands; Curly had plenty of river experience from his years spent trapping in northern Ontario. They repacked and continued to the Indian settlement at Grande Cache (a few kilometres southeast of the modern town). Nobody was around and all of the houses were locked or boarded up. They saw Ewan's house, wagon and cattle. There was a small chapel. They appropriated some fresh carrots and turnips from one garden that had been sown just like grass, with no attempt at cultivation or weeding. The fire protection signs were also written in English and Cree.

From Grande Cache they turned south to the Sulphur River, then crossed Hardscrabble Pass and followed Rockslide Creek back to the Smoky River. They had to wait until morning for the level of the Smoky River to drop enough to cross. They then headed upstream toward Mount Robson.

At Chown Creek they split up; Curly, Mary, Caroline, Arnold and David took a sidetrip to climb Mount Bess (3216 m). They had an uneventful but glorious day's climb. Theirs was the second ascent of the peak. As they returned to the Smoky they found Jasper National Park wardens fighting a forest fire. It had been started by four Indians who had been

7. Ewan Moberly was a Metis homesteader in the Athabasca Valley when Jasper National Park was established in 1907. Bought out, he moved to the Grande Cache area in 1910. The cash he had received from the government enabled him to buy cattle and equipment for his new location.

hunting goats illegally in the park and let their campfire get away. The culprits were caught.

Back at the railway they were met by Curly's father, who had brought fresh fruit and vegetables from Jasper as a treat for them. The final dinner was served on two new white pack mantles for a tablecloth. The women found it quite entertaining to get dressed up in civilized clothing again.

The following winter was the last one that Mary spent teaching in New York City. In 1916 she started Camp Mystic (near Mystic, Connecticut), which was a summer camp for girls aged 8 to 18. She believed deeply in encouraging young girls to participate in outdoor living and adventure. Her ideal was to "utilize what was usually considered two lost or wasted months in a young girl's life and coin this time into health, character development, love of out-of-doors, fearlessness that enhances womanliness and self-reliance that comes from the ability to help one's self in the emergencies of life." The camp

From the New York "Times," September 25, 1909

Miss Mary L. Jobe, an instructor in history at the Normal College of this city, and in her student days an athletic Bryn Mawr girl, was a member of the recent Canadian Topographical Survey expedition, exploring in the Big Bend of the Columbia and Mt. Sandford, British Columbia, the highest of the Selkirks.

The party traveled over uncharted rivers, cut through a primeval forest and explored dangerous glacier-clad mountains, bringing back scientific data and a picture history of a region never before penetrated by white men.

While admitting that the trip was strenuous, Miss Jobe says that it was altogether delightful, and that she never felt overtaxed even after a twelve hours climb. She says it is not too difficult for any woman of courage used to outdoor sports and exercise.

MISS JOBE USES *PETER'S MILK CHOCOLATE* ON ALL HER EXPEDITIONS

Page from Mary Jobe Akeley's Camp Mystic brochure.

Mystic River Historical Society

provided training in camp craft, swimming, diving, life saving, boating, arts and crafts, nature study, dramatics, music, horseback riding, dancing, and athletics.

Mary owned a 30-m launch, the "Northern Light," which was rumored to have previously belonged to one of the Canadian railways. She used the boat to transport campers from her site on the Mystic River to Mystic Island (which she owned), in Fishers Island Sound. The island had wonderful beaches and they sometimes camped there.

In her elaborate camp catalogues Mary referred to her background and experience as an explorer and mountain climber in Canada as her qualifications for camp director. Her "camp uniform" was very similar to what she considered the "proper climbing costume" that she wore on her trips. Both were fairly revolutionary for the times. Camp Mystic flourished until 1930.

Mary was also a proponent of nature study for children. "My special plea is that young people should be aroused not only to an added appreciation of our wild animals and the beauties of nature but also to an understanding of the rapid and unfortunate changes which are occurring in our world today."

With the establishment and operation of Camp Mystic, Mary was too busy in the summers to go to Canada at that time of the year. But she was back in Jasper again in the autumn of 1917. She accompanied Curly and Jack Hargreaves on an early-winter trip to cache supplies on the Wapiti River. A few months later Curly was to take William Rindfoos, a photographer from the Smithsonian Institution, on a trapping expedition there.

After four days spent gathering all of their provisions in Jasper they boarded the train for Robson Station. At Curly's corrals they spent two more days shoeing the horses and making up the packs. Finally, on October 10, they got away in the late afternoon. They arrived at the campsite in Robson Pass by starlight and the northern lights.

Their trail led them over familiar territory along the Smoky River over Bess Shoulder and Jackpine Pass, then down the

Jackpine River. From there they traversed the headwaters of the Muddywater River and crossed Sheep Creek Pass to the Porcupine River. Skirting the headwaters of Providence Creek they approached Mount Sir Alexander (Mary's "Mount Kitchi," officially named in 1916) from the northeast.[8] From there they traveled north to the Wapiti River. They returned via Compton Creek and the Smoky to Grande Cache. They then followed a provincial forestry trail along the Muskeg, Baptiste and Wildhay Rivers to Entrance, west of Hinton.

Just over Jackpine Pass they were delayed by a snowstorm. The storm was spectacular as "big fleecy snow clouds roiled up to the mountain tops." The Jackpine Valley was the "old, familiar, unending trail of roots, bumps, streams, mud holes and then stretches of muskeg." Mary's horse, Pet, broke into a beaver burrow in a riverbank and she had to jump off and roll away as he plunged through it. The valley was an oft-flooded network of beaver houses, trails and burrows. Curly had to tear a hole in one beaver dam to lower the water level so that they could cross the middle fork of the Jackpine.

On the early part of the trip there were berries in abundance. The horses loved the dry stocks of the fireweed plant. An occasional brave flower still survived through the fall frosts. There were few birds, most having already migrated south.

While trying to reach a good camp over the Great Divide late one day, they were caught in a snow squall on the pass. While plunging through snowdrifts, leading her horse, Mary became fearful of getting stepped on so she drove him on ahead. The snow was so thick she could only see a few metres. Some horses refused to go and had to be tailed (the halter shank from one horse tied to the tail of the horse in front). "Never before had I pulled a horse uphill backwards," said Jack. In the blizzard Curly went ahead to locate the trail off the ridge and broke through a snow cornice. He dangled at the end of the halter rope and was only saved by the horse pulling back. Fearful of more such occurrences he led them off the ridge back to

8. The name Mount Kitchi has been transferred to a peak about four kilometres north of Mount Sir Alexander.

the Jackpine side. In the dark Mary fell headlong time and again. Hearing the thud Jack would stop and "patiently enquire if I were still alive and coming." They made a late, wet camp just below treeline. In the morning, as on many others, they had to thaw out the ropes and pack mantles before they could pack up the horses.

By morning the weather had cleared somewhat and they were able to cross the summit and descend the steep shale slope on the further side. They still battled waist-deep drifts that would have caused serious problems in the dark. Curly "surged ahead like a moose," breaking trail for man and beast alike. Their traction was aided by wearing "rough locks": lengths of trapping chain on the soles of their oil-tanned boots. It was an invention of Curly's.

After two weeks of snow and rain they reached the Wapiti River, north of Mount Sir Alexander, on October 27. The weather cleared. The grass was still green and the willows still had leaves — a welcome change from the wintry conditions on the divide. Curly and Jack immediately set to work to build a cabin in which to cache the provisions. Mary was kept busy in camp, with endless rounds of cooking and cleaning for the hungry crew. After having seen so much beaver activity she thought it would be great to have a family of trained beavers in camp to get in the boughs for beds and to cut the firewood supply.

The weather held well for the construction. In the full moon "peak after peak piled up in a long line and rising from black wooded depths looked like a caravan of huge white camels enroute across a desert of darkness."

Two weeks later the cabin was complete and all of the provisions were hung from wires or placed in tin containers out of the reach of rodents. On November 10 they left the Wapiti for home.

This marked a turning point in Mary's life. She turned her back on the Canadian west. Curly visited in New York, ostensibly to promote his business, but probably to see Mary. It is rumored that Curly asked her to marry him and she

Jasper-Yellowhead Historical Society

Jack Hargreaves, Curly Phillips and Mary Jobe, upon their return from Mount Sir Alexander, 1917.

declined.[9] If so, that may have had somewhat to do with her not returning to Canada. She also became very involved with running Camp Mystic.

At about this time Mary met Carl Akeley through a mutual friend. Akeley was an explorer, scientist, sculptor, taxidermist and inventor. While working at the Field Museum of Natural History in Chicago, he developed the modern method of taxidermy, whereby specimens are mounted and displayed in life-like poses. When Mary met him, Carl was an employee of the American Museum of Natural History in New York City. He was an African specialist and had done a lot of exploring and collecting on that continent for the museum. Mary became enamored of the man and of his work. His involvement in dangerous travel in exotic places undoubtedly appealed to her own sense of adventure.

Mary and Carl were married on October 18, 1924. She was his second wife. His first, Delia Akeley, became an African

9. In 1923 Curly married Grace Inkster, the daughter of an Edmonton-area homesteader.

explorer in her own right after their divorce. Two years later Mary joined Carl on his fifth expedition to Africa. While they were in the Kivu district of the eastern Belgian Congo (now Zaire) Carl fell ill from a tropical disease and died on November 17, 1926. After burying her husband in the Congo, Mary stayed on to complete the work of the expedition. Upon her return to America the museum's authorities named her to succeed Akeley as adviser in the development of the African Hall, a position she held until 1938. This hall was later renamed the Akeley African Hall.

Mary immersed herself in Africa and Carl Akeley's work. She became a vocal crusader for the establishment of game preserves on the African continent. "Today the wild animals of Africa are making a losing fight," she said in 1929. "The great problem of the student of wildlife traveling in Africa today is not to defend himself against wild animals but to actually see them." She was instrumental in carrying on Carl's struggle to form Parc National Albert in the Belgian Congo. For her work in establishing and promoting this and other game preserves in the Congo, Mary was made a Knight of the Order of the Crown by King Albert of Belgium.

In 1935 she traveled to Zululand (now part of Natal state, Republic of South Africa), Swaziland and to Kruger National Park in South Africa, under the aegis of General Jan Christian Smuts. She studied and wrote about the tribal people, particularly the Zulu and Swazi. In 1946, and again in 1951, she returned to the Congo to see the new parks and to visit her husband's grave.

Mary wrote many books and magazine articles about Africa. Her book titles include *The Wilderness Lives Again, Carl Akeley's Africa, Adventures in the African Jungle, Lions, Gorillas and their Neighbors, Restless Jungle* and *Congo Eden.* Through the 1930s and 1940s Mary gave frequent radio lectures and interviews, mostly on her African expeditions. She also lectured widely to all types of organizations, clubs and schools throughout the eastern and mid-eastern states.

In 1937 Mary made one last trip to Canada. She returned

to the big Bend of the Columbia River, and traveled by canoe, reliving her 1909 adventure.

Mary had been voted a fellow of the Royal Geographical Society in 1915 and belonged to the American Geographical Sociey, too. She was also a member of the American Association for the Advancement of Science, Alpine Club of Canada, American Alpine Club and Club Alpin Français. She also belonged to numerous other societies, such as the American Game Protective Association and American Society of Mammalogists. In 1930 Mary received an honorary Doctor of Literature from Mount Union College.

Mary Jobe Akeley died on July 19, 1966, at a nursing home in Mystic, Connecticut.

Mount Jobe (2271 m), located southeast of Mount Sir Alexander, was named for her in the summer of 1923 by members of the Alberta-British Columbia Boundary Commission. The name was officially adopted by the Geographic Board of Canada on September 1, 1925, to commemorate the woman who had done so much exploring in the Canadian west. Mary was undoubtedly pleased by this recognition.

Caroline Hinman
(1884-1966)

> *Let us probe the silent places,*
> *Let us seek what luck betide us,*
> *Let us journey to a lonely land I know.*
> *Robert Service*

What do Egypt, the Sahara Desert, Tunisia and Guatemala have in common with the Canadian Rockies? The answer is an enthusiastic, energetic woman by the name of Caroline Hinman, who arranged and led her "Off the Beaten Track" tours to all of these places and many more.

But Caroline's first and foremost love was the Rocky Mountain wilderness and the freedom and relaxation of trail life. To this beloved area she brought groups of girls from the eastern American cities, who "did not know of even the existence of this wonderland," and she introduced them to the joys of outdoor life.

Caroline Borden Hinman was born in Cincinnati, Ohio, on November 8, 1884, to Russell and Marie (Erwin) Hinman. She was the eldest of four children: Katherine, Russell and Eunice. Her father was a book editor. At the age of six she moved with her family to Chatham, New Jersey for two years. They then moved to nearby Summit, where she lived the rest of her life. She graduated from Kent Place School in 1902 and immediately entered Smith College, in Northampton, Massachusetts. She graduated in 1906 with a four-year Bachelor of Arts degree. During college she was involved in many clubs and was on the golf team.

In December of 1906 she went to California to be a bridesmaid for a schoolmate. She stayed there until March and spent a further two months traveling home to New Jersey. It was the beginning of an irrepressible urge to explore and travel. Caroline always referred to herself as having "a one-track mind": she was totally absorbed by anything to do with travel or camping.

Caroline's father believed that each of his daughters should have a profession, regardless of need. Expanding upon Caroline's longing to travel, he sent her on a trip to Europe in the summer of 1909, under the tutelage of an able and experienced woman who was conducting the party of eight. Russell Hinman suggested that Caroline observe the woman's methods. The trip awoke "the Wanderlust which had slumbered until then, and which has pursued me ever since." The following summer Caroline led a party of four personal friends to Europe. She had a much bettter time "bossing" than she had "following" the year before.

But before Caroline could get down to serious business conducting tours abroad, she took a trip to the Canadian Rockies that was to set her life's course.

Caroline spent the early summer of 1913 with Bess and Albert MacCarthy at their ranch in British Columbia. She joined them for a further three weeks at the Alpine Club of Canada camps at Lake O'Hara in Yoho National Park and at Mount Robson, west of Jasper. Here she was introduced to mountain climbing by the Swiss guides. While at the Robson camp she participated in a five-day trip over passes and glaciers led by Curly Phillips. They made the first ascent of Mount Pamm (2829 m), near Moose Pass, which Caroline named. To Caroline it was "a first and unforgettable experience of the joy and beauty of mountain travel."

This early experience in the Rockies made an indelible impression upon Caroline.

> So deep an impression did that experience make upon me, so much benefit did I derive therefrom, physically, mentally and spiritually, that before the following winter had half begun, I had determined to go back and to take with me others who, without being led, might never find the way to that health-bringing wonderland of upolluted air, warm sunshine and brilliant flowers.

Caroline's second European tour was the following summer, when she led a party of six in partnership with another woman. They were in the Austrian Tyrol when the First World War broke out and they had quite an exciting time reaching Zurich, Switzerland. After three weeks there they traveled across France, often in the company of soldiers and carrying their own food. Their return ocean journey was delayed by a week because their ship was redirected to the war effort.

Caroline's second Canadian trip catered more to her spirit of adventure. In 1915 she accompanied Mary Jobe, a woman she had met at the 1913 Robson camp, on an expedition to climb Mount Kitchi (now Mount Sir Alexander), a remote unclimbed peak to the north of Jasper National Park (see chapter on Mary Jobe Akely, page 91). They were outfitted by Curly Phillips who had been the chief packer at the 1913 camp. Caroline was to become Curly's friend and enthusiastic supporter until his death in an avalanche in 1938.

Caroline and Mary left Edmonton for Jasper on June 28, 1915. Here they met the rest of the outfit. Curly had five men assisting him. It was certainly unusual, if not downright scandalous, for two attractive young women to set off on a two-month adventure with six men unrelated to them.

The expedition life agreed with Caroline, who returned home "so brown and fat and healthy" that her family hardly recognized her.

A few months after returning from her 1915 trip Caroline was bemoaning the fact that the war had shut off further European tours, and that she had no way of going north, when her non-venturous mother said mildly, "I don't see why you don't lead parties out there then."

Plans were made, and the following year Caroline led her first conducted tour to the west, to Glacier National Park, Montana. She had decided that for her first trip she'd stay in her own country. During the month-long trip the group stayed in comfortable chalets — with the exception of a ten-day camping trip into Waterton Lakes National Park over the international boundary in Canada. The venture was a complete success. The girls were bubbling with enthusiasm over the trip and their parents were likewise delighted.

From such inauspicious beginnings Caroline's *Off the*

Beaten Track tours expanded to three different outings each summer, first by packhorse and later including boat trips and auto tours. With the exception of three seasons during the Second World War, Caroline returned to the Canadian Rockies each year for over four decades.

Most of Caroline's tours were for well-educated teenage girls from wealthy American families. Each group averaged ten or twelve girls. Caroline personally screened the applicants from her home in New Jersey or interviewed them in New York. She furnished references from former clients and expected the same from prospective campers who were unknown to her. Occasionally the tours did include mixed groups of both men and women, and of all ages.

In 1917 Caroline led her first trip entirely in the Canadian Rockies, beginning in Banff. They traveled by horse south to Mount Assiniboine, then back to the Pipestone Valley west of Banff and finished at Lake Louise. Legendary Jimmy Simpson was the outfitter, Ulysses LaCasse was the head guide and Jim Boyce was the "good-natured" cook. One of Caroline's clients, Mavis Benedict, wrote that LaCasse's friends gave him a hard time about guiding a group of girls — there was an article in the Banff Crag and Canyon "that showed pretty well what freaks we [the guides] were considered."

During her early years as a tour operator, from 1915 to 1921, Caroline was working full-time as a secretary for the Board of Education in Summit (she landed the job the day after returning from her Mount Sir Alexander trip). Then she quit her job to engage in her chosen avocation full-time. This enabled her to lead overseas trips in the winter as well as to organize her summer trips to the Rockies.

Enthusiastic as she was about her chosen occupation, Caroline didn't particularly recommend conducting independent parties as an occupation for women who had no other source of income. Although the returns were often good, the organization of such trips was obviously full of uncertainties and the income was variable.

During the winter Caroline sometimes taught a travel course to which guest speakers were occasionally invited. Her desk was often a "delightful confusion" of maps, timetables and correspondence with prospective clients.

Caroline Hinman.

In 1920 Caroline was again back in Jasper. Curly Phillips led their tour south from Jasper to the Columbia Icefield area, then back through the Tonquin Valley to Mount Robson.

In 1921 she took a group of 12 people north of Jasper. Because the Snake Indian River was in flood Curly did not want to risk fording it, so he transported the whole outfit — 47 horses and about 2300 kg of equipment — by train to Bedson Station where they disembarked. The riders followed on the evening train and there was a tremendous commotion as they packed up the horses in the moonlight.

Over the next few weeks they followed a zigzag pattern across mountains and valleys to the north of Jasper. They left the Snake Indian Valley by Willow Creek to Rock Lake. After fishing for a couple of days they headed north over numerous small passes of the front ranges to the headwaters of the Sulphur River, from which they crossed over to Hardscrabble Creek. Then it was over Hardscrabble Pass to Blue Creek, a tributary of the Snake Indian River. Once they were back in that drainage they followed the Snake Indian to its headwaters and then into the Smoky River valley.

After making a food cache they took a four-day sidetrip up the Short River. On the first day they had to oust a black bear with two cubs in order to set up camp. The next day they explored the glacier at the head of the valley and chose a route by which they hoped to ascend the as-yet-unclimbed Mount Chown (3381 m). Unfortunately their route took them to a different summit, and when they realized their error there was no time left to try again. A few days later they were on the opposite side of Chown, from where five of them again planned to climb the mountain.

Throughout the morning the weather was unsettled. As they plodded slowly up the long expanse of the Chown Glacier, periodic views of the summit enticed them ever onwards. But shortly past noon the sun was obliterated, the snow came down heavily and ''we were enveloped in a rather terrible and silent whiteness.'' In deteriorating conditions they turned back at the bergschrund (the crevasse between the head of a glacier and the bedrock wall). The falling snow obliterated their tracks and hid the crevasses. About fifteen minutes after turning back, Curly fell into a crevasse, but the others were able to arrest his fall.

> We pulled as though expecting to lift our one hundred and eighty pound
> guide bodily from the crevasse in which he dangled. A muffled voice
> then reached us "Give me slack. You are cutting me in two." ... He
> was in a narrow crevasse which he could straddle. Using his ice axe,
> he hacked out a toe-rest in the straight ice sides of the crevasse, shouted
> to us to pull, and bracing himself got his toe in the niche. Then he
> hacked another hole in the other side and through his own ingenuity
> and what little aid we could give by hauling, he emerged in five minutes
> time, breathless and with a broken rib, but otherwise unhurt.

Less than half an hour later another party member fell into a crevasse, but she was quickly rescued. The progress slowed to a crawl as they negotiated the rest of the crevasses back to the safety of the moraine. Camp was a welcome sight. "I suppose it is the danger and the excitement of mountain climbing that helps make it so interesting, and surely it is the contrast from the cold, snowy glaciers, with their treacherous creavasses that makes camp in the friendly timber seem like the most comfortable home on earth."

A few days later, on September first, they arrived back at Robson Station with another adventure behind them.

During the summer of 1923 Curly again guided Caroline's group, this time on a six-week trek through little-explored country along the continental divide southwest of Jasper. Caroline's party of ten men and women, including her sister Kate, boarded a train in New York on July 17. In Montreal the women spent a day shopping and then boarded another train for the west. In Winnipeg another woman joined their party and brought with her a mangy little airedale dog named Dusty, who became a full member of the expedition. Then it was on to Jasper, where they changed into their trail clothes, leaving their civilized togs behind.

First they visited Maligne Lake, then they crossed the Maligne Range and followed the Athabasca and Chaba Rivers to Fortress Lake. The previous winter Curly had cached canoes at both of the lakes, hauling them in by dogteam 50 km to Maligne and 80 km to Fortress, over rough country.

On their way to Fortress Lake they found a note nailed to a tree, addressed to the "Hinman-Phillips Party." It was a plea for help from a group of climbers: one of their party had been kicked in the knee by a horse weeks earlier; knowing that Curly was coming in, they wanted him to fetch the injured person from the far end of Fortress Lake with his canoe. As requested, Caroline's party took him back with them to the main Athabasca River trail and sent him on his way to medical help in Jasper. He was quite an entertaining fellow, and some of the women were sorry to see him leave!

From the Athabasca River they ascended the Whirlpool to Athabasca Pass, took the British Columbia side of the Great Divide to Fraser Pass, followed Tonquin Creek to the Tonquin Valley and then returned to Jasper. Much of this journey was through untracked wilderness, which required determination in cutting a trail through for the horses. As Curly had a lot of new, untried horses along, he would cut a tree for the tourists to cross streams on, rather than allowing them to ride the horses through and perhaps get into trouble.

Caroline considered Curly to be one of the best guides in the Rockies. "Energy, ardor, enthusiasm, thoroughness, skill marked everything he did, and the rougher and more unexplored the country, the more his spirit thrilled to the task of making a way thru it possible for the string of 'tenderfeet' behind him."

Jim Boyce of Banff had cooked for Jimmy Simpson on Caroline's first trip, because in order to get a national park guide's license, a candidate had to cook for one season. He then guided for Simpson the following year. Boyce left Simpson's employ in 1921 to start his own outfit. Caroline had been so impressed by his skills that when Boyce started his own outfit she rarely booked with anyone else in the Banff area. Boyce guided Caroline for 16 years, two months every July and August. His head packer was Charlie Hunter. On one trip they had 55 head of horses for 18 people. Boyce said that Caroline was a good customer and "a good traveler — she knew what she wanted." Of course, the tours were quite novel for the guides and packers. They were required to camp some distance away from the girls, in order to head off any hanky-panky, and they sometimes came under the scrutiny of the chaperones. On one occasion a packer accompanied a few of the girls boating on a lake, when he thought he noticed the glint of the sun shining on glass on a nearby ridge. Using his binoculars, he was amazed to see someone observing their every move from that high point! Ed Feuz, Jr. described meeting a Hinman group when he was with a climbing party:

> We were on the north side of the Saskatchewan River ... we had a camp there. All at once ... this boy came running down behind the tent and said 'Here are the girls! Here are the girls!' Here was a whole string of girls ... right in the middle of the river ... it was the prettiest sight I ever saw in my life! ... No climbing today!

Such events added to the carefree character of trail life. Three or four packers took care of all of the horses and the camp chores. After breakfast each camper was required to make up her own bedroll and duffle bag and prepare a lunch for the day. The head guide would then lead off, followed by the girls; the men with the packhorses would start as soon as they were assembled. On an average day they would ride for a few hours and then stop for lunch beside a stream or high on a hillside or pass. Then they would ride for another two or three hours before making camp for the evening. The first thing upon arriving in camp, Caroline would lie down in every likely looking spot to find a comfortable sleeping platform. She usually slept out under the stars, only retreating to the tent when it rained or snowed.

Caroline received the nickname "Timberline Kate" from Jim Boyce because of her desire to always camp where there was a good view, usually near timberline or in a pass. The nickname seemed to please her. Lillian Gest, one of her frequent clients and a close friend, always said the camps were so high that there "wasn't enough water to brush your teeth!"

Every few days they would stop for a day, to rest the horses and give the men time to catch up on camp chores and to rest as well. The girls would spend the day reading, writing diaries, playing games, swimming, fishing, hiking or taking pictures. Sometimes they had a sports day. One sports day included three-legged races, obstacle races and cowboy races (dressed-up foot races), bareback riding, orange-spearing, bucking contests, wrestling on horseback, stunt-riding and even an Indian parade. At other times there were baseball and darts. Each evening there was a large campfire, around which stories were told, poetry read and hot chocolate shared by all. They once celebrated a guide's birthday by dancing the Virginia Reel to a humming accompaniment, with pots and pans serving as intruments!

The girls made quite a stir when they hit town, a

circumstance that Caroline took pains to avoid. Neither were they beyond carrying a small flask of whisky hidden from her in their saddlebags, for fortitude on cold days!

One of Caroline's favorite tricks was to leave something behind in camp or on the trail, on purpose or not, and she then took great pleasure in finding these relics on later trips. Once it was a jacknife and another time a hometown newspaper. They always carried small calibre rifles and sometimes pistols, which were sealed when in the parks. Outside of the park boundaries they practised their target shooting.

Although the group was usually far from civilization, arrangements had been made so that every so often they would meet up with someone for supplies or mail, or if they met a party on the trail that was "heading in" they would send some mail. Such events, of course, were always a cause for great excitement — and probably homesickness to some.

Caroline seldom traveled over familiar ground if an alternative route seemed feasible. She was always looking for new areas to explore, having the utmost confidence in herself and her guides in taking inexperienced people out in the wilderness. With the head guide she would pore over maps around the campfire, marking all of the trails and linking up areas unknown to her to form a trip. Over the years she traveled many thousands of kilometres on horseback, covering the length and breadth of the Canadian Rockies, from Waterton Park in the south to the uncharted country north of Jasper National Park.

Caroline was very fit physically and could spend many hours in the saddle or walking through the mountains. She was tall and strong, although not conspicuously athletic, poised and "absolutely fearless." Lillian Gest, who participated in many of Caroline's tours, wrote of meeting Caroline on the trail at Lake O'Hara in 1921. She "trotted along the trail with the greatest of ease and apparently was unaware that it was uphill." She always wanted to see what was "on the other side." Although mountaineering was never a trip objective, she did climb Castleguard Mountain (3090 m), mounts Temple (3543 m), Bess (3216 m), Magog (3095 m) and Mumm (2962m) and several lesser peaks in the Rockies. Besides belonging to the Alpine Club of Canada she was a member of the Appalachian

Mountain Club and the Club Suisse de Femmes Alpinistes. She attended many ACC camps in the Rockies.

Her first really exotic overseas tour was in January, 1924, when she spent three months in Sicily, Naples, northern Algeria and Tunisia — including a nine-day camping trip by camel across the Sahara — a unique venture for a party of six women, unaccompanied by men. The entire trip cost $1600 per person. A year later she traveled by new six-wheeled desert motor cars in the same area.

The Trail Riders of the Canadian Rockies organization was born in the summer of 1924. Jim Boyce signed up both Caroline Hinman and Lillian Gest as charter members. She attended many of their camps and also served on the executive.

That autumn, Caroline went on a five-week hunting trip north of Jasper with her friend Wiffie Lewis. They were guided by Bert Wilkins (Curly Phillips's brother-in-law and partner) and Rufe Neighbor; Joe Soper was again their cook. They had five saddlehorsesand eighteen packhorses. She had never hunted before, but the party bagged two each of sheep, goats, moose and caribou, and they killed one grizzly. She shot a ram. Her attitude toward hunting had changed from ten years before, when she had watched Frank Doucette kill a moose: she had written with horror that the "poor old moose was a pathetic sight lying there motionless when he had been so full of grace & freedom a minute ago." The experience of making comfortable camps in the snow increased her respect for the resourcefulness and skill of the guides.

In the autumn of 1925 Caroline went hunting again with Wiffie, and this time Lillian Gest joined them. They journeyed north of Lake Louise with Max Brooks, Bill Potts and Soapy Smith as guides. On the last day before heading south into the park Caroline had still shot no game. She was hunting with Bill when they spotted two grizzlies from their lunch stop. They stalked them for two hours through the snow before Caroline shot and wounded the smaller one, and Bill shot the mother when it stood up. There were some tense moments when the rifle muzzle plugged with snow while reloading.

She was on two more hunting trips in the next three years, with Charlie Hunter and Lillian Gest north of Lake Louise. (See chapter on Lillian Gest, page 202, for more details.)

White Museum of the Canadian Rockies

Caroline Hinman with Rocky Mountain goat that she shot, 1925.

Caroline's first trip to Mount Assiniboine was in 1926. The 12 members of the group detrained at Seebe, where they were met by Jim Boyce's outfit. They traveled via the Kananaskis River, Marvel Lake, and Wonder Pass to Magog Lake, where they set up camp.

The day after arriving at Assiniboine they formed an ambitious, but inexperienced, party to climb Mount Magog. Jim Boyce led Caroline, Lillian Gest and a 16-year-old boy on one lariat. Their alpenstocks were cut from nearby bushes. Charlie Hunter followed with another 16-year-old boy and his uncle. Charlie put his climbers in front of him, so that he could "see what the dudes were doing." They ascended an icy couloir to the summit (3095 m) without incident. Descending, though, required step-cutting — for which they had no ice axe, simply a Boy Scout hatchet that one of the girls had given Jim as they were leaving camp. After some debate they unroped and tied Jim to Charlie's lariat and he went down to cut the steps. One by one they descended and traversed to saftey. After returning to camp Jim's only comment was "we'll never do anything like that again." Caroline led trips to the Assiniboine area many more times in the following years.

On that trip the party headed out to Windermere in the

Columbia River Valley of British Columbia, via the Mitchell and Cross rivers. Trails were often indistinct and the men frequently scouted ahead of the group, blazing and cutting out a trail. While riding down the Cross River the packtrain was ahead; one man dropped a matchhead and a small fire had already started by the time the riders came along. With some difficulty they were able to put it out using their horse blankets. They were much chastened by the event.

At Windermere they stopped for laundry, mail, ice cream, and other amenities. Caroline had her hair bobbed at the hairdresser's. They visited Caroline's friend, Bess MacCarthy, at her ranch. She gave them a much-welcomed crate of fresh eggs.

On their way through Kootenay Park they stopped at Wolverine Pass for several days. Eyeing a nearby glacier, the men made a toboggan and hitched four of Jim's dogs to it. They went full-speed across the glacier until they dumped into a small crevasse sideways, which put an end to the event.

When they ended the trip at Lake Louise everyone had baths and shampoos. They dressed up, dined, danced and generally enjoyed the excitement of civilization. But after weeks in the open air the hotel was hot and stifling.

Caroline had ambitious plans for a trip to the Rockies for the winter of 1927-28. A tour would take in the Banff Winter Carnival, the hot springs, a snowshoe trip to Lake O'Hara Lodge, skiing and dog team trips at O'Hara, and a dog team trip from Banff to Lake Minnewanka. Participants could then accompany her motoring in southern Califonia and cruising through the Panama Canal. However, the trip was cancelled due to lack of interest.

Starting in 1929 Caroline began hiring some of her former campers to lead trips in the Rockies for her. That freed her to lead other tours or to enjoy a visit on her own. In that particular year she led a walking tour to the Alps. She climbed the Ortler (3902 m) in the Austrian Tyrol and the Jungfrau (4158 m) in the Swiss Alps, but was turned back on several other climbs, including the Matterhorn, by inclement weather. Caroline was 45.

Meanwhile her *Off the Beaten Track* tours had expanded to include exotic destinations.

Horseback and Canoe Trip in the Canadian Northwest

June 27 - September 4, 1930

One of Donald Phillips' canoes

I'm glad there is always a Land of Beyond
For us who are true to the trail,
A vision to seek, a beckoning peak,
A farness that never will fail;
A pride in our soul that mocks at a goal
A manhood that irks at a bond,
And try how we will, unattainable still
Behold it, our Land of Beyond!
— ROBERT SERVICE.

Sixteenth camping trip in the Canadian Rockies

CAROLINE HINMAN

80 PROSPECT STREET, SUMMIT, NEW JERSEY

I and my parties have wandered through Europe, through Morocco, Algeria, Tunisia, we have camped on the Sahara, we have visited the Sudan, we have crossed the Arabian Desert from Damascus to Bagdad. We have flown across Persia from Tehran to Ispahan, Shiraz and Bushire; we have traveled through Soviet Russia from Leningrad and Moscow to the Black Sea Riviera and over the Caucasus Mountains to Caspian Sea ports. We have seen the big caravan from Kabul come down the Khyber Pass in India, we have house-boated in the Vale of Cashmere [Kashmir] and camped in the Himalayas above Darjeeling on the border of Sikkim and the Nepal; we have crossed India from north to south and reveled in the tropical beauty of Ceylon, Burma, Sumatra, Java, Bali, Siam and Indo-China. We have climbed the hills of Hong Kong and marveled at the cherry blossom season in Japan.

During the winter of 1932-33 Caroline led a six-month around-the-world tour that visited Syria, Iraq, India, Siam, Cambodia, China and Japan. While in Darjeeling they took a five-day horseback trip toward Mount Everest, and later a week's tour around Mount Fuji in Japan. During the 1930s she led numerous winter trips to Guatemala, Mexico and the Yucatan Peninsula.

Whether in her beloved Rocky Mountains or on the other side of the world, Caroline searched for places far from the crowds, where there was silence and beauty, and "stillness that fills one with peace."

As was often the case, in 1933 Caroline offered two separate packtrips in Canada. In July she went first to the Mount Assiniboine area and then via Egypt Lake to Prospector Valley in Kootenay National Park, continuing to Lake Louise via Paradise Valley. On the second trip, begun immediately afterward, she rode north from Lake Louise to the Red Deer River and back to Banff via the Cascade River Valley.

At Assiniboine, Caroline and Lillian Gest went off with their rucksacks and ice axes for a delightful day scrambling the ridges and small peaks, enjoying the gorgeous views. When moving camp from Simpson Pass to Egypt Lake, the two women again set off on foot across country. Having started late, and forced to change their route due to cliffs and cornices, they arrived in camp about six o'clock, much later than the rest of the outfit. Caroline "felt the thrill of facing the unknown alone." At Egypt Lake Jimmy Simpson brought in their mail and newspapers. Caroline had bills to pay and letters from prospective clients to answer. She sent back a couple of night letters, or telegrams, with Simpson, booking clients for the next packtrip.

The ACC was holding its annual camp in Paradise Valley that year, not far from Caroline's camp. She was asked to speak at their campfire about her trips. She was very nervous about giving the talk and went off in the woods alone to plan it. The tension and extreme heat made her feel sick all day. But once she was on her feet talking she did fine.

The changeover day, from one trip to the next, was understandably hectic. They left Paradise Valley for the Lake Louise train station, stopping at Chateau Lake Louise for mail. At the station she had to meet the new arrivals and send off those who were going home. The outfitter then took the new duffel on to the first night's camp. She went back up to the hotel for lunch, and then on to the trail to reach their Pipestone River Camp.

While Caroline's group was camped on the Siffleur River, Sampson Beaver and his wife Leah rode through camp. (See chapter on Mary Schäffer Warren, page 62, for more on Sampson Beaver.) He stayed to talk and have supper while she rode down the trail to set up camp. The next morning they gave him some extra food supplies. Coming back to the Pipestone they saw a group of 50 Indians heading back to their homes on the North Saskatchewan River from the Banff Indian Days

On most evenings Caroline enjoyed going out fishing, often alone. For bait she used almost anything, from grasshoppers to fresh meat. The fish were a welcome and necessary addition to their food supplies. Outside of the national and provincial parks the men sometimes hunted game in an effort to supplement dwindling food supplies. So as not to disturb the girls, they often did it at night. One day some of the girls saw a dog playing with a deer leg and Caroline tried to pretend it was a coyote that the dogs had killed. Another time she pretended that the shots they heard were really a rockslide.

Glacier Park, Montana, was again visited in 1934, this time on a four-week sojourn along the continental divide from Banff. A second party did the trip in reverse. The trip, one way, cost $595 per person, including train fare from New York. In 1936 Caroline held a four-week camp based at Skoki Lodge (then managed by Jim Boyce), with day rides, mountain climbing and hiking over three weeks. They were the first guests at the newly-enlarged lodge — the roof wasn't quite completed and some guests slept in teepees.

In 1937 Caroline booked one of Curly Phillips's 800-km boat trips down the Peace River. It was a route "full of interest and variety with its Hudson's Bay trading posts, Indian villages, gold prospectors camps, fur trader's cabins and trout fishing everywhere." From Jasper they boarded the train for Prince George, British Columbia. Then it was by truck to Summit Lake on the Great Divide. From there they boated down the Crooked River to Lake McLeod, then onto the Pack River to the Parsnip and finally on to Finlay Forks and the main Peace River. When they came to rapids the group would walk around, while the men ran them in the flat-bottomed boats. Near Hudson's Hope they had to portage everything, including the boats, 22 km around a canyon (where the Bennett Dam is located now). Then it was on to Fort St. John and down to the town of Peace River, Alberta where they boarded the train for Edmonton. The trip cost $350. She led three more river tours after this, all with Curly's brother Harry, after Curly was killed.

By the 1940's Caroline was using all modes of travel in the Rockies. In 1941 she offered the following trips: four weeks by car from Jasper to Banff, three weeks on horseback in the Mount Assiniboine area, and a boat trip on the Peace River.

Caroline attended the Skyline Trail Hikers camp in Citadel Pass in 1948 and was elected to the council in the same year. The following year she served as a vice-president, in 1950 as

Whyte Museum of the Canadian Rockies

Lunch time on one of Curly Phillips's boat trips on the Peace River, ca. 1935.

president.

Throughout her life Caroline was deeply involved in civic and welfare projects in Summit, New Jersey, acting as secretary for the Volunteer Services of Overlook Hospital during the Second World War and serving with the Red Cross for some ten years. She was involved in various capacities with the Summit Convalescent Home for Children, Women's Alliance, Summit Playhouse Association, various Smith College Clubs, the Unitarian Church and the United Campaign.

Caroline was apologetic about not writing books on her travels but she did keep detailed diaries, which are filled with her enthusiasm and her love of nature and beauty. Her writings capture the immediate joy of sparkling sunshine on a mountaintop as well as the misery of cold, driving rain. They faithfully record the little details of camp life and the personalities of her fellow travelers. She also left many photographs and moving pictures of trail life. Most of her energy was spent conducting her independent travel tours, and they were her "greatest pleasure."

Caroline retired in 1960 from organizing and conducting tours. She lived quietly in Summit, dying there on July 12, 1966, at the age of 82.

Perhaps Caroline herself summed up her life best, when she wrote the following for a college reunion book in 1931:

> As I look back over the past twenty-five years I feel I have accomplished very little. I have no husband, I have no children, I have no home of my own, I have written no books, I have amassed no fortune, I have distinguished myself in no way whatsoever ... but I have been extremely happy, extremely busy, utterly contented and absorbed in my job of taking people to out-of-the-way places in the world.... This has absorbed me for twenty-five years ... Where have they gone? and what have I done with them? I might have done better — and I might have done worse.

Gertrude Benham
(1867-1938)

Gertrude Benham, an untiring English mountaineer, had climbed many of the famous peaks in the Alps—Mont Blanc (4807m), the Matterhorn (4478m), Monte Rosa (4634m)—before coming to the Canadian Rockies. She was reported to have had over 130 ascents to her credit when she attempted Mount Assiniboine, the "Matterhorn of the Rockies," in 1904.

Gertrude was born in 1867, the youngest of six children of a London family. Her father died on June 13, 1891, and her mother on April 2, 1903, leaving her a small inheritance. On an early visit to Switzerland with her father, she felt at once that she had "come home" and fell in love with mountains: "I think that I am naturally a mountaineer, for I have no fear of heights, [and] I am a good walker." She eventually went climbing in Switzerland 17 times.

Her first journey outside of Europe was to Canada. She arrived in Banff in early June, 1904, intending to climb until October and then go off to New Zealand. She was one of the first serious woman climbers in Canada.

In the Rockies Gertrude based herself at the Lake Louise Chalet. As it was a late season and there was still a lot of snow on the mountains she contented herself with tramping the lower elevations and "flower-hunting." Then, on June 27 Gertrude and a Mr. Frost were guided up Mount Lefroy (3423m) by the Swiss guides Hans and Christian Kaufmann. They made the approach to Abbot Pass from the Plain of Six Glaciers at Lake Louise. Although the morning began clear, soon clouds moved in and it began to rain. As they reached the Death Trap it began to snow. The snow was soft, and a driving wind and snow reduced the visibility. It was a tiring ascent. When leaving the glacier Christian fell into the bergschrund, but was quite easily rescued. They did not remain on the summit long because of the fierce wind. In an article in the *Banff Crag and Canyon* Gertrude wrote, "My hair was covered with little icicles that jingled when I shook my head, and the snow, driven by the wind, stung our faces like needles." Their tracks were quickly obliterated, and "the thick mist gave a most curious sensation of walking into nothingness." A few days later, she climbed Mount Victoria (3464m) in perfect weather.

Gertrude spent most of July in the Lake Louise area, climbing under the guidance of the Kaufmanns. They climbed Mount Whyte (2983m), Mount Temple (3543m), and Popes Peak (3162m).

From Lake Louise Gertrude and Christian moved to a camp at Moraine Lake, in the Valley of the Ten Peaks. Gertrude noted that the ten peaks were named after the Indian numerals one to ten, and "in this country, where nearly all the peaks are named after persons, it is a relief to find a few with other names." She desired to make the first ascent of "Heejee Peak," (she spelled it Hiji) which was Peak One.

On July 19, she and Christian ascended the couloir between Peaks Three and Four to gain the ridge. After a long and tiring trudge through soft snow they ascended the summit of loose rock. On their return to Moraine Lake they stopped at Walter Wilcox's camp. From him they learned that the peak they had ascended was not Heejee, but an unnamed one. Disappointed, but still determined, they planned an ascent for the next day.

But Christian's brother Hans was guiding Professor Charles Fay in the same attempt. Fay was a founding member

American Alpine Journal

131

Christian Kaufmann has accompanied me as guide on the following expeditions,—Mount Lefroy, Mount Victoria, Pope's Peak, Mount Whyte, Mount Stephen (from Lake Louise to Field), Aiji, Mount Temple, N° 3 & N° 6 & Mount Assiniboine, also another peak whose name I do not know. Of these expeditions, four were first ascents & our route up Mount Stephen was by an unclimbed ridge. On rocks, ice & snow Christian shews the greatest care & skill & is a very agreeable companion, which adds much to the pleasure of climbing, & I hope to have some more climbs with him, in the future.

Gertrude E. Benham

∴ Lake Louise. Aug. 8 /04

Gertrude Benham's entry in Christian Kaufmann's fuhrerbuch (guide's book).

of the Appalachian Mountain Club in Boston, Massachusetts, and later a president of the American Alpine Club. The Geographic Names Board had asked Fay which mountain he would like named for himself in recognition of his mountaineering achievements in Canada—he chose Peak One.

The drama unfolded on July 20, when both parties made a summit bid. Hans led Fay up a couloir from Consolation Lake on the east side of the mountain. They were forced to turn back because of dangerous snow conditions and heavy rockfall. Meanwhile, Christian again guided Gertrude up the 3-4 couloir from Moraine Lake, and, by staying farther to the left on the snowfield than they had the previous day, they ascended the

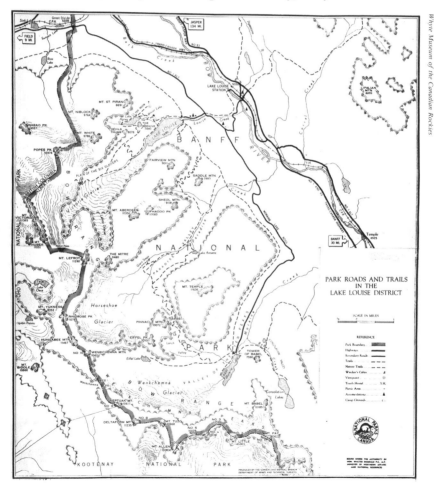

right peak (3235m). They also made the first ascent of Mount Allen (3310m), then known as Peak Three.

Two days later, on July 22, Gertrude and Christian made the first ascent of Mount Bowlen (3072m), or Peak Six. While descending they saw smoke in the valley and feared that their camp was on fire. Although they soon saw flames across almost the entire hillside, they found that their camp was safe. They spent a restless night, fearing a change in wind direction, and escaped in the morning.

It was rumored that Fay requested that his name be given to another peak, but when he found that it too had already been climbed (perhaps by Gertrude), he reluctantly accepted the designation of Peak One. Fay was greatly disappointed, but made the second ascent on Aug 5—but guided by Christian Häsler, Sr. and Frederick Michel, not Hans Kaufmann.[1]

It was generally believed that Fay wrote with indignation to the Canadian Pacific Railway, demanding that they dismiss the Kaufmanns from their service. Perhaps he did get Hans fired, as at the end of the season Hans returned to Switzerland, never to return to Canada. Christian, though, continued to guide in Canada for at least a few more seasons. To be fair to Gertrude, there is no evidence that she was aware of the guides' duplicity. Hans and Christian were known to be fond of a practical joke, particularly at someone else's expense, but that time it may have backfired.

After her successful stay at Moraine Lake, Gertrude moved back to Lake Louise, before deciding to move on to Yoho park. Guided by Christian and Hans she tramped from Lake Louise to Field in one day, by a novel route. Leaving Lake Louise at midnight, they crossed Abbot Pass to Lake O'Hara, then skirted Mount Odaray to the Cataract Valley. By ascending a previously unclimbed ridge of Mount Stephen they attained its summit (3199m) at 7:30 p.m. After descending for a time they stopped for a short rest and sleep, then continued on by lantern light. They arrived in Field at three in the morning. This is no mean feat, as the distance is some 35 km, with a total elevation gain

---

1. Both successful ascents were made from Moraine Lake via the couloir between Peaks Three and Four. Fay had also chosen that route for his first attempt, but Hans had refused to take it, likely because he knew that Christian and Gertrude were climbing there.

and loss of 5300 m. It's no wonder that she was reputed to have exhausted her guides!

In the Yoho, Gertrude climbed mounts Gordon (3203m), Balfour (3272m) and Collie (3116m), all by new routes.

On the first of August, Gertrude set out for Mount Assiniboine, still guided by the Kaufmanns. They were outfitted by the legendary Bill Peyto, who sent Jimmy Wood and Jesse Trot to pack for them. Gertrude walked for the first ten kilometres, which astonished Wood, who kept enquiring every kilometre if she was tired yet.

It wasn't until the third day on the trail that they caught sight of Mount Assiniboine in all its grandeur and beauty. "It stands on an undulating, grassy upland, dotted here and there with groups of pine-trees, with a beautiful lake lying at its foot, while the lower peaks around seem to add to the height and majesty." They were delighted with the scenery, and with the weather, but they were tormented by mosquitoes and horseflies: "I suppose they do not get many visitors, so they make the most of those who do come."

They started their summit bid at three o'clock in the morning. Gertrude groped and felt for her clothes and gear in the dark as they had forgotten to bring candles. Much of the climb was over steep snow and ice slopes, then loose stones and steep rock slabs. On the summit ridge they found the remains of a small mammal, which Gertrude supposed had been inadvertently dropped by a bird of prey.

Although the day was cloudless their view from the summit (3618m) was unfortunately obscured by smoke from distant forest fires. Gertrude's ascent was the third of the mountain, and the first by a woman. She had succeeded in conquering the "Matterhorns" of two continents.

Through late August and early September, Gertrude made a number of ascents from Glacier House: mounts Sir Donald (3297m), Sifton (2942m), Dawson (3390m), Deville (now Selwyn, 3360m), Bonney (3107m), Rogers Peak (3214m), and the Swiss Peaks (3208m). The Truda Peaks (3117m) may have been named for Gertrude.

After her successful climbing season in Canada, Gertrude went on to climb in New Zealand and Japan. She also visited Australia, India, Egypt and Corsica before returning to England.

Gertrude never returned to Canada, although she wrote that she often thought of the good times she had in the Rockies, but the rising prices made traveling and climbing there "almost impossible."

To say that Gertrude travelled extensively over the next three decades would be an understatement—she traveled around the world eight times! On one trip she was away from England for four years. Two of her favorite locales were Central Africa, which she crossed four times, and the Himalayas. She traveled alone to every corner of the British Empire except Tristan da Cunha and some small islands. Journeying as much as possible on foot, she traversed thousands of miles "studying nature" and walking "for pleasure." Only when absolutely necessary did she travel by steamer, railway or motor car.

On her first trip to Africa, in 1909, she covered nearly 5000 km. On that trip she reached the summit of famous Mount Kilimanjaro (5843m), in Tanganyika. In a 1928 article in the *Daily Mail* of London, Gertrude described her ascent:[2]

> I was told by the Germans at Moschi, the little hill town, (it was German territory then), that the mountain had never been climbed by any Britisher, man or woman, and very seldom by anyone else. Though Kilimanjaro is enormously high, the actual climb is not very steep, the chief difficulties being the rareified [sic] air, the intense cold and the powers of endurance that are needed. I started from Moschi with 5 porters, 2 guides and a cook boy. The lower part of the mountain is thick forest, and the guides had to hack their way through it. Our first stop was at the limit of the forest area, where we set our tent and had a good rest. We were 10,000 feet up now and the view was indescribably pretty. Below me was the sweltering African plain, but all round were wild flowers and the coolness of an English spring. We left the tent behind and started from the forest area with as little luggage as possible. The air was becoming rareified now and we had to take it easy. After two hours walking I met with my first setback. The boys discovered two skeletons of members of a previous expedition who had died from cold and exposure. This unnerved them and they refused to go on. I had expected trouble of this sort—the plains people mistrusted mountains and believed them to be the dwelling place of evil spirits. I argued, threatened, and bribed, but nothing would move them. It was impossible to proceed without the loads of firewood, provisions and blankets, and yet there was no one to carry them. But when I found my entreaties were no good, I put my white woman's prestige in my pocket and shouldered the bags myself. This shamed

---

2. This is an unsubstantiated claim. The *Guide to Mount Kenya and Kilimanjaro* lists Frau von Ruckteschell as being the first woman on the mountain, making an incomplete ascent in 1914.

the cook boy, who said he would follow me. Then 2 of the braver boys decided to come. So after I had sent the remaining boys to guard the camp our depleted party set out. The next incident was when we reached the snow line (about 1200 m below the summit). There is a little plateau here before the ice, and in it is a cave where previous expeditions had made their camp. One of the boys found some drifted snow, and never having seen it before he picked it up and played with it like a child. He became so excited that he said he would carry it back to show to his Bwana, his English master. We put the snow into a cup and kindled a fire, because of course it was very cold. This soon melted the snow and caused more trouble, because when the guides saw the snow disappearing they thought it bewitched and refused resolutely to go further. I saw that it was useless this time and made the remainder of the journey alone. The ascent did not take me so very long, and I actually looked inside the crater, being careful to step on rocks in case the snow was treacherous and merely overlapping the cavity. My first feeling up there was that of being absolutely on top of the world.

A couple of years later Gertrude walked from South Africa to Kenya. In 1913 she was again back in Africa. This time she crossed the African continent from west to east in 11 months, tramping over 6000 km. She started in northern Nigeria. She was accompanied by seven or eight native bearers at any one time, hired in different areas, and had no other companions. Her chief difficulty, she said, was not wild beasts but teaching the native bearers to cook. She carried calico, needles and other items to trade for food. After reaching the Kenyan coast, she went on to India, and was in the Himalayas when the First World War broke out. She returned to England.

In camp, Gertrude engaged in "that very feminine pastime" of embroidery and knitting. In this way, she was able to finance, or perhaps by exchange arrange, the purchase of native curios. According to Bob Campbell, a Banff outfitter, Gertrude's parents had disapproved of her mountaineering, insisting that she finance her own expeditions, which she did by selling her embroidery work.

Gertrude also made her own clothes, and a great deal of time was spent in darning and repair work when traveling through the bush. She wore a khaki skirt, puttees (strips of khaki fabric wrapped over the boot tops and around each leg, acting as gaiters), strong shoes, and a pith helmet. She traveled unarmed, carrying only a sunshade and an umbrella, "not very warlike weapons." By one newspaper account she also carried a Bible, a pocket Shakespeare, *Lorna Doone*, and Kipling's *Kim*.

When in camp Gertrude also sketched and painted mountains and landscapes extensively. She was elected to the Royal Geographical Society in 1916 because of the topographical value of her mountain sketches. She apparently resigned later in the same year with ill feeling over an unrecorded incident. She painted many peaks around the world that had not been painted before, and considered them portraits rather than pictures. Although an accomplished watercolorist, Gertrude's interest in mountains was more geographic than artistic.

Mountain climbing was again one of her activities in Africa in 1922. In that year she climbed Mount Elgin (over 4300m) twice, and circumnavigated Mount Kenya. When asked about the fears of medical problems in Africa, Gertrude replied, "I am convinced there is little risk if plenty of exercise is taken, no alcohol drunk, and the native food of the country exclusively eaten."

Between her world travels, Gertrude would return briefly to England. But "London boarding houses are not a pleasure and I am longing to get away."

In 1927 Gertrude was once again in Africa. From there she continued for four years, journeying to Madagascar, Egypt, Arabia, Syria, Nepal, Tibet, Malaysia, New Zealand, Guatemala, British Honduras (now Belize), the West Indies, and South America. The only time that she was ever robbed was in South America. Many of her valuables were taken from her gear while it was stored at a customs house.

In the 1930s Gertrude spent many summers in the Himalayas. She collected over 11,000 flowers there, but many of them were ruined when she descended to lower elevations.

In 1934 Gertrude gave an informal talk to the Ladies' Alpine Club of England, illustrated with sketches mounted on an easel. Not previously a member of the club, she was nonetheless elected to honorary status in 1935.

Gertrude Benham died at sea in February 1938, while returning to Britain from yet another solo trip across Africa. She was 71 years old.

Gertrude had previously donated her vast collection of curios from around the world to the City of Plymouth Museum, in England, where it is on display today. Unfortunately, her collection of over 300 mountain paintings has been lost.

Gertrude was a woman who wandered the globe, defying the traditions of the day.

> I am a lone wanderer. I have no home in the sense that is generally understood, and so there is nothing to prevent me enjoying to the utmost the spirit of wanderlust that has entered my soul. I am never lonely. How can I be when there is so much to see and admire in the world?

Henrietta Tuzo Wilson
(1873-1955)

Henrietta Tuzo made a number of ascents in the Selkirks and Rocky Mountains just after the turn of the century. These climbs were more difficult than those of other lady alpinists of the time. One was a first ascent, and most were first ascents for women. She considered mountain climbing "a glorious sport."

Henrietta "Hettie" Loetitia Tuzo was born in Victoria, British Columbia, on May 6, 1873. Her father, H.A. Tuzo, was one of British Columbia's pioneer doctors; he had traveled west with the fur brigades. He was born in Trinidad but grew up in Quebec. In 1853, after he graduated as a medical doctor, he immediately joined the Hudson's Bay Company as a clerk. He journeyed through Canada with Sir George Simpson in the same year, crossing the Rocky Mountains via Athabasca Pass.

In Victoria, Dr. Tuzo worked first for the Hudson's Bay Company and then for various banks. In 1874 he moved to New York City, where he worked as a bank manager. Hettie's only sibling, Jack, was born there on September 15, 1874. The family moved to England two years later, where Dr. Tuzo died on August 14, 1890.

At 17 years of age Hettie was left to look after her mother. The latter was a domineering woman, and Hettie "escaped" from her by engaging in outdoor pursuits such as tennis and, later, mountain climbing. Hettie and her mother lived a genteel life in the country near Warlingham in Surrey. They had a garden and raised a few chickens. Hettie developed a keen interest in botany and gardening. One of her school scribblers was filled with notes on flower families, with accurate watercolor drawings. Her days were frequently spent playing tennis, badminton, croquet or grass hockey. Sedentary activities included chess and the Amateur Dramatic Club. Her social consciousness was raised by attending lectures on the suffragette movement and becoming an active member of the Humanitarian League.

Hettie was educated at a girls' school in Croydon. She later pursued some medical studies through university extension lectures at the University College in London and at Oxford. She also attended classes in Egyptology, political science, theology and literature. She dropped her studies, though, because of the difficulty of attending classes so far from home. She was tutored in French.

In 1893 Hettie made her first trip after moving to England. With her mother and brother she journeyed to Norway and Sweden. A few years later, in 1896, they traveled on the continent. Hettie's first climbing experience came when she climbed the Ortler (3902 m) in the Tyrol.

In late 1897 Hettie began to learn the rudiments of photography and sketching in preparation to going abroad the next year. She eventually mastered photo processing as well.

The following summer she and her mother traveled to Canada to visit her brother Jack, who had moved there in 1897. He worked as a mining engineer near Nelson, in southeastern British Columbia. She described the visit as "an epoch-making event" in her life. Upon her return to England she found Britain "cramped and small and so tidy" and it was with a "sore heart" that she took up her old life again. She found it difficult to exist as a spirited woman in Victorian England.

In 1898 Hettie discovered Banff. She and her mother arrived there on July 16 for a brief stop on their way to visit Jack again. On their return they stayed at Glacier House. She fell in love with the mountains and prairies of western Canada.

Being "deadly bored" with her life in England, Hettie in 1900 again traveled to the continent with her mother. They visited the Alps at Innsbruck, Austria and Cortina, Italy.

But in 1901 Hettie and her mother were back in Canada. Her mother always accompanied Hettie and they stayed at the Canadian Pacific Railway hotels. From Glacier House, on September 18, Edward Feuz, Sr., guided Henrietta to the summit of Eagle Peak (2819 m). He also led her up the Illecillewaet Glacier and to Look-out Point. These were her first climbing adventures in Canada.

Then came an extensive tour of the Far East in 1902—Japan, Malaysia, Singapore and Hong Kong—and a year spent at home.

In 1904 Hettie returned to Canada. She and her mother spent a month at the Banff Springs Hotel, visiting all of the local haunts: Lake Minnewanka, Sulphur Mountain, Sundance Canyon. The highlight came when she and three others were guided to the summit of Mount Rundle (2949 m) by a waiter from the hotel. From Banff, Hettie and her mother moved on to Laggan (now Lake Louise). There she scrambled up Mount Fairview (2744 m) with Jack and a few others. She also became reacquainted with Julia Henshaw, who was taking photographs for her upcoming book on mountain flowers. They shared common interests in botany and photography.

Hettie also met Gertrude Benham, who was just heading off to climb Mount Assiniboine. Miss Benham was the only serious woman climber in Canada at the time, and Hettie was undoubtedly impressed by her achievements (see page 125). They met again later in the summer at Glacier House, where they did some climbing together. At Field she and Jack visited Emerald Lake and went on horseback to the Yoho Valley.

After returning from a few weeks spent in Vancouver, Hettie and her mother stopped again at Glacier House. On the first of September Hettie climbed Mount Afton (2545 m) with Swiss guide Christian Bohren. Nearby Mount Bonney looked so "superlatively beautiful" that they decided to climb it the next day.

By 3:15 a.m. they were on horseback for the approach. The wrangler refused to let her ride sidesaddle so Hettie rode astride for the first time in her life. The route had been frequented by grizzlies, which made them very nervous, and they saw huge tracks in the snow. She regretted not being able to linger in the wonderful alpine meadows, abloom with luxuriant flowers. After crossing the Lily Glacier and reaching the foot of Bonney Glacier, they had to choose their route, for Christian had not climbed Mount Bonney before. They elected to head for the saddle far ahead of them. At one difficult point she waited in a "safe" place—"that is, my toes were in chinks and my hands had tiny bits of rock to hold"—while Christian searched out a route. After ascending a steep snow slope onto some rocks, a large avalanche roared down to cover their tracks, and "snow did not seem so interesting for a little while." After ascending what they thought was the peak, they were disappointed to see a higher summit some way off. They traversed snowfields and yet another peak before reaching the actual summit (3107 m). For their descent Christian chose a more direct route via the north face although it turned out to be no quicker than their earlier route. The homeward scramble became "somewhat severe" after dark, with Christian encouraging Hettie and urging her on. When they returned to the hotel, exhausted, Hettie's mother had a wonderful supper waiting. They were out nineteen hours. Theirs was the second ascent of the peak.

The following day, Hettie rested from her climb and planned an ascent of Mount Sir Donald. Unfortunately the next two days her mother was unwell and unable to leave her room so Hettie postponed the climb. But on September 6 Hettie and Christian arose at 2:30 a.m. for their climb. With the coming of dawn Christian put the candle out, and Hettie set her skirt "to working length." At one point they had an "amusing scramble" under an ice bridge, where Christian had said there were good steps, but Hettie found herself scrambling on her elbows and knees and relying on a good pull up by Christian. They reached the summit at nine o'clock and after enjoying the view for half an hour, started their descent. They had climbed Mount Sir Donald (3297 m) in a near-record 9-1/2 hours.

On September 9 Hettie and Gertrude Benham arrived at Rogers Hut, again with Christian Bohren guiding. The two women "started as housemaids, made the pine bough beds and swept up and then turned cooks." Strangely, Hettie does not

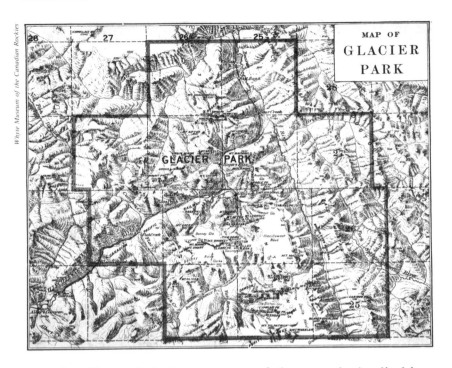

mention Gertrude in her account of the next day's climbing, which she wrote in the Glacier House Scrapbook, even though Gertrude did accompany them. From the summit of Rogers Peak (3214 m) they traversed the Swiss Peaks (3208 m) which Hettie wrote were "certainly not a Piccadilly saunter." They returned to the hut via the Hermit Glacier. Throughout her climbs with Christian she praised his patience and skill.

Shortly thereafter Hettie moved on to the Chateau Lake Louise. On September 15 she climbed Mount Victoria (3464 m) with Christian Kaufmann as her guide. From Lake Louise she returned to eastern Canada and thence to England.

In 1906 Hettie again arrived in Banff in early June. That year she spent a lot of time going about with Mary Schäffer. She found Mary to be a most pleasant companion who shared her interests in the wilderness and wildflowers. Mary even insisted that they paint together. Hettie joined Mary and botanist Stewardson Brown (who was helping her finish her late husband's treatise on wildflowers) on small excursions to collect botanical specimens. One trip was to Ptarmigan Valley, and another was in the Pipestone River drainage.

Hettie became a founding member of the Alpine Club of Canada in 1906, and she attended their first camp in the Yoho Valley. While at the camp she climbed Wapta Mountain (2778 m) with Christian Kaufmann, via the previously-unclimbed northeast face. As they descended the south face of the mountain they met the official climbing party from the camp going up. The following day they made the second ascent of Mount Collie (3116 m). While at the camp her interest was piqued by stories about the wonderful mountains of the Valley of the Ten Peaks near Moraine Lake, particularly Peak Seven, which was as yet unclimbed. Undoubtedly Christian was able to regale her with stories of the climbs to be done there.

Henrietta's red-letter day came on July 21, 1906, when she and Christian made the first ascent of Peak Seven, now called Mount Tuzo (3245 m). It was the last of the Ten Peaks to be conquered. From their camp at Moraine Lake their route took them up the couloir between Peaks Three and Four (now Mount Little and Mount Bowlen) then across a snowfield behind Peaks Four, Five, and Six (mounts Bowlen, Perren and Allen) to reach Peak Seven. At the summit Hettie was so "deadly tired" that she had a nap while Christian built a cairn to commemorate their first ascent. On the descent they were threatened by an avalanche, this time even more closely than on Mount Bonney: while on a treacherous snow slope they heard a report, "looked up to see a mass of rock coming," and in spite of the steepness, tore back from whence they had come as "huge boulders ploughed down over our tracks." After the avalanche settled they still had to cross the slope, which they did with trepidation and much haste, to the safety of the rocks on the other side. By the time they arrived back in camp they had been out twenty-one and a half hours. After only a few hours sleep they were on their way back to the railway station at Lake Louise, via the Chateau. Although she felt fresh Hettie thought she probably "looked tough."

Three days later, on July 24, Hettie joined four other women on a 17-day pack trip to the Kootenay Plains on the North Saskatchewan River. The other women were Mary Schäffer, Mollie Adams, Dorothea Sharp and Zephine Humphrey. Mollie, who was "an enigma" to Hettie, became Mary's regular traveling companion after this trip. They were outfitted by Billy Warren and Bob Campbell. At Laggan they spread out on the station platform with such "a mess of food & dogs pack saddles & covers cameras ropes & miscellaneous" that it was some time before the confusion was straightened out. It seems that her friendship with Mary Schäffer became somewhat strained over the next two weeks. Hettie found Mary to be quite domineering and getting unnecessarily upset about things. (For a different version refer to the chapter on Mary Schäffer Warren, page 57.)

Hettie had met her future husband, John Armitstead Wilson, in Banff in June of the same year. He was working at the Exshaw cement plant and often spent his days off in Banff. Wilson was born in Scotland on November 2, 1879, and came to Canada in 1905. John and Henrietta were married in England the following year, on November 14, 1907.

Immediately after their marriage the Wilsons moved to Ottawa, where they lived for the rest of their lives. For many years Wilson was the director of air services in the Department of Transport and is often referred to as the father of civil aviation in Canada. They had three children: John Tuzo,[1] Mary Loetitia and William Henry Tuzo.

The Wilsons attended the 1911 ACC camp at Vermilion Pass together, as John had business to attend to in Vancouver. Although she afterwards remained active in the Ottawa Section of the ACC, Hettie did not return to mountain climbing after her marriage. She maintained an interest is the outdoors and concern for it by serving with the Canadian National Parks Association, which was formed in 1923 to support the preservation of national parks.

Henrietta was a prime mover in civic affairs in Ottawa. In 1928 she was elected president of the National Council of Women, a post which she held for five years. At various times she also held executive positions on the National Council of Education, the Imperial Order of the Daughters of the Empire (I.O.D.E.), Ottawa Welfare Bureau, National Council of Education and the Royal Ottawa Golf Club. She was also a

---

1. Hettie's son, John Tuzo Wilson, is perhaps Canada's most well-known geologist: he discovered the mechanism of sea-floor spreading, thus explaining part of the theory of plate tectonics.

member of many other organizations: Ottawa Women's Canadian Club, Ottawa branch of League of Nations, Ottawa Horticultural Society and the Red Cross Society. In recognition of her civic contributions, Hettie was awarded the King's Jubilee Medal in 1935 and the Coronation Medal in 1937.

Henrietta Tuzo Wilson died on January 11, 1955, only a few months after her husband.

Henrietta Tuzo Wilson, in her climbing outfit, with Swiss guide Christian Bohren at Glacier House, 1904.

Elizabeth Larned MacCarthy (1877-1944)

Bess MacCarthy was a shy, unassuming woman whose mountaineering accomplishments have been overshadowed by her husband's. Albert MacCarthy made both of Canada's very dramatic first ascents: Mount Robson, highest peak in the Rockies, in 1913 and Mount Logan, highest peak in Canada, in 1925. But it was Bess who discovered the joys of mountain climbing first and introduced Albert to its joys. They climbed together throughout the Rockies, Purcells and Bugaboos. Bess made 26 first ascents in the process (the third most after Katie Gardiner and Georgia Engelhard). Albert is credited with 30.

Elizabeth (Bess) Larned was born February 1, 1877, to a prominent family in Summit, New Jersey. She had three brothers, one of whom, William, was the American national tennis champion for seven consecutive years. Bess was a skilled tennis player also and grew up skating, skiing, riding and climbing—a trend away from feminine things and toward athletic sports. The family spent long summers at Lake Placid in the Adirondacks of New York state, where she became a lover of nature and a denizen of the outdoors. She climbed all of the major peaks in the Adirondacks, some of them many times.

Bess was attracted to Captain Albert "Mack" H. MacCarthy, a friend of William's, who shared her outdoor and athletic interests. He was born in Ames, Iowa in 1876. He entered the United States Naval Academy at Annapolis, Maryland, in 1893 and graduated in 1897. They were married on May 30, 1905. The union brought together wealth, intellect and athletics. Albert resigned his naval commission in 1907 after serving ten years of active duty; he returned briefly to the navy during World War I and afterward served in the Naval Reserve.

In the early 1900s Bess was introduced to mountain climbing in the Andes and in Japan. Her first trip to Canada was in 1909 when she and Mary Jobe accompanied Herschel Parker and Howard Palmer on a mapping expedition to Mount Sir Sandford, in British Columbia's Selkirk Mountains (see "Mary Jobe Akeley," page 82). After that ten-day trip the two women spent five more weeks camping and canoeing in the Big Bend area of the Columbia River north of Golden. They then went climbing at the Alpine Club of Canada's Lake O'Hara camp. At O'Hara Bess qualified for active membership in the club by climbing Mount Stephen (3199m). She also climbed Mount Schaffer (2692m) and was on the first ascent of Mount Victoria (3464 m) from the south side. In later years she climbed Victoria a number of times. She and Mary also did a three-day circuit from O'Hara over Opabin, Wenkchemna and Wastach Passes, Mitre Col and Abbot Pass, and back to O'Hara.

After the camp six members traveled by horse up the Beaverfoot River to the Ice River, south of Field in Yoho park. Dr. A. Eggers had hired Ed Feuz, Sr. to guide him on his second attempt on the unclimbed North Tower of Mount Goodsir (3525m). On the day of the ascent, nearing the summit, Eggers was unable to continue, but J.P. Forde and P.D. McTavish succeeded in making the first ascent with Feuz. Bess "longed to accompany them, even while realizing that it was beyond me." Within a few years, though, she was making even more difficult ascents than that.

Forde, McTavish and Bess returned to Field on foot, over Wilson and Duschesnay passes. The monotonous struggle through dense underbrush to Wilson Pass was relieved only by the frequent patches of strawberries, raspberries and blueberries. Expecting to make the trip in one long day, they carried only scanty provisions; Bess brought a quilt. Soon realizing that they would be spending the night out, they stopped early to gather enough firewood for warmth. The men took turns feeding the fire throughout the night. In the morning they left the quilt behind "to decorate a tree and mayhap gladden the eye of some belated traveller."

At the confluence of the Ottertail River and Goodsir Creek they caught some much-appreciated trout. While struggling through more tangled brush on McArthur Creek Bess fell into a deep pool from which she was "most unceremoniously" plucked by her companions. The extra weight of wet clothes tired her during the day. They missed finding Duchesnay Pass and were confronted instead by an impassable wall of rotten rock. Retracing their steps, they traversed the ridge between mounts Duchesnay and Odaray and "crawled" onto the Duchesnay Glacier, crossing it to the proper pass. From there they traversed the shoulder of Mount Stephen until they reached the summit of Dennis Pass. At 7:30 p.m. they caught sight of the lights of Field, still 1000m below. While crossing another creek on the descent Bess managed to pull Forde into it, although she didn't fall in herself. Two hours later they reached Stephen House (CPR hotel) and sat down to a late supper. "Even the remarks of the tourists in the hotel upon my costume having no effect on my appetite," wrote Bess, "which had been growing keener every minute since noon." She had undoubtedly proved her traveling abilities on this outing.

Bess introduced Albert to mountain climbing two years later, at the 1911 ACC camp at Sherbrooke Lake. He did his qualifying climb on Mount Daly (3152m) and together they climbed a number of other peaks in the area. It was here that they met Winthrop and Margaret Stone. Dr. Stone was the president of Purdue University in Indiana and an ardent mountain disciple. The two couples were to spend seven seasons climbing together, at ACC camps and on private expeditions.

Both Bess and Albert were members of the Alpine Club of Canada (he became an honorary member) and the American Alpine Club. Bess was also a member of the French Alpine Club, and Albert of the Appalachian Mountain Club and The Alpine Club of London, England.

After the Sherbrooke Lake camp the MacCarthys joined

Colonel William W. Foster, Deputy Minister of Public Lands of British Columbia, on an inspection trip over the proposed route of the new Banff-Windermere Highway. At that time it was only a lightly blazed trail from the Bow Valley to Lake Windermere in the Columbia Valley. Although they were plagued by continuous fog and rain for the five-day trip, Bess and Albert were entranced by the "magnificent and unknown country." When they reached Radium they had a delightful moonlight swim in the hot springs and then went to a houseboat on Lake Windermere. They fell so in love with the valley that they bought a ranch, which they named "Karmax," on the benchlands above the village of Wilmer. From the ranch there was an encompassing view of the Columbia Valley. This was their summer home and retreat from eastern civilization for 15 years.

During this time they usually spent the winters in the east, sometimes living in Summit, New Jersey, and sometimes in New York City. Albert was trying his hand at a number of business ventures, including textiles, law, banking, real estate and even hotel operation. He grew to hate business more and more, wanting to return to Karmax where they could again "call our souls our own."

On their ranch they cleared land, planted, irrigated and harvested crops, and tended cattle. Bess loved the outdoor life; riding and repairing fence lines, checking irrigation ditches. She had a great affinity for animals and two large dogs were her constant companions. A few times she and Albert would plan an overseas trip but it would invariably be cancelled because in the end Bess would refuse to leave the dogs. The dogs were even taken to Alpine Club camps. She was an insatiable reader, and the bookshelves were piled high with the classics, as well as books on nature, travel and exploration around the world. She also enjoyed working on pottery. Bess was a shy, introverted woman who found the frenetic, but conventional, life of the Eastern cities repressive, always longing to return to the peaceful freedom of outdoor life.

While at the ACC's 1913 Robson Pass camp Albert made the coveted first ascent of Mount Robson (3954m) with Austrian guide Conrad Kain, and his friend Bill Foster.

Flush with the excitement of the Robson camp the

Albert and Bess MacCarthy.

MacCarthys started looking for new challenges and first ascents. Climbers had just returned from the Purcell Mountains west of Karmax, pronouncing Mount Farnham (3457m), the highest peak, as "absolutely unclimbable." Here was a challenge in their backyard. With a wagon and three saddle horses the MacCarthys, accompanied by a Miss Broadbent and a packer, reconnoitred the mountain from Karmax. They set up a fly camp (temporary shelter) at the base of the northeast ridge, planning a climb for the morrow, but an overnight snow made an attempt impossible. But before returning they made the third ascent of Nelson Peak (3283m).

Sometimes Bess stayed on at Karmax after Albert went east to take care of business. In the fall of 1913 she joined Conrad Kain on two successful goat hunts. They spent an "exceedingly strenuous week" on one hunt. They walked and led packhorses. She had also planned a third hunt for some New York friends but this was canceled by a cold snap and heavy snow.

The following year the MacCarthys attended the ACC's Little Yoho camp. Following the camp Conrad was to sail to New Zealand. He wired Albert that the steamer was delayed and that he could spare them a few days if he was needed. They jumped at the chance and returned with Conrad to confront Mount Farnham. They took a couple of men along as packers, one of whom was their gardener.

On August 10 they set out for the big climb. It proved to be nine-and-a-half hours of very tricky rock and snow work to the summit. Mack noted that several very interesting spots were encountered on the first of two arêtes. These "were negotiated by the gymnastic stunt of extending the arms and legs to the extreme limit and then gradually shifting the balance from the rear to the forward supports, while the sheer drop of a thousand or more feet directly below strongly suggested the advisability of the right hand and foot letting the left hand and foot know just what they were doing before the responsibility was actually shifted."

It was only after that that "the real interest and difficulties" of the climb began, and soon "no muscle of the body felt that it had been neglected." There were many hours of ascending broken ledges, followed by nearly 150m of exciting chimney climbing. New snow and a cold wind hampered their efforts, but did not deter them. As they approached the summit, Conrad, "reaffirming his allegiance to the suffragette," dropped to the rear and invited Bess to lead the last section.

They had used up their water, but on the summit the ever-resourceful Kain placed large slabs of rock at an angle to the sun and melted some snow. They were inspired by the views of unclimbed and unexplored peaks to the north, west and south. All too soon they knew they had to descend, with little chance of reaching camp before dark. Extreme care was called for in negotiating the steep ledges and keeping the rope clear of the sharp rocks—Conrad had declared that they should treat the rope like their own mother! When they did arrive back in camp they had been out for 22 hours and 15 minutes; they enjoyed "last night's supper and to-day's breakfast in one and the same dish." Their successful ascent of Mount Farnham was a testament to Conrad's skill and to everyone's climbing abilities.

After their exertions they enjoyed a rest day in camp listening to Conrad's tales of life, from snaring mice in Siberia to the intricate problems of government! He was a complex individual, who believed in being a free man. This led him to guide independently from the guides' organizations created by the Canadian Pacific and the Canadian National railways. The next day they climbed Mount Farnham Tower (3329m), with Bess again leading on the summit stretch.

After such successful climbing seasons with Conrad in 1913 and again in 1914 the MacCarthys decided to hire him exclusively for the summer of 1915. It was an extremely successful season during which they made many first ascents in the Purcells. Conrad had a tremendous influence on both of them, honing their mountaineering skills to a fine art.

Besides the MacCarthys and Kain, the 1915 climbing party included Winthrop and Margaret Stone, and newcomer Otto Frind. Frind was a Canadian who climbed with Conrad in New Zealand. The last week in July was spent working their way up to the base of Mount Ethelbert (3158m). It was an enchanted valley in which to camp, with a charming lake nestled between the crags and precipices of Ethelbert and Mount Horeb. The hanging valley above camp was dotted with lakes. The ascent itself was uneventful; it provided tempting views of the rest of the Purcells.

After their return there was an interlude of a few days before they set out to explore Horsethief Creek, to the northwest of Karmax. As well as the Stones and Frind they were joined by their friend Beatrice Schultz, and assisted by a packer and a cook. They left Karmax in two farm wagons and at the end of the road they took to packhorses. After the first night's camp Bess was called upon to use eight stitches to close a deep gash on one of the horses, which had cut itself in scrambling through the timber. She performed her veterinary task ably.

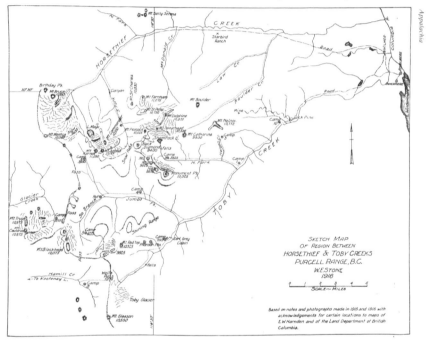

On the second night they established a base camp on the south fork of Horsethief Creek, only ten minutes from the snout of the glacier and within striking distance of a dozen or so first-class peaks.

On the first day's climb they ascended Commander Mountain (3362m). Although it was late in the day when they reached the summit, rather than retrace their steps they traversed Jumbo Peak (3399m) on their return to camp. The next day was much easier, with only a small climb of Mount Peter (3354m). On the sixth of August they climbed Mount Delphine (3376m), which was a second ascent, and then traversed

Spearhead Peak (3231m) and "Peacock" (3208m), now called Mount McCoubrey. They reached the summit of Peacock at seven o'clock in the evening, so with little daylight remaining they glissaded down a long snow-filled chimney, dropping some 1400 m in a short time. Stone remembered descending at "a speed resulting disastrously to the garments of one member of the party, who in consequence was ordered to the rear for the rest of the march." In three days they had accomplished five first ascents and one second ascent.

After the Stones left for civilization the MacCarthys and Kain also made a second ascent of Eyebrow Peak (3380m) and a first ascent of Birthday Peak (3207m), the latter so named because it was climbed on Conrad's birthday.

Having climbed most of the big peaks in the southern part of the Purcells the MacCarthys turned their attention north in 1916, to what was known as the "Spillimacheen Spires" (now the Bugaboo Spires). From the high peaks to the east, and from the Purcells themselves, Bess and Albert had seen this group of massive granite towers north of Horsethief Creek. Although the area had been visited by miners searching for copper and galena, it was a virgin area for climbers. Conrad had seen the

A photograph of the Bugaboos, as seen from the southwest, annotated by Albert MacCarthy.

remarkable spires, rising thousands of vertical metres out of the icefield, in 1910 while guiding the Longstaff-Wheeler Expedition, but he had done no climbing then. Tom Longstaff described them as looking "like arctic nunataks out of an icecap: quite sheer, without a speck of snow," to which Conrad replied, "There be no ledges there to catch that snow." In the intervening years Conrad had undoubtedly regaled the MacCarthys with stories of "the Nunataks," and they were eager to see them up close.

Thus, on August 25, 1916, the MacCarthys, Kain, Frind, Mrs. George Vincent and her son John, with the aid of two packers, made camp in the valley below what would later be known as the Bugaboo Glacier. The next morning they ascended the glacier for their own firsthand look at the awesome spires. From a col between two of the spires they looked out upon a broad glacier along whose west side ran "the walls of a lofty ridge that stood in a semi-circle with five sharp peaks vying with each other for leadership." After some time spent discussing the peaks, their possible lines of attack and which might be highest, they finally chose the tallest of the western ramparts, the North Howser Spire. They crossed the glacier and gained the ridge by a steep couloir. Then followed some fine rock and snow work to reach the summit (3400m), which they did at four o'clock. "True to habit," Conrad led them down a different route an hour later. As they were coming off the glacier at 9:30 p.m., they were rewarded with a shifting display of the northern lights. Mack described the scene:

> For a moment the sky would be black, then a bright spot would appear and from it would radiate shafts of light in all directions. These shafts would quiver, contract and then expand until they almost met, then contract and from their common centre quivering rings of light would run out with incredible speed like waves and cross-bar the heavens: suddenly all would be darkness again, only to be broken in a moment when the display would take on still other forms.

Two days later, on August 28, they made a traverse of Sextet Ridge on the west side of the Bugaboo Glacier. This involved climbing over the summits of Anniversary Peak (2912m) and Howser Peak (3095m). But their gaze kept returning to the three spires just above camp. They decided that "Peak Three" was the highest, partly because the sheer walls of "Peak Two" were very ominous. At 6:30 a.m. on the twenty-ninth, Albert, Bess, John and Conrad left camp for Peak Three.

The climb went well until the group reached an elevation of about 3050 m, at which point they encountered a most formidable gendarme.[1] It was "a veritable bugaboo" which immediately suggested a most appropriate name—Bugaboo Spire—which came to be applied to the whole range. There being no safer line of ascent, Conrad decided that the face of the gendarme itself was their only hope. It was the crux of the climb.

Mack described Conrad's determined efforts to surmount this obstacle:

> He gradually worked up this face by means of several diagonal cracks until he succeeded in getting both arms over the top edge, and here he stuck for a long time, feeling about and looking for some little thing that might afford him a hold long enough to pull himself over; at last he found it, although it was not apparent to us when we followed, and slowly crept over the edge. Half an hour we waited while Conrad's body disappeared and reappeared at the edge; after each disappearance we expected to hear a shout that we could prepare to follow, but each time Conrad's fingers would slowly come into sight and then he would appear again to survey the situation and make a fresh start It was impossible to throw the rope over anything to give him support . . . all we could do was to tend the useless rope, giving him slack and pulling it in again when he came back into view. Just how he finally got into the crack is a mystery to us but, after a dozen reappearances, he smiled and said: "I make it," and soon began to call for rope, until about sixty feet had run out and he called from the top of the ridge above the gendarme.

"The endurance required in balancing one's whole weight on the toes should be cultivated," commented the self-effacing Conrad. It had taken him an hour and a half to overcome the hurdle. The group then proceeded rather uneventfully to the summit (3185m). Eyeballing a second summit as perhaps being higher, they set off for it. After two hours they succeeded in reaching it—according to their barometer it was the same height as the first, to which they returned.

As a rule Conrad never worried about a descent but this time he was not confident of descending the gendarme without too much risk. On the way up he had heard Mack whisper to

---

1. This term means literally "a policeman." It is descriptive of a pinnacle along a ridge.

Whyte Museum of the Canadian Rockies — ACC collection

Bess MacCarthy descending on Bugaboo Spire, 1916.

the others that he was confident Conrad would not descend the same way if any other route was to be found. "I concealed my fear carefully," Conrad wrote to Frind. Instead, they rappelled down the cliff back of the gendarme, to a small ledge which led back to the ridge below the gendarme. In Mack's view the ledge was a rather "insignificant edge above a 2,000-foot drop" where "no one cared to linger." After that they were virtually home free. Conrad rated the climb of Bugaboo Spire as his most interesting in seven years of climbing in Canada.

After their time in this unique area Frind and Mack advocated park status for the Bugaboos but it was many years before it was achieved. (Bugaboo Glacier Provincial Park was declared in 1969.) Although Frind did not particularly like the MacCarthys' fast-paced climbing he admitted that he would have done far fewer ascents in the Bugaboos without their "well-known strenuosity."

Part way through the First World War the MacCarthys bought a second ranch, named "K2," on the east, or Rocky Mountains, side of the Columbia River. Needing more help with their holdings, Albert hired Conrad to work for him full-time. He was particularly needed when the MacCarthys were not at the ranch in the winter. Conrad's future wife, Hetta Ferreira, was the MacCarthys' maid.

In 1917 Albert got his Navy commission again for a few short years, which precluded much climbing aside from the ACC camps. The following year Bess assisted in the war effort by running a soldiers' and sailors' restaurant in the state armory at Annapolis, Maryland, where they were then living.

The MacCarthys were Conrad's close friends and he sought their advice on many things. Conrad wrote Dr. Thorington about sending some of his furs to Bess to sell in New York for him, hoping that she would be honest with him for "I know she is very fond of making a cent or two if she possibly can do it."

During the winter of 1915-16 Albert and Bess had a journey to New Zealand planned. Everything was booked and paid for but important business came up that caused them to cancel the trip. They had sent Conrad ahead to search out some climbing and had to wire him to cancel. Their only excursion was to go skiing and skating in Quebec and the Adirondacks.

That summer Bess and Albert did more exploring in the Purcells. They were packed in by Bill Williams, an Indian guide, with his six horses. The MacCarthys and Stones were accompanied by three local novices, Elise and Elinor Hopkins and Madelaine Turnor. They were guided by Kain. The novices participated in the expedition with enthusiasm, but they did no serious climbing.[2]

By the second night the group had established a base camp. From it they traversed a ridge of four peaks that culminated in Monument Peak (3094m). As they intended to continue their traverse and descend by a different route, they dallied on the summit. Ten minutes into the descent, though, they came to an impassable cliff. Conrad disappeared and a little later found a new route and called up, "It is all right," but Stone felt that "his expression was not altogether reassuring." After great difficulty and five hours of hard going they finally reached the glacier below. Daylight passed quickly, and they stumbled back to the camp in the dark.

Two days later they climbed Black Diamond Mountain (3094m). Then they moved camp down the valley. Here Mrs. Vincent and John arrived, bringing with them fresh supplies. In spite of prevailing snow squalls on August 3 they ascended Mount Nelson (3294m).

When they moved camp to the "Jumbo Fork" of Toby Creek, Frind joined them, bringing yet more welcome food. They had taken only enough provisions for two weeks but it seemed they were going to be staying longer (they were eventually out 25 days), so Mack had sent Bill out by "pony express" with a note for Frind to bring in more supplies: a folding stove, three five-pound tins each of greengrape and raspberry jam, fifty pounds of potatoes, six more cups, and ten loaves of bread, which were to be baked by Hetta.

On August 7 most of the group ascended Blockhead Mountain (3063m). Having seen a great snow-clad peak to the

---

2. Madelaine was a local girl who was working for the MacCarthys on their ranch. She helped Bess with the cooking on this trip. They had previously taken her to the ACC camp at Little Yoho in 1914. It was Conrad who later taught her how to pack horses and she spent the rest of her life working as a guide and outfitter in the Columbia Valley.

northwest, seven of them backpacked up another tributary and bivouacked below it. On the ascent they were caught for an hour in a snow and electrical storm, during which their ice axes buzzed ominously. When the storm passed, the cloud curtain was swept aside, revealing a snowy plain ahead of them. They quickly chose a route up the north arête before the clouds again enveloped them. Albert and Bess alternately led to the summit. They named it Truce Mountain (3246m). From its summit they traversed to Cauldron Mountain (3216m). A pleasant glissade down quickly changed to panic when they hit ice—luckily within 60m it was again covered by snow.

A long hard day on the mountains brought weariness after exhilaration. As Stone put it, "The end of a day on the mountains is invariably an anticlimax. The ascent is inspiring; it whips every energy into action; but the return is dull and without zest. The heights are behind, enthusiasm has spent itself, and before are the darkening valleys and the weary way over scree and rough moraine."

On the evening of August 10 they celebrated Conrad's birthday. On the following day Bess and Albert joined Conrad in ascending Redtop Mountain (3109m). Then came a few days spent moving their camp to Wells Gray Pass, where they were stormbound for two days by rain, which turned to snow. When the storm finally passed they left the valley; the fresh snow had made climbing too hazardous. Descending from the pass, a packhorse slipped and fell over a cliff to the glacier below. It had to be shot and its load redistributed among the other horses.

In all they climbed thirteen peaks, twelve of which were first ascents (six over 3050m), and they traversed five passes.

In June of 1917 there was a happy event at Karmax—the marriage of Conrad and Hetta. For the next three years they continued to live on the ranch. Albert and Bess spent the 1917 summer building, fencing and clearing land at the ranches. They relied on Conrad's help, as labor was scarce in the valley. The only climbing they did was at the ACC Cataract Valley camp, with Conrad as their personal guide. Bess was the first woman to climb Mount Hungabee (3493m). This was the last season that Conrad climbed with them. His wife was sick and he did not wish to leave her alone.

The MacCarthys had many visitors from among their

friends in the east. One elderly lady, who ran a family hotel in Maryland for them, had never been on a horse before. While wading her first creek she fell into the water. Madeline Turnor could never understand why they dragged their "unfortunate friends" along in an effort to introduce them to the outdoors.

Bess and Mack continued to attend the annual Alpine Club camps faithfully. In 1918 they were at the Paradise Valley camp, for the first time without Conrad in six years. After the ACC Victory camp (the First World War was over) in the Yoho Valley in 1919 they climbed Mount Lefroy (3423m). Later in the summer they climbed Mount Sir Donald (3297m) in the Selkirks, via the northwest ridge. In 1920 they were at the Mount Assiniboine camp.

In 1920 Conrad bought his own small homestead in the Columbia Valley, from which he operated a guiding and outfitting business augmented by trapping in the winter.

The MacCarthys and the Stones had spent seven seasons climbing together. Margaret Stone made 23 first ascents, mostly with Bess and Albert, while Winthrop made 18. Theirs was a congenial and able group. This all changed when Winthrop died on July 17, 1921, during the first ascent of Mount Eon (3310m) with his wife.

The Stones had nearly reached the summit when Winthrop detached himself from the rope to explore beyond a small chimney. It appears that he worked his way over rotten rock until he reached the summit, from which he fell some 250m when a hold gave way. Margaret saw him fall but did not at first realize that he had taken the rope off. With great courage she followed their ascent route back down the mountain, until her way was blocked by a cliff. She then anchored the rope and lowered herself. As she was still short of the ledge below she let go of the rope and dropped to the ground. To her horror she discovered that she could proceed no further, and the rope was now out of her reach. She spent the next six days on this narrow ledge, wearing only a flannel shirt and knickers. Fortunately there was a very slight trickle of water. Margaret was finally rescued on July 24, seven days after her husband had fallen, by a search party made up of Swiss guide Rudolph Aemmer, outfitter Bill Peyto and a Royal Canadian Mounted Police officer. Winthrop's body wasn't recovered until August

Winthrop and Margaret Stone on the summit of Wapta Peak, 1919.

5, by a second search party. Albert and Conrad were members of that group; after locating the body of their long-time friend they continued to the summit, where they built a cairn and left a note.

The death of Winthrop Stone had a tremendous impact on the climbing community, especially on Albert MacCarthy. His friend's death, and the resulting anguish to Stone's family and friends, caused Albert to pause and reflect on the price that is sometimes paid for mountain adventure. He did not climb for a year, but his interest was revived again in 1923 with plans for an expedition to Mount Logan (6050m), the highest peak in Canada and yet unclimbed.

The idea of climbing Mount Logan had surfaced in 1913 after the euphoria of making the first ascent of Mount Robson, but the plans had been put on hold because of the war. The suggestion was made again in 1923 and Albert was elected leader of the expedition. Then followed two years of planning and a reconnaissance in 1924, made by Albert at his own expense. In the spring of 1925 Albert made food caches and on June 23, 1925, he made the first ascent accompanied by Bill Foster, Fred Lambart, Allen Carpé, Hamilton Laing and Norm Read. Albert was back in the Rockies in time to attend the ACC's annual camp at Lake O'Hara with Bess.

In the summer of 1926 Albert traveled overseas. He made 101 ascents in 63 elapsed days in the Alps, of which only 45 were climbing days! Mack wrote to Dr. J. Monroe Thorington[3] that exploring and climbing in Canada was "far more interesting and absorbing than anything that the European Alps afforded in its highly developed and stereotyped climbs," so he did as much as he could in one year. He then went on to do some minor climbs in New Zealand. Bess had promised Albert that she would go with him but in the end she wouldn't leave her dogs behind.

In 1926 Albert made major changes in his business affairs. They sold the ranches and moved to Denver, where he joined a brother involved with the La Plata Mines Company. Then

---

3. Thorington was a Philadelphia eye doctor, climbing historian and author of the first editions of the climbing guides, the book *The Glittering Mountains of Canada* and editor of Kain's biography, *Where the Clouds Can Go.*

in 1932 they moved back to Annapolis, where they lived in an apartment at a hotel called "Carvel Hall," which was a Larned-family corporation. When William Larned, an architect, had been working on renovations at the Naval Academy many years earlier, he could not find a place to live. His father had suggested that they buy an old house in the area and start their own hotel. William chose "Paca House" and drew the designs to convert it to Carvel Hall. When he found himself too busy to manage it, Albert took over as president. He maintained this position until the property was sold to the Sheraton chain in 1944.

The MacCarthys became very active in the Annapolis area. Because of their fondness for dogs and other animals they formed a local chapter of the Society for the Prevention of Cruelty to Animals (SPCA). Albert served as its president for 20 years until his death.

On February 2, 1934, the MacCarthys' old friend and guide, Conrad Kain, passed away. He died of equine encephalitis—Canada's greatest guide, killed by a mosquito bite. His wife had died a year previously. A well-known and respected guide during his lifetime, Conrad has since become a legend in Canada.

In October, 1942, Bess suffered a stroke and Albert underwent blood transfusions twice because of stomach hemorrhages. His persistent stomach problems were thought to have resulted from the hardships encountered during the Logan Expedition. That winter they went south to a cottage at Camden, South Carolina.

Bess died on February 10, 1944. Albert never climbed again. He did continue his annual excursions to the Alpine Club of Canada camps until 1952, when declining health prohibited the lengthy journey across the continent. He also attended some camps of the Skyline Hikers of the Canadian Rockies. He died on October 11, 1956, at the age of 80 years.

Two peaks in the Purcell Mountains have been named for the two couples who pioneered many first ascents there: Mount MacCarthy (3063m) and Mount Stone (3033m)—fitting memorials both.

Phyllis James Munday
(1894-1990)

Fair dreamer of the upper air,
Embodiment of the mountain calm,
Grant us thy heights release from care,
Thy solitudes unfailing balm.
—W.A.D. Munday

In the early spring of 1925, Phyllis and Don Munday joined a friend, Tom Ingram, on an early-season attempt of Mount Arrowsmith (1817 m), near Port Alberni on Vancouver Island. While stopped for lunch and casually scanning the horizon with binoculars, Phyllis spotted a high peak in the Coast Mountains across the Strait of Georgia. It was shining like a beacon through a break in the clouds that hugged the mountains. She pointed it out to Don, who immediately took a compass bearing before the clouds obscured it once again. To them, it was the "far off finger of destiny beckoning."

The mountain lay due north on a line passing near the head of Bute Inlet. They guessed the mountain to lie about 240 km away, in a virtually unknown and unmapped area. It seemed to dwarf the surrounding peaks. Could it be a monarch, never before discovered? Don wrote that "I do not recall that Phyl or I suggested in words to each other that there lay our future goal ... we took that for granted from the moment we first spotted it." They christened it "Mystery Mountain." Their search for it and attempts to ascend it are unequaled in mountaineering circles.

Phyllis and Don Munday were the premier husband-and-wife mountaineering team in the world. In Don's words, "She and I formed a climbing unit something more than the sum of our worth apart." Over a period of nearly 35 years they explored the mountainous regions of Alberta and British Columbia, coming to know the Coast Mountains like no one else has before or since and claiming many first ascents in the process. "Phyl," as she was known to all, had no equal among women mountaineers, and few even among men.

Phyllis Beatrice James was born to Frank and Beatrice James in Ceylon (now Sri Lanka) on September 24, 1894. Her father managed Lipton's, and later Ridgeway's, tea estates there. Her sister, Esmeé (Betty), was also born in Ceylon.

Her family loved the outdoors, taking frequent Sunday afternoon walks. Phyl credits her mother with curing her bad habit of turning her ankle; Beatrice would touch the offending ankle with her walking stick whenever it started to go wrong.

The Jameses traveled back and forth to their native England and returned there to live when the girls were very young. A few years later their parents emigrated to Canada, leaving Phyl and her sister behind for the time being. The girls came over later. Phyl had her seventh birthday in her new homeland; her brother Richard was born after the family moved to Canada.

Initially they settled in Manitoba, where Frank James worked as an accountant in various towns: Carberry, Brandon and Virden. From the prairies the family moved to near Nelson, in the West Kootenay area of British Columbia. Phyl always marveled at how her mother adapted to the early, rough life in Canada. After all, in Ceylon they had many servants and a nurse or nanny for every child. She had been brought up as a lady, and had hardly even seen the kitchen before. Beatrice was determined, though, that her daughters should learn how to cook and how to manage a household.

While in the Kootenays Phyl was a real tomboy, always clambering about the hillsides. Her chief joy, to her mother's horror, was walking along the fallen logs that crisscrossed the ravines. "My poor mother, she'd have had a thousand fits if she'd known some of the logs that I'd crossed over," chuckled Phyl. This early surefootedness was of great benefit in many of Phyl's later adventures. Her parents had given her a 22-calibre rifle and she practically kept the family in food in the fall by shooting grouse — a good excuse to go off in the bush. She had a bony old horse named Titus, which she rode bare-back everywhere, which is probably why she always loved the packtrips included in some of her mountaineering expeditions.

When they left the Kootenays in 1906 the Jameses were actually headed for New Zealand, but they got only as far as Vancouver and never left the country. Although she had attended school in Nelson for a while, Phyl received most of her education in Vancouver. Her real education, though, was received in the outdoors in all seasons, and she studied all growing things.

Phyl's father had been a tennis champion for many years in both Ceylon and in Vancouver; he felt that with proper help and guidance his daughter could be a tennis star — but Phyllis had other ideas. Her eyes were forever turning towards the hills around Vancouver. She wanted to climb mountains, for "there was something about getting away often, in the wilds, as we used to call it that appealed to me more than anything else, and I wanted to go up to the mountains."

Phyl's outdoor interests found an outlet when she asked her mother to form a Girl Scout group in 1910. A Boy Scout troop had just been formed, and she couldn't understand why girls shouldn't be able to enjoy the same activities. Not knowing of the Girl Guide movement, they thought they were being "very daring and wonderful" to suggest such a scout group. The Girl Guide movement in England had been founded only the previous year, when Lord Baden-Powell discovered that over 8000 girls had joined the Boy Scouts by using only their initials when enrolling. Their Girl Scout group soon became part of the Girl Guide organization.

One of the guide leaders encouraged outdoor interests, taking them to Bowen Island or into the mountains. Although her mother was a leader, she never went along on these outings, and her father thought they were all "quite crazy." They also had picnics and summer camps, made Christmas donations to needy families, and during the Great War they did much for the Red Cross and the troops.

Phyl served with the Guides for the rest of her active years, holding at different times every office open to her. She established the Lone Guides Company, which allowed girl guides who lived in isolated areas to keep in touch with others via a monthly company letter. At the time, Phyl was living on Grouse Mountain and was too far away to attend meetings regularly.

She was a particularly keen instructor in campcraft and served as nature advisor for the British Columbia Girl Guides for years, until failing health left her unable to continue. She was awarded the Bronze Cross, the highest decoration of the Guides, for her part in the rescue of a youth who fell down a precipice on Grouse Mountain. He had suffered head injuries and could not be moved, so she nursed him for three weeks in their isolated cabin, in midwinter. Phyl is the only mountaineer on the continent to have been so recognized. Another time she carried a 50-kg injured teen-aged girl partway down Grouse Mountain on her back, unaided.

Phyl was also deeply involved with St. John's Ambulance, the volunteer first-aid organization. She first came into contact with St. John's Ambulance during the First World War. She had falsified her age in an attempt to get overseas but was rejected. She then joined the St. John's organization. She formed the St. John's Ambulance Brigade Nursing Division in North Vancouver, and later she served as Provincial Lady Superintendent. She was in charge of first aiders during the Fraser Valley Flood of 1948. In 1967 she was named Dame of Grace of the Order of St. John in recognition of her unselfish service. She frequently manned the "blister tent" at Alpine of Canada camps, bandaging the many cuts and bruises.

As a teenager, Phyl hiked and scrambled a lot at Grouse Mountain (1211 m) on Vancouver's north shore. After leaving the streetcar, she used to take about three hours to reach the summit. She would go up Grouse on her own or with other guides. "Going up Grouse Mountain," Phyl remembered, "I thought I'd conquered the world."

Her first real climb was of the Lions (1646 m), near Vancouver, with the British Columbia Mountaineering Club (BCMC) when she was about 16 years old. After the climb her father asked, "You've climbed one mountain, why do you want to climb more?" Phyl infuriated him by pointing out that "he'd played more than one game of tennis"!

She had become interested in the BCMC through a friend

in a women's war reserve group, and they'd go out to all the local mountains on weekends.[1]

The club had a "drawer" in a photo shop on Granville Street, and members could sign up there for trips. Later they would check back and find out what group they were in, and what they had to bring for food. She was frequently the only woman on club outings in those early years.

When Phyl first started climbing, women wore bloomers. "We'd start off from home with a skirt on — you were never seen on the street with a bloomer, or a pair of pants.... It just wasn't done in those days." They would take the streetcar from home, and as they started hiking up the trail they'd cache their skirts under a log. This meant, of course, that they always had to return the same way, or they couldn't go home on the streetcar! Once she was climbing over a great log, which was on a slope, and as she stepped off it the elastic in her bloomer broke and caught on a snag. She was only a few inches off the ground, but she couldn't get up or down. Finally she was rescued by one of the men. They never let her live the incident down.

Near the end of the First World War Phyl was employed as a clerical worker in the orderly room of the Military Annex of the New Westminster General Hospital. She also served with its Voluntary Aid Detachment. It was here, in 1918, that she met Don Munday, a 28-year-old soldier and mountaineer who was recovering from a war injury. His nurse was a good friend of hers.

Don had been born in Portage la Prairie, Manitoba, on March 16, 1890 and lived there until he finished high school. He moved to Vancouver in 1909. Don had started climbing before the war, and he joined the BCMC in 1910. When the war started he signed up with the Scout Section of the Canadian 47th Infantry batallion, in June, 1915. It was his job to get the men at the front to the right places and back again, so he

---

1. The Vancouver Mountaineering Club was a small organization founded in 1907, just after the Alpine Club of Canada was formed. It became the British Columbia Mountaineering Club in 1909. The BCMC offered regular weekend outings in the Coast Range mountains. These were inexpensive and informal. The trips usually began on Saturday afternoons, which meant that even those people who had to work on Saturday mornings (most factory and office employees) could join the outings.

became very proficient with a compass. In October of 1917, while he was returning from one of those postings, he was hit with a shell. It tore through his left arm from the wrist to the elbow, where it exited. After being awarded the Military Medal, he was invalided home a year later. He spent considerable time convalescing in the hospital.

Don was very determined not to let the injury interfere with his life. Through the years he frequently exercised his arm, rolling a wad of paper in his pocket. The hardest things for him to do were to tie his boot laces or carve meat, because he found it difficult to bring his fingers together.

Phyl had heard a great deal about Don from people in the BCMC, but "hadn't a clue what he was like." Although Phyl did not like Don very much at first, he was "very persistent," and soon his quiet, gentlemanly ways and his love of the mountains, won her over. After the war, they were on the club executive and climbed a lot together, which was "a sure way of quickly getting to know what a person is like." They made at least two first ascents near Vancouver in 1918: Coquitlam Mountain (1583 m) and Blanshard Peak (1558 m).

On one of their earliest climbs together, Don stood on some unsafe rocks, which broke away and fell toward a glacier. He skidded to a ledge and Phyl jumped below him, with the intention of breaking his fall. Her footing gave away, but he was able to support her briefly while she gained a foothold, before his ledge also crumbled. He wrote that

> the incident lends itself readily to being given a romatic aspect — like other occasions when we had stood together undismayed by the appraising eyes of danger — but it has mountaineering significance in showing how even at that time we relied on each other for rightness of action in emergencies, often without audible language between us.

Phyl and Don were married on February 4, 1920. Phyl's mother hosted a gala wedding for Phyl and Don, but she was exasperated when they bypassed the reception to rush home to exchange wedding clothes for knickers and boots. Two hours later they were off to their beloved mountains. They spent their one-week honeymoon at a cabin on Grouse Mountain north of Vancouver.

Later in 1920 Phyl and Don spent some time climbing in the Mount Robson area. They climbed Lynx Mountain (3170

m) and made a first ascent of the north ridge of Mount
Resplendent (3426 m). Although they didn't climb Robson itself,
they set their sights on it for the future.

They lived on Grouse Mountain, which was accessible only
by foot or by horse from the end of the Lonsdale streetcar line.
They lived in a tent (even in winter) while building a rough log
house overlooking Vancouver. After many years they left the
site because it didn't live up to its promise. The lot was part
of a promotional affair that they "got hoodwinked into" —
they were to be managers of a resort, but the financing for it
fell through. Their cabin, the oldest one on the plateau, was
later destroyed by fire. While living at Grouse, the Mundays
were the first in the area to take up skiing.

Their only daughter, Edith, was born on March 26, 1921.
A few weeks later they took her up to the cabin. Edith was only
11 weeks old when she accompanied them up Crown Mountain
(1503 m). On the first of July the same year they traversed the
Seymour Valley and continued down the Stawamus Valley into
Squamish with Edith along. She also attended a BCMC
climbing camp in the Selkirk Mountains the same year.

At first Don carried Edith in a hammock across his
shoulders, so that he could support her head with his arm.
When she got bigger he made a papoose-style canvas carrier,
with a hood and mosquito netting. She used to hum with the
rhythm of his walking.

On the trip through the Seymour Valley, the Mundays stayed
in a cabin owned by the Britannia Mining Company. A
monstrous baking pan was perfect for bathing the baby. When
three geologists from the mine came along they were stunned
to see a baby in a bread pan on the oven door!

In the mid-20s the family moved to North Vancouver, so
that Edith could go to school and they could still be close to
the mountains. They spent most weekends at the cabin on
Grouse, or, later, at a cabin on Mount Seymour.

In her early childhood, Edith was always having an
imaginary packtrain, which she would treat like a seasoned old
packer. Now and then she'd throw a stone ahead of her, call
out a horse's name and tell him to get moving!

The Mundays raised their daughter to be thoroughly
comfortable and unafraid in the outdoors. Edith remembers

being a happy child, but "sometimes in retrospect I wonder if I didn't take second place to a mountain!" While growing up she didn't realize how much she had absorbed from her parents, which is so much a part of her life now: a love of nature and photography, and a keen interest in maps.

Don was a freelance journalist, mostly writing stories of mountaineering and outdoor exploration for magazines and newspapers. At various times he wrote for and edited the RCMP magazine *Scarlet and Gold,* the British Columbia Provincial Police magazine *Shoulder Strap,* and the *Veterans' Weekly.* He was a Fellow of the Royal Geographical Society and president of the Canadian Authors Association. He wrote a book about wildflowers shortly before his death, but a similar book had recently been published, which left little market for his own.

From 1921 through 1923 the Mundays continued to explore and climb in their own backyard mountains, including Garibaldi Park and the Spearhead and Fitzsimmons Ranges. They made six easy first ascents of moderate elevation: Stewart Peak, Mount Foley, Isosceles Peak (2486 m), Parapet Peak (2439 m), Overlord Mountain (2621 m) and Blackcomb Peak (2473 m). Don led many expeditions to rescue skiers and mountaineers who were injured or lost, and his judgment, experience and endurance were invaluable to the success of these missions.

Four years after their first visit to the Mount Robson area, the Mundays were back, at the ACC's annual camp at Robson Pass in 1924. They had just returned from an ascent of Mumm Peak (2962 m) when club president A.O. Wheeler announced that they would have the opportunity to climb Mount Robson (3954 m), Phyl's "first love." This was despite the prevailing impression that no women would be allowed to attempt the "big climb," which was regarded as being beyond the physical endurance and mountaineering skill of women. The group included the Mundays, Fred Lambart, A.W. Drinnan, Annette Buck, J.F. Porter, Austrian climbing guide Conrad Kain and his assistant, Joe Saladana. Phyl wanted no favored treatment. "Having seen my lady companion's pack lightened, unbeknown to her, of the supplies she was going to carry, led me to guard mine closely."

High camp was located at timberline on the southwest face, above Kinney Lake. There were three tents, a stove, cooking utensils and bedding. Although it rained during the night, the weather was good when Conrad woke them well before daylight.

Conrad called us at 2.30 a.m.; at 3.30 we were on our way to test the perils of the climb for ourselves. At about 8,000 feet we gained the ridge behind the little black peak of the west face, in time to see the ice front of the southwest face discharge a mass of ice down cliffs where exceptionally big avalanches are somtimes hurled 5,000 feet into the valley of the Little Fork. Nearly a thousand feet higher the same glacier has broken through the ridge to fling ice down bare cliffs for 6,000 feet almost to the trail along Lake Kinney.

What concerned us more intimately was that we had to cross the cliffs for nearly 100 yards directly under the glistening and shattered wall which, 100 feet in height, hung far out over the way we must go.

From this and the greater wall somewhere above, tremendous avalanches had fallen just after the previous party passed — some assurance that less remained to threaten us. A few stray blocks came down with crashing reports as they shattered on the rocks, but we passed safely.

More good rock climbing followed for about 2,000 feet, the shining white peak in sight most of the time, and seemingly close at hand. So far we had performed so that Conrad had not roped us, but now we had to work across the cliffs 200 yards under the upper ice-wall, and then actually climb its 150-foot face. The wall extends for more than a quarter of a mile, sloping diagonally upwards — close to Lake Kinney we had passed remains of an avalanche fallen 8,000 feet from this wall.

The ice cliff, amazingly overhanging, fantastically sculptured, grunted uneasily. Conrad coached both rope parties carefully; we gathered up the slack of the ropes, and worked out along a protruding shelf. Perhaps a fairly steady head and foot is needed for one to trot rapidly along a ledge with 8,000 feet of thin air immediately below; nevertheless it is fairly certain that no one in the party actually saw just then the void below or the ice menace above.

In one place the ice sloped back slightly, and here Conrad decided to force a passage, and plied his ice axe vigorously, working out diagonally far beyond the base of the ice wall — surely the dizziest place imaginable, but obviously the only way. Cutting small handholds, he stood on one foot and chopped the final step to surmount the crest of the ice, over which he disappeared. I had anchored him with the rope around my ice axe thrust in a hole in the ice. Now it was my turn to follow — without a professional guide I had scaled as difficult ice walls before, but never with such an excess of nothingness under my heels, or so much impending above.

Just above this point they were held up on the glacier when Saladana fell through a snowbridge. He was quickly extricated, but he had lost his ice axe, which took an hour to recover. This delay proved costly later when they were trying to descend before dark. On the main ridge, the ice terraces reminded Phyl of

"breakers on a rough sea."

The slope above is unlike anything elsewhere in the Rockies — an absolute chaos of ice blocks on a slope of not less than 45 degrees; domed with snow, and bristling with gleaming icicles, they were a never to be forgotten sight, fairylike perhaps, but sinister, hostile, menacing. Even in the bright sunlight, we shivered if we stopped. When a cloud crossed the sun the cold was intense.

Around, between, under the ice blocks we climbed, the rotted snow often subsiding beneath us, necessitating the use of the rope to get the rest of the party across the holes. Sometimes we crawled on hands and knees across doubtful places, or even lay down and wriggled. Utmost care was required to avoid giving some of the shattered masses just the jar which might set them going, probably to disrupt the whole slope.

It was late in the afternoon before Conrad negotiated the last, short face section, disappeared from view, then pulled the rope in quickly. Phyl climbed onto the summit and was greeted by Conrad, who extended his hand and said, "There, Lady! You are the first woman on top of Mount Robson," and almost pumped her arm off in congratulations. For her it was the achievement of a four-year ambition.

Alpine Club members who climbed Mount Robson from the 1924 camp. Front row (l-r): Joe Saladana (assistant guide), Don Munday, Phyl Munday, Albert MacCarthy, Annette Buck, Harry Pollard. Back row: Malcolm Geddes, Thomas Moffat, Fred Lambart, A.W. Drinnan, James Porter.

Whyte Museum of the Canadian Rockies

Darkness overtook them on the descent. They sought shelter in some rocks, but they were all cold. They reached their high camp at five o'clock the next morning, and the other climbers welcomed them with soup, toast and tea. Two hours later they left for the long tramp back to base camp at Robson Pass. Theirs was the third ascent of the magnificent peak.

Phyl had climbed next to Kain on the rope, and she cherished her memories of the famous guide: his humor, fits of laughter and his cursing. "He could swear more, and never use the same word twice, than anybody else I ever came across!"

In July 1925, Phyl and Don climbed in the Premier Range of the Cariboo Mountains, west of Mount Robson. They were the third party to explore the area. They made a first ascent of Mount Sir John Thompson (3246 m) and the second ascent of Mount Sir Wilfred Laurier (3520 m), the highest peak. Their camp was plagued with porcupines. One "perfect pest" molested their belongings at every opportunity, and it even followed them to the snow line when they went climbing. The salt-hungry porcupine was waiting there for them when they returned! The rest of the time it spent high in a tree alongside the creek by which they camped, observing everything. Finally, Don decided to put an end to this harrassment and felled the tree. The top of the tree, and the porcupine, crashed on the opposite bank, where the climbers hoped it would stay. But they hadn't counted on the persistence of the critter, which merely plopped into the creek and swam back.

Later still that summer the Mundays attended the ACC camp at Lake O'Hara, climbing mounts Hungabee (3493 m) and Victoria (3464 m). They then returned home to plan an autumn expedition to their recently discovered Mystery Mountain.

It seems amazing that the Coast Range had remained unexplored for so long compared to everywhere else in Canada. But there were no roads or railways in the area, nor aircraft landing sites, so it remained unknown. They had seen the mountain, but the problem was to find out exactly where it was and how to get there. No one knew anything about it.

The Coast Mountains are a formidable, savage range. As their name implies, they lie parallel to the Pacific Ocean, extending north of Vancouver some 1500 km. The wet, stormy climate, all but impenetrable forests and raging rivers keep them isolated even today.

In 1922, Capt. R. P. Bishop, land surveyor, reported seeing high peaks to the northwest of Chilko Lake. He thought the peaks might rise over 4000 m. In 1924, Dr. Dolinage, a geological surveyor, also reported 4000-m peaks in the area. The Mundays firmly believed that the unknown and unmapped heart of the Coast Range might still offer rewards equal to those granted the pioneer climbers in the Rockies and Selkirks. The early explorations in the Selkirks and Rockies had been by Britishers or Americans, but it was left to Canadians to explore the Coast Range.

And large peaks there were! To make a comparison: in the 180,000 km² of the Canadian Rockies there are only 14 summits that exceed 3500 m, a few of which have a vertical rise of only 1500-1800 m. In an area barely 5% of that, between the Homathko and the Kliniklini Rivers, where Mystery Mountain was situated, there are six. And the vertical rise is consistently over 3000 m.

During 11 trips in 12 years, the Mundays spent a total of 15 months exploring in the area. They attempted to climb Mystery Mountain itself 16 times. They did gain the northwest peak, and they once came within 18 m of the summit.

In September of 1925 they set out to reconnoitre Mystery Mountain, accompanied by Tom Ingram and Athol Agur. They traveled on the *S.S. Chelohsin*, a Union Steamship Company boat, to Orford Bay in Bute Inlet. A trapper took them another 40 km in his motorboat to the head of the inlet. After toiling straight up from sea level, they gained the summit of Mount Rodney (2391 m). On the skyline one peak towered over all the others: Mystery Mountain. Who would believe their estimate of its height of over 4000 m? At 3954 m, Mount Robson was still believed highest in the province. "At least Phyl and I knew we must return again," wrote Don, "not as assailants, but in a spirit closer to veneration."

The only plausible access route seemed to be via the Homathko Valley. This was a 50-km-long trench, with steep flanks 2400 m high, and the head seemed blocked by a large glacier. The scene was anything but encouraging.

But during May of 1926, they made two trips to the

Homathko. The first trip was a reconnaissance to see if the route was feasible. On the second one they spent a week freighting five week's worth of supplies as far up the Homathko River as they could, using a four-metre rowboat with a "kicker" (outboard motor), and a canoe. On May 31 the whole party set out together: Phyl, Don, Tom, Athol, Johnnie Johnson and Don's brother Bert. Edith stayed at a logging camp on Bute Inlet with a woman and her daughter.

As they headed into Homathko Valley, Don wrote that it "lost itself in a cavernous gloom as unwelcoming as the dark lair of some unknown beast." The valley floor was awash from heavy rain and flooding glacial streams; they crossed and recrossed creeks, usually on narrow, sagging tree trunks. Willows, alder, brush, silt, rotting trees and devil's-club, "the most diabolical plant in North America," threatened to bar their passage every step of the way. Phyl summed it up as "an awful fight" through "a heart-breaking barrier." After 13 days they had traveled only 48 km from tidewater, and were a meagre 100 m above it. Don estimated that they had averaged over 160 km per person relaying their supplies in three trips.

For another week they battled their way up the Waddington

A Munday party traveling through the dense jungle of the British Columbia rain forest.

Glacier, attempting to get as close as possible to their goal. After climbing a peak to scout the area, Phyl became snow-blind. Although the affliction was painful, fortunately it was temporary. Tea poultices placed over her eyes eased the burning sensation somewhat, but for days Phyl was led by hand as they moved camp. Still, she continued to carry her share of the loads.

With a scant four days' food rations left, they decided on June 23 to make a final push for the mountain. They left camp at nine o'clock in the evening, aided by generous moonlight and an acetylene lamp. At 5:15 a.m., in the glorious sunrise, they crested "Mystery Pass" and had their first full view of Mystery Mountain. They spent the next 12 hours working their way closer to the mountain, but alas, time had run out. They returned to tidewater.

They were running severely short of food on their return to the boat and Phyl spent a lot of time picking berries to supplement their low rations. One slim breakfast consisted of a can of sardines, and a "thin bannock" — for six people! Another breakfast was one pancake each: no baking powder, butter or sugar to go with it.

In the spring of 1927 the Mundays were struck with the tragic loss of their friend Athol Agur, who had shared so much with them. He was killed in an avalanche on Grouse Mountain. Johnnie Johnson had been skiing with him but had survived.

Hoping for an easier route to Mystery Mountain, the Mundays tried an approach from Knight Inlet in July of 1927. Knight Inlet was fed by the mighty Kliniklini River and the outflow of the Franklin Glacier. They traveled on the *S.S. Venture* to the Glendale Cove cannery and voyaged the last 55 km in their own open boat. They were joined by Phyl's sister, Betty McCallum. The struggle along the valley was much less trying than that along the Homathko the year before. They made three unsuccessful attempts on Mystery Mountain, the final time being chased down from a subsidiary summit by a severe storm. Lightning stabbed around them and "weird blue coronas of electricity played about the rocks, our boots, our ice axes and even our hair, but we didn't feel a thing." Appropriately, they named the mountain Fireworks Peak (3200 m). Betty returned to her family in Vancouver on the next steamer. Phyl and Don returned to the Franklin Glacier, but they were stormed in for a week. When the weather lifted, the new blanket of snow made the mountain too treacherous to climb. They returned to Vancouver, disappointed but not defeated. They had learned, though, that the Knight Inlet access was excellent, and it became their usual approach to the area.

And always they outran the mapmakers. When weather made it impossible to try for the main tower of Mystery Mountain, their objective, they would explore the surrounding area. Phyl's philosophy was that "there isn't any one mountain worth throwing your life away on. So if it [the condition of Mystery Mountain] wasn't good, we'd go off and do something else . . . but every time — it doesn't matter whether it's storm or sunshine — it's always worth it."

It was also in 1927 when J. T. Underhill's survey party established the height of Mystery Mountain as 4016 m. Don and Phyl were vindicated in their belief of its height. Within months the Canadian Permanent Committee on Geographic Names had officially named it Mount Waddington.[1]

The Waddington area was previously unknown, but it did not remain that way long once the height of the massif was established. A. O. Wheeler, director of the Alpine Club of Canada and surveyor of the Great Divide, including Mount Robson, would not believe that Waddington was higher than Robson until he was permitted to check the surveyor's calculations.

Phyl missed Edith terribly on these extended climbing trips. She would glue Edith's picture in the front of her diary, and she enjoyed reading Edith's letters. Mail would be left for them at their boat or at a logging camp nearby.

Don and Phyl returned again in 1928, accompanied by

---

1. Their first choice had been "Mount George Dawson," for the great Canadian geologist, but others felt it should reflect the history of the area and suggested Mount Waddington. Alfred Waddington seemed to have a penchant for championing unsuccessful causes. He vehemently opposed the Fraser Canyon route to the Cariboo goldfields and formed his own company to build a road overland from Bute Inlet (accessible by steamer from Vancouver), through the Homathko Valley and across the Chilcotin Plateau. Only a few kilometres of road in the Homathko was ever built, as the forests and canyon were virtually impenetrable. The Mundays were following in his footsteps. Other people, though, thought the mountain should have honored the Mundays, who had done the pioneer exploration of the area. The Mundays were in favor of the chosen name.

Don's brother Bert. They climbed intermittently due to poor weather, making only two first ascents, of Mount Whitetip and Mount Myrtle. On July 8 they arose at 1:15 a.m. for yet another attempt on Waddington. After hours of struggling along the northwest ridge they topped what appeared to be the final peak — only to discover the soaring main tower across a gap to the east. It was adorned with huge feathers of ice, like "ostrich plumes," formed by rain and snow freezing in the high winds off the Pacific. It was "a nightmare molded in rock" and seemed impossible to climb. Don wrote in his diary that it was "thrilling to see a so uncompromising face" on Waddington. Soaking wet, and with darkness approaching, they were forced to turn back. More than five years would pass before they could attempt Waddington again.

Don and Phyl would frequently return from the Waddington area with just enough time to wash and pack up for the annual ACC camp, which they always tried to attend.

Phyl's mother, Beatrice, died the following year, which precluded any expeditions that summer. But they returned to mountaineering again in 1930. The use of skis made their travels on the glaciers much less troublesome than in previous years. Don concocted the wax for their skis. They made first ascents of four lesser peaks, then prepared to attempt the mountain that had been recently named for them. Poor weather had prevented a first ascent the previous year.

Mount Munday was on the long southeast ridge of the Waddington massif. They skied to Mystery Pass and up the slope as far as they could. At the bergschrund they each poked a foot and ski through into the chasm, but the snowbridge did not collapse. A cold wind precluded much time on the summit (3505 m), and they were soon enjoying the ski run back down the glacier. After removing their skis in a crevassed area, they continued trekking through the night, keenly atune to the "disturbingly brilliant" stars and Milky Way. They felt themselves fortunate to be abroad on such a night.

In 1931 the Mundays forsook the Union Steamship boat and traveled the 400 km from Vancouver to Knight Inlet in their small outboard motorboat. The trip was "quite hairy at times," to say the least. Bad weather again plagued them, although they climbed Mount Jubilee (2748 m), Sockeye Peak and Dauntless

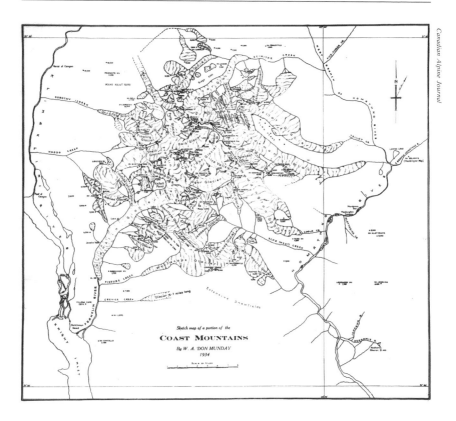

Canadian Alpine Journal

Mountain, and they filled in more blanks on their maps. Conditions were so bad the following year that they made only one small ascent in the area, Bezel Peak.

In 1933 the Mundays joined Bostonian Henry S. Hall, Jr., in an assault on Mount Waddington from the northeast, via Tatla Lake. Hall, with Swiss guide Hans Fuhrer (a former CNR guide now guiding independently) from Jasper, Alberta, had made inroads that way the previous year, and although it was rough going he was convinced that this was the best route by which to approach the mountain. Hall offhandedly complimented Don and Phyl when he wrote, "Back packers would have a hard time of it in this valley — even the Mundays." Alfred E. Roovers and Donald W. Brown rounded out the party of six climbers.

They were outfitted and guided by Pete McCormick, Harvey J. Valleu and Pete Evjen. McCormick had misgivings about taking a woman on such an arduous trip. Valleu carried a loaded revolver in his shirt, and he slept with a sawed off shotgun under his pillow. Nevertheless Phyl felt thoroughly spoiled on this trip, as she did not have to do the cooking for a change, and horses did all of the packing! At one camp Valleu added some "doubtful" dried eggs to soup made from "resilient" goat remnants — none of them felt very well the next day.

With seventeen horses they set off on the 45-km journey to the snout of the Scimitar Glacier, their access to the mountain. They crashed through flooded thickets, floundered through swamps, fought rockslides and feared for their horses' lives and their own on raging creek crossings. A mere 11 km from the glacier their way was blocked by fallen timber as the result of a recent fire that had ravaged the Scimitar Valley. It took the men five days to cut a mere five kilometres of treacherous trail through the canyon.

They wanted to use the horses to pack their gear to base camp on the glacier, so they cut a staircase up onto the ice. As the horses naturally shunned the clear ice, Phyl used Don's hat to carry gravel to mask it. Two horses were very reluctantly led upward, and they set up a camp at the base of Mount Hickson. After nearly three weeks of tough traveling, they were finally within reach of their destination — only to discover that Hall's "easy route" from Mount Tiedemann to Waddington did not exist. Upon close inspection they all agreed that Waddington was unapproachable from that side.

On July 14, though, they made a first ascent of Mount Combatant (3701 m), finding it necessary to bivouac on a shelf below the summit. As usual, Hans melted snow on his alcohol stove and made cocoa from a piece of Bakers unsweetened chocolate. Although they had no milk or sugar the hot drink revived them considerably. Henry, Don and Phyl, roped together, sat with their legs over the precipice, trying to keep from being pushed off by Alf and Hans behind them. One member of the party suggested "shivering singly" lest shivering in unison should cause their ledge to collapse. All the same, Phyl reveled in the beauty of the night and the coming dawn. The descent was uneventful.

For the next three days their camp was buffeted by very high winds. After Phyl and Don's tent ripped in four places, they moved into the cook tent with Hans, but it too was soon torn

Montage of Mount Waddington, annotated by Phyl Munday. The main tower of Waddington is on the left.

in several places and became soaked in the rain. They decided to move their camp down the valley, and after a horribly cold time packing up, they retreated from the glacier. After rejoining the packers, they battled their way back to Tatla Lake. The party threatened to break up as McCormick and Valleu revived their long-standing dispute over horses and "ownership" of the valley. A few months later Valleu was charged with assaulting McCormick.

In the spring of 1934, four climbing parties entered the Waddington area. And on June 26 Alec Dalgleish, the leader of a party from Vancouver, fell nearly 300 m to his death — the first fatality on Mount Waddington.

That same July, Phyl and Don were again joined by Hall and Fuhrer, who brought along Phillip (Pip) Brock and Ronald Munro. With so many in their party, they chose the *S.S. Venture* for their sea approach. Again they were turned back on Waddington, once by weather and once by technical difficulties requiring more pitons and rope. As consolation, a few days later they made the first ascent of Finality Mountain (2833 m). They returned to Vancouver, defeated once more by Mount Waddington.

It was on this trip that Don and Pip wrote a limerick about Phyl's good cooking:

> There once was a lady called Phyllis,
> Who did her goldarndest to fill us,
> When we reached the last bite
> We were filled up so tight,
> That we thought she was trying to kill us.

In the summer of 1935, the Mundays explored the Kliniklini Glacier on the west side of the Kliniklini River, at the head of Knight Inlet. They were joined again by Pip, who brought along James Varley. A few days after starting up the river Pip had to return to his parent's funeral: they had both been killed in a plane crash.

Finding no way to bridge the torrent of Tumult Creek, the Mundays and Varley only glimpsed the main glacier from a high ridge and vowed to return again the following year.

This time they traveled up the coast in their homebuilt seven-metre launch, which Edith had named the "Edidonphyl," for the three of them. They called the boat engine "Olie," and how

Phyl longed to "hear Olie's voice" when it wasn't working, which seemed often. Due to Olie's stubbornness, Phyl had to row a lot, towing the boat while Don tinkered with the engine. On one such occasion she and a friend were rowing the dinghy, towing the boat, when Ollie inexplicably started, very nearly dragging the dinghy under! "Much as we wanted the boat to go, we had to yell to Don to stop her," Phyl wrote, "It was exasperating."

In July, 1936 Phyl and Don were once again battling upstream against the Kliniklini River. In tow were two of Hall's friends, William Hinton and Sherrett Chase. On August 1 they rendezvoused with Hall and Fuhrer, following the latter's first ascent of Monarch Mountain (3533 m) south of the Bella Coola Valley. Hall brought word that Fritz Wiessner[2] and Bill House had accomplished the long-coveted first ascent of Waddington on July 21, using pitons and extra rope. The Mundays took it well. "We seemed to manage and do all the climbing we needed without carrying all those things," says Phyl. "I suppose we could have done much more in the way of rock work if we had had more pitons. We had only two, but we never used them." House later admitted that he wouldn't want to repeat that climb.

To cross Tumult Creek, they constructed a cable crossing using wire cable, a clothesline pulley and a seat harness. Don and Phyl had traveled far up the canyon to find a place to cross and then came back down, spending the night out in the process. The others stayed on the opposite bank. Because of the roar of the river, they passed signals between the groups in Morse code — possible only because Phyl remembered it from her Girl Guide days and one of the fellows had been a Boy Scout.

While traversing a canyon on the edge of the Kliniklini Glacier itself, Don, Phyl and Henry saw a young grizzly below them. Thinking themselves at a safe distance, they took out their cameras. As the bear came toward them, an unseen sow with

---

2. One of the world's best climbers, Wiessner introduced many European techniques to the United States when he moved there from his native Germany. He was the leader of an ill-fated American attempt on K2, in 1939, during which one climber and three sherpas died. He resigned from the American Alpine Club in the furore that followed. In 1966 the club belatedly cleared his name and made him an honorary member.

two cubs charged from ten metres behind them. By yelling and waving their arms, they kept the bear from attacking. But on a second charge she went for Phyl. Don diverted her attention: he and the sow roared at each other until Don, "finding she had had more practice at roaring," flung his hat in her face and backed away. Unfortunatly, he tripped and fell to a rocky shelf. Expecting the bear to attack Don, Phyl rushed to his side, wielding her ice-axe courageously. Luckily for all, the bear chose to retreat.

Bears were frequently sighted on their journeys, and they were always anxious about the safety of their food caches. As they grouped together to avoid surprise, Sherry Chase observed that "grizzlies do promote sociability in a party."

At one camp, pikas[3] stole some home-dried apples that Phyl had jealously guarded for a surprise apple pie. Hans gallantly retaliated by heaving rocks off the cliff edge at some pikas!

A first ascent of Fang Peak (2347 m) allowed them to spot Silverthrone Mountain (2819 m), which they ascended on August 14. They beheld wondrous views to the headwaters of the Kliniklini River and to the Owikeno Lake area. On the approach to Silverthrone they carried skis, which Phyl "talked out loud to" Smany times while attempting to manoeuvre through trackless bush. With their destination achieved, they returned to tidewater.

Phyl was a very stong woman, frequently carrying a 30-kg pack, and she never took the lightest load. She was an excellent rower, and to her often fell the laborious and risky river and inlet crossings. Don and Phyl were fairly equal in climbing ability. They took turns leading, but in rock-climbing situations where there was a touchy left hand-hold, Phyl would lead because of Don's war-wounded left arm. They climbed on many different kinds of rock, and "always seemed to find a route somewhere or other where we didn't seem to need a piton." In 1948 Phyl received the ACC's Silver Rope Award in recognition of her leadership capabilities — the second woman so honored (Polly Prescott received hers in 1941).

On one particularly perilous creek crossing one of their climbing companions put his hand on Phyl's packstrap, and

---

3. Pikas are small mammals, related to rabbits and hares, that live among boulders in high mountain areas.

said, "I'll carry your pack across." She refused, saying that everyone must do his or her share. She didn't give in until he looked her straight in the eye and said, "Mrs. Munday, I'm single" — a reference to the danger involved. At this Phyl relented. He went across on all fours, with her pack, and then she followed.

Occasionally, when pressed for time, they made 20- or 30-hour scouting trips from their base camp. As they began to tire they sometimes had visions. Once Phyl thought that she was on a heather slope, and went to sit down, but actually she was on a glacier. Leading the party at such times was a sought-after position, as the extra responsibility made it easier for the leader to stay awake. About such occasions, Don commented that "my wife and I bring to this kind of night travel a glad confidence in each other that one not knowing us well might brand foolhardiness."

On all of their outings, the Mundays were meticulous in their observations and recordings. Don was a member of the International Commission on Snow and Glaciers; he served on the National Research Council's subcommittee on snow and ice research, and he made many glacier observations. He was also an associate member of the Arctic Institute of North America and a member of the British Glaciological Society. Don and Phyl also had the pleasure of naming most of the features in the Waddington area.

They kept detailed records of their climbs. They both photographed panoramas. From the panoramas and his compass readings, Don made photo-topographical maps. Phyl collected and pressed flowers, and she made an insect collection for the Provincial Museum of British Columbia in Victoria. The museum staff gave her chloroform in which to preserve the insects. Don also collected some geological specimens. Phyl never considered herself a botanist, just a lover of those "brave little things growing all on their own." She felt that her collecting and mapping made them see and observe a lot of things that they might have missed otherwise.

Once when Don stopped to pick up an insect for Phyl's collection, his leg sank full-length into a crevasse. Her sister, Betty, braced herself next on the rope. Phyl calmly came forward from the rear to stow the insect away without a word about

Don's safety. Betty berated her soundly for her callousness!

The Mundays made most of their own equipment, including sleeping bags of eiderdown and sail silk (commonly called Egyptian cotton), and also a three- person sail-silk tent. Don designed and cut, while Phyl sewed. The tent had a vestibule in front to cover their boots, and it used cod-line for guy ropes. It weighed just under two kilograms, which was very light in those days. Phyl put snaps on the peak of the tent so that in hot weather they could take up both sides like a verandah. Don also made custom-fitted packboards of slide alder and canvas, and he fastened Phyl's handsewn packbags on with eyelets and heavy wire. These packs were lighter than the common "Trapper Nelson" model popular at the time, and more convenient for bushwhacking as they didn't have protruding ends to catch on things.

One of their original lamps was homemade, fashioned out of an empty powdered milk can with a hole punched in its side to hold a candle. They called it a "bug" in humorous reference to the firefly. Days in camp were spent fixing gear, waterproofing boots with dubbin, washing, baking and so on.

Although Phyl spent the winters experimenting with drying different foods, they had little lightweight food. The menu was usually very simple. Bannock was a staple. Phyl would make

Provincial Archives of British Columbia/HP84024

Phyl Munday in camp.

it in a baking tin, put it on the fire, and then set up the reflector so that it would brown and cook on top. That way she didn't have to flip it, and she could attend to other chores while it was cooking. In camp Phyl would cook food for the next day's climb: boiled pudding, beans, rice. Chocolate, nuts and raisins served as "iron rations" when they were climbing. For one scouting foray from their base camp, Phyl cooked up a jam tin full of beans and made some "bone-dries," or pilot bread (a dry bisuit), the latter which they ate with jam.

The Mundays took the following supplies for six people on their 1934 forty-day trip to Mount Waddington. These were packed in boxes and shipped on the boat.

Flour — 96 lbs
Butter — 40 lbs
Tea — 5 lbs
Cocoa — 2 lbs
Dried prunes — 8 lbs
Dried pears — 4 lbs
Raisins — 10 lbs
Dates — 4 lbs
Porridge — 10 lbs
Bran — 5 lbs
Pearl barley — 5 lbs
Brown sugar — 10 lbs
Edam cheese — 20 lbs
Macaroni — 15 lbs
Shelled almonds — 3 lbs
Brown beans — 15 lbs
Pilotbread — 15 lbs
Klim powdered milk — 20 lbs
Coffee — 3 lbs
Dried apricots — 5 lbs
Dried peaches — 5 lbs
Black figs — 5 lbs
Dried Apples — 5 lbs
Cornmeal — 10 lbs
Rolled oats — 10 lbs
Rice — 20 lbs
White sugar — 50 lbs
Jam — 48 lbs

Chateau cheese — 10 lbs
Chocolate — 4 doz 5-cent bars
Walnuts — 3 lbs
Lima beans — 4 lbs
Salt — 4 lbs
Bacon — 50 lbs
Baking soda — 2 lbs
Custard powder — 3 tins
Dried potatoes — 4 lbs
Dried carrots — 6 lbs
Tomatoes — 6 large tins
Potatoes — 15 lbs
Peaches — 6 large tins
Meatballs — 3 tins
Soap — 2 cakes
Oil — 5, 2-gal cans
Ham — 30 lbs
Baking powder — 9 cups
Pink salmon — 6 tall tins
Dried eggs — 3 tins
Dried onions — 4 lbs
Sardines — 18 tins
Peas — 6 large tins
Pineapple — 6 tins
Corned beef — 3 lbs
Toilet paper — 6 rolls
Oxydol — 1 large pkg

Cotton bags originally filled with sugar or flour were used for storing food. Phyl would fill a baking pan with tallow, melt it on the oven door, and dip all of the bags in it to keep them waterproof. She'd sometimes can the butter in the ever-useful four-pound (1.8 kg) jam tins, with Edith packing it in the tins.

Arising from one of Phyl's less successful cooking experiments in camp were "panics." These were a cross between pancakes and bannock, thus "pannocks," which became shortened to panics. They were eagerly devoured nonetheless.

On rainy days in camp Phyl would do embroidery, sometimes hampered by near-freezing temperatures. At one such camp she arranged a collection of old tins for Don's inspection, with the suggestion that he make a stove and stove pipe for the shack they had built the previous year. He grudgingly went to work with a can-opener, and the next day they were able to move into the now-tropical hut. The stove was fashioned out of a biscuit tin, with square vegetable tins serving as a pipe. Phyl made curtains out of gauze bandage and a little cotton sack.

While backpacking they often wore ordinary shirts and pants, saving their knickers and puttees for climbing. Phyl made them each a pair of climbing knickers from an old wool blanket. They were windproof — and almost rainproof, too. Phyl and Don also had wool shirts, sweaters and "bone-dry" coats, which were made of canvas and had lots of pockets. She often fitted the coats with an extra layer over the back to cover the pack.

Climbing in the notoriously poor weather of the Coast Mountains, the Mundays were often caught in rain and snow storms. In such instances they would retreat as quickly as possible and bivouac if necessary. On one trip, they had 150 hours of rain out of 152 consecutive hours! These conditions undoubtedly aggravated Phyl's arthritis. Most nights she had to wrap her knees in cold towel compresses and cover them with light rubber sheets in an attempt to keep the swelling down. She made light of this process, calling it "a bit of a nuisance." In 1937 Don and Phyl, accompanied by their daughter Edith, Henry Hall and Hall's friend Hermann Ulrichs, took the *Edidonphyl* some 600 km north of Vancouver to Bella Coola in their search for a great peak that they had sighted from Mount Waddington. Phyl said that "just to mention a big mountain to either Don or I, was enough to make you want to go and find it, and climb it, if possible." The boat trip took ten days. The area was the most magnificent they had ever seen.

They made the first ascent of Mount Stupendous (2728 m), returning to camp in the dark with the dubious aid of a folding lantern that they had to "coerce" into staying unfolded. Edith was 16 years old, and this was the first time she had accompanied Phyl and Don for any serious climbing. They were very impressed with how well she handled the hard days on the mountains. The Mundays also attempted to climb Defiance Mountain, but to no avail, as the name they gave it implied.

The "discovery" of Mount Stupendous (named by Sir Alexander MacKenzie in 1793) received quite an airing in England. *The Post* summed up an article by saying that "it seems a tremendously bulky object to have been overlooked in a civilised territory." Such was exploration in the Coast Mountains as late at the 1930s.

Progress was slow in this untracked wilderness. The great depths of the valleys — rising some 2500 m or more from sea level — and their consistently steep sides made ascents difficult. The valley bottoms were often choked with tangles of alders. As Edith emerged from one such thicket, she remarked to her dad, "You nearly had to come and chop me out."

After returning from the climb they stopped at Tommy Walker's Stuie Lodge, where Phyl assisted in hosting a reception for Governor General Lord Tweedsmuir (John Buchan), who was making a visit to the new provincial park that had been named in his honor. They accomplished little other exploring; preparations for Tweedsmuir's visit had claimed all available transport, which hampered movement.

The same party of five — the three Mundays, Henry Hall and Hermann Ulrichs — returned the following year. This time, however, they traveled up from Vancouver on the *M.V. Venture*. They attempted Mount Saugstad twice, but could not reach the summit. On the second try they climbed and named Bastille Mountain (2286 m), an outlier of Mount Saugstad. They chose the name because it was the Bastille Day holiday in France.

Don, Phyl and Edith joined one of Walker's trail rides to the north of the Bella Coola Valley. Some of the route had been improved the previous year for Lord Tweedsmuir's visit. They were out for six days on this trip, and Phyl went on two more rides later.

That summer Don and Edith also went up the Caribou Mountain trail to Turner Lake and Hunlen Falls with Walter Radcliffe. Radcliffe was scouting out a trail for Walker to use for trail rides. They walked and took one packhorse, as they expected a lot of downed timber and little pasturage. It took them 3 days just to reach Turner Lake. Don had already seen the falls from below, when he had joined Walker and George Draney, who were outfitting a fishing party to Stillwater Lake.

The whole family assisted in fighting a small forest fire near Bella Coola. Women couldn't be included on the payroll, so Phyl and Edith listed only their initials. They received a small sum, such as a total of eight dollars, for their hard work!

They were back the following year to attempt once again the main peak of Mount Saugstad (2908 m). Don thought that Edith "showed needless industry in pointing out rocks poised too delicately on cliffs overhead!" They were turned back by difficult snow conditions. Phyl had a near-disastrous accident while battling the slide alder in Snootli Pass, when boulders hidden in the vegetation shifted to trap her leg such that she was unable to move without help. Fortunately, no bones were broken.

The Mundays were drawn to the Cariboos in 1940, but in 1941 they were back in the vicinity of Waddington — this time to the southeast, on the edge of the massive Homathko Icefield. Although some of its peaks had been named, the icefield remained unexplored. As they journeyed up Bute Inlet, "it was like re-visiting old friends to see those fine peaks," which they hadn't viewed since 1926. An American friend from the Alpine Club camps, Polly Prescott, joined them. It took ten days of horrendous bushwhacking to come even within sight of the glaciers, a job that they thought would take maybe five days. Polly sagely noted that "the Coast Range does not perform on a Rocky Mountains time schedule." Instead of "counting their blessings one by one," the bedtime diversion of the women was to compare the days new pattern of bruises and abrasions. To Polly the trip was "a thorough course in camp-craft, camp making, cooking and trail-breaking carried to a degree of efficiency never experienced, nor found necessary, in the Rockies." Their only major climb was the first ascent of Mount Grenville (3079 m) on the southern edge of the icefield.

Mount Queen Bess, on the northern limit of the Homathko Icefield, is the highest mountain between Vancouver and Mount Waddington, and the Mundays feared some other party would climb it before they did. Twice they had planned trips but were unable to follow through. So in 1942, with Henry Hall accompanying them, they hired outfitters Ken Moore and Lou Haynes, and Ken's daughter Isabelle, to pack them in from Tatlayoko Lake in the Chilcotin area.

As on any packtrip the horses began to show their individual characters. One of these was "The Horse Without Brains," whose pre-dawn arrival one morning was signaled by the sound of scattering pots and pans. Clad only in stockinged feet, Don eventually routed him from camp.

Their forward progress with the horses was slowed, and eventually halted, by almost-inpenetrable second-growth timber. At their farthest point the horses could be turned around and unloaded only after chopping out a clearing.

With Lou's aid, the three climbers backpacked their supplies to the head of the valley. The only approach onto the glacier was fraught with danger; rocks were melting out from the ice and falling down their route.

Finally, on July 20, they reached the long-sought-after summit of Mount Queen Bess (3313 m). The climb was treacherous because of poor snow-and-ice cohesion on rock slabs. But from the summit they were treated to an extraordinary view extending from the seaward side of the range to the Chilcotin plateau. They returned to camp some 25 hours after their departure.

With the outbreak of the Second World War, Don tried to rejoin the army but was rejected because of his previous injury and his age. He was almost 50. To do his part in the war effort, though, he took regular employment in a Vancouver shipyard. Along with other Alpine Club members, Don taught skiing and rock climbing to Canadian troops during the summers of 1942 and 1943 in Yoho National Park. One of the prairie boys, after seeing the rugged mountains, commented: "Good God, is this what we're fighting for?" During the 1943 annual ACC camp at Lake O'Hara, Phyl led many of the climbs because most of the men were instructors at the army camp.

In 1946 and 1947 the Mundays were back on the Homathko. Their 1946 explorations gave them the first ascent of Reliance Mountain (3134 m). In 1947 Phyl went in from the Chilcotin Plateau with two outfitters and nine horses. Don and five other members of the Vancouver section of the ACC flew in and met them at Tatlayako Lake. The purpose of this trip was to test the feasibility of getting horses to the base of the mountain, with the future idea of an ACC camp there. Unfortunately they used up most of their good weather in clearing a packtrail up Reliance Creek and could do no climbing. Phyl flew home with the others, which was her first airplane flight. Less than 24 hours after returning to Vancouver, Don was off to the Waddington area with a rescue team to recover the body of a member of the Harvard University Mountaineering Club.

Although Reliance Mountain was their final first ascent, the Mundays continued to climb in the Coast Mountains and in the Rockies. They also continued to enjoy skiing. When the conditions were excellent, it "made the marrow in my bones bubble," according to Phyl.

In 1947 Don was encouraging the Alpine Club of Canada to sponsor an expedition to Ellesmere Island in the Arctic. He wanted to supercede any American interest, as "we cannot help feeling a bit of secret regret that Canadians have not been more to the fore in mountaineering in their own country." He was disappointed that the expedition did not get organized.

While on the 1948 ACC camp they climbed Mount Athabasca (3491 m) at the Columbia Icefield. They also climbed the north face of Mount Thompson (3065 m), near Peyto Lake, the same year.

Don and Phyl shared their last Alpine Club camp in the Freshfield group in 1949, where they climbed Mount Freshfield (3336 m). Phyl was 55 and Don 59. In November that year Don fell ill; six months later, on June 12, 1950, he died at Vancouver Military Hospital. While he was ill, Phyl had taken the bus every day from their home in North Vancouver to visit him (in her seventies she learned to drive and bought a car).

Don Munday had loved the wild country near Mount Waddington so much that he had requested that his ashes be spread there. A plane was duly chartered, but it did not appear to be a good day: clouds covered the mountains. However, as they neared Mount Munday, the clouds opened to reveal the mountain which had held them in thrall for so many years. The plane circled as the pilot looked for a favorable location, and then Phyl, Don's "chief push" and partner in life and climbing, dropped the package. She had put Don's old climbing cap around it. Another circuit of the mountain was made, but already the clouds were returning to obscure the area. Some of Don's ashes were also spread in Garibaldi Park, and a small rock memorial was built there by friends.

In 1955 Phyl had the pleasure of re-visiting the Waddington region with Sir Edmund Hillary. They spent many hours flying over the mountains and glaciers she knew so intimately.

After Don died, Phyl continued to do the easier climbs into her 60s and to attend the annual ACC camps. She served as hostess for eight summers during the 1960s at the ACC Clubhouse in Banff. In 1982 Phyl returned to Banff and at 88 years of age succeeded in walking up a few modest hills. She continued to get inquiries about the Waddington area from people who were planning trips, and her correspondence was full of requests for opinions and photographs — more than she could fulfill. She was truly the Grande Dame of the Coast Mountains.

Phyl always found it difficult to find words to describe her love of climbing: "There just aren't any words, but on a mountain you are so very close to nature. Mother Nature can be severe with the careless, but I always feel a friendship with mountains, almost as if they were human."

Phyl really enjoyed snow and ice climbing, because conditions change all the time, whereas "rock is rock." The thrill of exploration and discovery was the main factor for Phyl "I'm not a rock monkey as such, not at all like the rock climbers today. I wouldn't want to hang on a string for hours and hours feeling around for something. I'd want to get going and get on the mountain. I'd rather have an easier mountain and get on top."

Phyl had only scorn for some of the modern climbers and mountaineers, who rush in, bag peaks, and rush home again. "They don't have any reverence for it all, love for it all, adoration for it. It's just accomplishment and nothing else." Phyl and Don were not only mountaineers, but true pioneers and explorers.

Besides the British Columbia Mountaineering Club and the Alpine Club of Canada (she joined the latter in 1920), Phyl was also a member of the Ladies' Alpine Club, the American Alpine Club, the Carlisle Mountaineering Club of England, the

Appalachian Mountain Club, and the Varsity Outdoors Club of Vancouver. She and Don were elected to the Appalachian Mountain Club for "outstanding feats of climbing and exploration in the coast range of British Columbia, and for vision and efforts which have opened up a spectacular new region to mountaineers." Phyl is the only mountaineer to be the recipient of honorary membership in three international mountaineering clubs: the Ladies' Alpine Club (1936), the Alpine Club of Canada (1938) and the American Alpine Club (1967). She was the only woman so honored by the American club. In 1970 she received the ACC's badge for outstanding service, and the following year she was named honorary president. She had trained ACC members in ice and snow climbing, and in mountain first aid. Phyl was also the editor of the *Canadian Alpine Journal* from 1953 until 1969.

Her crowning honor came in 1973, when she was named a member of the Order of Canada. She was also conferred with the title and degree of Honorary Doctor of Laws from the University of Victoria.

Phyl loved photography. She started with an ordinary Brownie, but soon graduated to a good bellows camera and finally to an Exakta, which was her favorite. "It's so exciting when you're focusing on something very small — the centre of a flower or even the veins and petals." Her color and black-and-white photographs of mountain scenery had won her acclaim in mountaineering circles. She always regretted not having color film on their Waddington trips. Don did the developing of their films and she did the printing, with Edith frequently helping. He built an enlarger from water pipe and an old camera. Don made lantern slides, and Phyl colored them under a magnifying glass. In the late 1920s they began shooting movie footage of their explorations.

Phyl loved to give lectures, showing her slides to many, many groups around the province, as well as to her friends. She showed a variety of photos, depending upon the audience. Many of her lectures were about flowers — she liked to start just when they poked through the ground and to take them right through the flowering stage to seeding — the whole cycle. One of her favorite lectures was titled "Tidewater to Timberline." After one such lecture, however, Phyl wrote in her lecture book that "they only really see the photographs and not the deep beauty of nature."

Phyl and her camera were at most of the ACC annual camps (she attended over 30 in all). She always brought an array of lenses. She had great patience and would take hours to compose only a few shots. Phyl was Honorary Photographic Secretary of the ACC for a number of years, and the position involved organizing competitions. During club photo exhibits, the photographs were hung in the main tent and a panel of judges awarded prizes at the end of the camp. She stressed the importance of public photographic exhibits to bring knowledge of mountains and nature to others.

Phyl's kinship with the outdoors was very special, and she frequently berated the general public because "they just go up there and they see the mountains away off in the distance, and come down like it was the last moment they had to live . . . . They just don't see anything . . . people today don't seem to respect nature." She loved nature in all its forms, from the wonderful cloud effects to the most minute spider or ant. "Nothing appealed to me like it [nature]," Phyl said, "and for a long time I didn't go to church because the mountains were my great cathedral."

In August of 1982, Phyl realized her dream of once again seeing Mount Waddington. Fifty-six years had passed since her first visit. While being interviewed for *Beautiful British Columbia* magazine, she said that she would be thrilled to land on the Homathko Icefield and see Mount Waddington once again. A reader of the article contacted the CTV television network, which was looking for ideas for its "Thrill of a Lifetime" program. With the participation of the British Columbia government, Phyl was flown to Mount Waddington. The trip was a complete surprise to her. On the Homathko Icefield she left the helicopter, firmly planted the ice axe that served as her walking stick, and shot a few photos on her ancient Exakta camera. A television crew photographed her in many poses on the Icefield. It was a dream come true, as she had given up hope of ever seeing "Mystery Mountain" again.

Phyl never considered whether she was a role model for other women climbers "I don't know what women really thought of me . . . . If a person enjoys it [mountaineering] and you are strong enough, and well enough to do it, and you can hold your own with a party . . . then there is no reason in the world why a woman can't do it." She felt that the reason a lot of women are discouraged in mountaineering is because the group sometimes travels off too quickly to start with, and they can't keep up. Her secret was to travel at a steady pace, one which she could hold to all day. As she grew older gracefully, it was obvious from Phyl's tremendous vigor that she had paced herself properly, when others had burnt themselves out. "She gave to everybody a sense that you don't go beyond your limits, your capabilities, that you had to think of the team, the others, of the party," remembered one Vancouver climber.

Phyl climbed some 100 peaks, nearly a third of which were first ascents. Many others were first ascents for women.

A young climber once asked Phyl why she and Don went into the Mount Waddington area so many times and didn't even reach the summit of the main tower of Waddington. She replied that

> we didn't go into the Waddington country just to climb one mountain and run out and leave it. We went in . . . to find out all we possibly could about glaciers and mountains and animals and nature and everything about that particular area — completely unknown before we went into it — so that we could bring out the information for the interest of other people as well as ourselves.

"What a life we've had," said Phyl, when I interviewed her in 1988 in Nanaimo, British Columbia. "Nothing can take away our mountain memories." Phyl passed away on April 11, 1990.

Lillian Gest
(1898-1986)

"How would you like to go to Banff and Lake Louise this summer?"

"Where are they?" I asked casually. Mother and I were sitting on the porch at our home in Pennsylvania one afternoon discussing summer plans. Neither of us liked Philadelphia's hot summers and were accustomed to go away for some weeks. We had tried various places in the east and once had gone to Wyoming but none quite called for return visits year after year.

So we went to the Canadian Rockies. The year was 1921 and I little suspected that I would return again and again until I came to look upon it as my summer home.

Lillian's mother had traveled through the Canadian Rockies in the 1880s, but it had rained most of the time and she had always harbored a desire to see them again in the sunshine. And so they came to Banff for the summer. With the exception of a couple of summers spent in the Alps, Lillian returned to the Rockies every summer for the rest of her life — riding, climbing and hiking to her heart's content. She jokingly told her friends that she was a Canadian every July and August.

On their first trip to Banff, in 1921, Lillian and her mother stayed at the Banff Springs Hotel for the first few weeks. There, they met an aunt, uncle and cousin who had already arrived. They took the regularly scheduled drives around Banff — to Tunnel Mountain, Lake Minnewanka, Johnston Canyon and Vermilion Lakes. They loved the daily walk to town to shop or to visit the Banff Zoo, being especially enamored of the polar bear. Years later, when the zoo was discontinued and the animals shipped to Calgary, Lillian felt as if she'd lost a friend.

She met another Philadelphia girl and they began to ride the local trails almost every morning, taking horses to Sundance Canyon, the Hoodoos or Sulphur Mountain. When the other girl suggested riding up Sulphur Mountain, Lillian thought they were being very adventuresome. She wore riding boots that were laced across the ankle and came up to just below the knee.

They then moved on to Lake Louise by train. They stayed at the Chateau Lake Louise and explored the area: strolling along the trails to Big Beehive and Little Beehive, hiking to the Saddleback and Plain of the Six Glaciers. And Lillian climbed Mount St. Piran (2649 m). They took the bus to Moraine Lake and hiked in that area as well.

From Lake Louise they traveled the few miles by train to Hector Station. A launch took them across Wapta Lake to the Wapta Bungalow Camp. While staying there Lillian rode to Lake O'Hara for the day. It was the beginning of a lifelong passion for the area. After a few days they left Wapta and moved on to Emerald Lake, going by car from Field.

Later they boarded the train for Glacier National Park, British Columbia. On the way to Glacier House in Rogers Pass they rode in the open observation car "in spite of cinders from the coal-burning engines and the two storms which we went through." They didn't want to miss the magnificent scenery. Lillian's father, William, joined them there and was happy that it was raining when he came from Banff so that he didn't **have** to ride outside! It was while at Glacier House that guide Ernest Feuz led Lillian onto her first glacier; she looked into a crevasse, threw stones down a moulin (water-worn shaft in the ice) and saw pink snow (caused by the presence of red algae). They also went by horse and wagon to Nakimu Cave. At the hotel Lillian met mountain climbers who regaled her with their stories. She "counted no day lost" when she could talk to them about their climbing.

In 1923 Lillian and her mother were back at Banff, Lake Louise and Glacier House.[1] Ernest Feuz put hob-nails in her walking boots, which improved her confidence and sure-

---

1. In 1916 the newly-built Connaught Tunnel lowered the railway grade through the Selkirks, eliminating the use of Rogers Pass. With the train no longer stopping in front of the hotel, the number of visitors declined steadily, and it was closed in 1924.

footedness so much that she went up the Illecillewaet Glacier by herself, worrying her mother to no end. She wore a divided skirt and high boots. She read Howard Palmer's *Mountaineering and Exploration in the Selkirks* from cover to cover, devouring his wonderful descriptions of the mountains, glaciers and forests.

They went to Lake O'Hara again, but staying overnight this time. Lillian went to visit Caroline Hinman, who was camped nearby with a tour group. She had been introduced to Caroline in the east by a friend who knew their mutual enthusiasm for the Rockies. Lillian was to have traveled with Caroline on this trip but a bout with whooping cough in the spring had caused her to cancel out.

The following year, 1924, Lillian did go out to the mountains with Caroline. Although she had camped in New Brunswick on a canoeing and fishing expedition, and one other summer in the White Mountains of New Hampshire, this was her first real introduction to the outdoors. For the next decade Lillian joined at least one of Caroline's trips each summer. They

A Caroline Hinman tour group on the summit of Mount Castleguard. Guide Charlie Hunter is on the right, holding the rope.

became very close friends, traveling around the Rockies and attending Alpine Club of Canada camps together. (Refer to chapter on Caroline Hinman, page 107 , for more details.)

On this first trip the 18 clients and 6 guides started in the Yoho Valley. They went over Yoho Pass to Emerald Lake, up the Amiskwi River Valley and over Howse Pass to the North Saskatchewan River. From there they headed north to the Alexandra River and Castleguard Meadows. They climbed Castleguard Mountain (3090 m) using lariats for ropes, tying far too many people on each one. Their alpenstocks were cut from tree branches. They explored a little way into the cave, using flashlights and lanterns made by putting candles in big jam tins. They also rode to Thompson Pass and onto the Saskatchewan Glacier before returning to Lake Louise via Pinto Lake and the Cline, Whiterabbit, Clearwater and Cascade rivers. At the end of the trip Jim Boyce, their outfitter, signed both Caroline and Lillian up as charter members of the new Trail Riders of the Canadian Rockies.

In 1925 Lillian spent two months on the trail with Caroline. One of the novices on this trip was Marguerite Schnellbacher, who later became an avid climber.

They left Lake Louise and headed north along the Pipestone

Whyte Museum of the Canadian Rockies — Gest collection

Hinman party crossing the North Saskatchewan River in "The Bucket," 1924.

and Siffleur rivers to the North Saskatchewan River. Lillian was riding a horse named Brownie, "Whom I find I don't like — rough and stumbles and has a mouth of cast iron, a pack horse's soul and all seems donkey or mule but the first 10 inches of her tail." When two of their packhorses drowned fording the North Saskatchewan River they took the others a few kilometres downriver to a different ford. The girls were ferried across the river in a primitive cable car called "The Bucket."

On the Kootenay Plains of the North Saskatchewan River they met a group of Indians who were getting ready to go to the Banff Indian Days. Some of the Indians watched the guides set up camp, but they did not encourage conversation. Finally, some of the girls boldly asked if they could visit the Indian camp, which was duly arranged.

It was a strange party; eleven of us American women in knickerbockers and flannel shirts with bright kerchiefs about our necks and five Indians — not quite the romantic figures sometimes pictured but interesting. They wore old trousers with bright colored shirts not too clean, a once bright but now soiled and faded kerchief about their necks, their coarse black hair in tight braids one on each side of their bronzed and stolid faces. They all wore mocassins some elaborately beaded in bright colors. Five minutes walk brought us to their camp. Their tepees were scattered through a little grove of poplar trees. We could count seven or eight but there may have been as many more which we did not see. The leaders among them were our former acquaintance Silas Abrahams known as Monkeyface also and his brother-in-law Peter Beaver. Their squaws were squatted outside their respective tents, large fat women who put their hands over their faces and giggled when we spoke to them. One of the women was engaged in cutting out a pair of mocassins and others occupied in various duties about the camp. The Indian women do all the work, even to saddling and packing the horses and pitching the tents. I saw one of them, a girl who looked about 15 with a papoose strapped to a board on her back, packing a horse. I have heard too that when a man shoots a deer his wife must go out and bring it back to camp. The women make all the articles one finds for sale in the shops and these we met made many pairs of mocassins that they sold to us when we camped nearby. They were friendly though silent and allowed us to look into their tepees which were smoky and crowded. The children of which there were many about were very shy and peaked at us surreptitiously from the tents. One tiny boy was quite friendly and allowed us to hold him while he listened to our watches tick and other things that generally amuse children.

While we were talking to the women, the men had gathered in a circle for some athletic contests. There was a pole vaulting contest using the small trunk of a tree; the shot put was played with a big stone. Two of our guides entered into the sport wearing mocassins lent to them by the Indians. Two stolid faced Indians held a string for a high jump and some of the Indians cleared it very easily and gracefully. As it grew dark the tepees lighted by the fires within shone out through the trees, making a very picturesque scene. Soon after we were again around our own campfire, we heard the beat of a tom-tom and stole out to listen in the meadow that separated the two camps. The rhythmic thud of this Indian drum kept on at intervals for some time occasionally accompanied by sharp cries of Ky-Ay. We hesitated to intrude and finally crept to bed while the strange sounds still continued.

From the Saskatchewan the group headed north up the Cline River and over into the Brazeau River drainage, thence over Poboktan Pass to Maligne Lake. One evening the mosquitoes were so bad that the girls wore veils, which prompted them to stage a mock wedding. They elected a minister, and Jim Boyce dressed up as a woman with a pillow for an expanded chest. He also wore a shawl.

When they arrived in Jasper they enjoyed a day of shopping, made merrier with treats such as ice cream sundaes. Leaving the outfit behind they boarded the Canadian National Railways train west and disembarked at Robson Station. The Hargreaves outfitted them for a few days' trip up to Berg Lake. Some of the more adventurous girls joined the guides in climbing Mumm Peak (2962 m). Lillian was a very reluctant climber and did not really enjoy being "dangled on a rope" in the chimney they had to negotiate.

Back on the trail at Jasper, they headed south along the Athabasca River, then over Little Shovel Pass and back to Maligne Lake. Rather than return to the Brazeau they traversed Jonas and Nigel passes to the headwaters of the North Saskatchewan River. Boyce carefully chose a path for horses and dudes up the Saskatchewan Glacier and they arrived safely at Castleguard Meadows. Once again they explored a short way into Castleguard Cave. She and Caroline had heard that a stream would appear from the cave; they waited for it but were disappointed. The party returned to Lake Louise via the Alexandra and Bow rivers.

During the next three summers Lillian again joined Caroline for her "Off the Beaten Track" packtrips. Always keen for a new adventure, they added a fall hunting trip each year. In 1926 Caroline invited Lillian to join her and two friends on a hunt. They were outfitted by Jim Boyce, who hired Charlie Hunter

Crossing the Saskatchewan Glacier, ca. 1924.

A Hinman party at the toe of the Saskatchewan Glacier, 1926.

as their main guide and three other men to assist him.

On the first hunting day Caroline and Lillian went out with Charlie. They were on the Siffleur River side of Pipestone Pass (at that time outside the national park) and decided to hunt in the Dolomite Valley, on the other side of the ridge. After ascending the ridge, though, they discovered that they were too far south, and wound up in a valley that was still in the park. Rather than turn back so early in the day, they descended into this valley and headed for the correct one. After crossing the pass joining the two they were surprised to find a glacier. They crossed it, using their rifles like ice axes, "driving the stocks into the snow with no regard to their lovely new appearance or possible future usefulness." They saw some goats high on the mountainside, but inaccessible. Realizing how late in the day it was, they decided to forego any further hunting and head back to camp. The first route over the ridge that they tried proved to be impractical and they had to turn back. It being too late to reach camp by then, they decided they had better retreat into the timber to bivouac for the night. They gathered boughs for a bed and Charlie hauled in enough firewood to warm them through the night, but they got little sleep. At first daylight the next morning they found a different route over the ridge. Once they were on the way Charlie went ahead to get the others from camp and bring back some food. Other than feeling weak from their exertion and lack of food they arrived in camp safely. Lillian did shoot a goat later in the trip.

A few days later they began to get snow, which lasted for the rest of the trip. They wore stout forestry-cloth knickers and heavy underwear, and "if it was very cold we just put on two of everything." Their sleeping bags were constructed of several layers of blankets and a down quilt enclosed by a heavy canvas cover.

The next autumn Lillian and Marguerite Schnellbacher went hunting again with Charlie. One day Lillian fired several shots at a big buck, but he disappeared over the hill. Knowing that she had wounded it they followed its tracks, and soon found it lying in some bushes.

> He was a lovely creature, lying down but with his head erect and looking straight at us. I didn't want to shoot, but he was wounded badly I knew and I had to. It is one thing to shoot an animal at a distance, quite another to do it at close range — I hated it all . . . Charlie offered to shoot him for me but I couldn't allow that. I had to finish what I had begun. So I fired, but I don't know where that bullet landed. I doubt if it hit the deer . . . I rather think it landed somewhere across the meadow . . . I sat down out of sight of the dead deer and resolved never to shoot deer, moose or goat again.

As she hated bears, her vow did not include them. And she didn't include sheep because she desperately wanted a bighorn ram's-head trophy.

Marguerite was also affected by the killing of animals. One day Lillian returned to camp to find that Marguerite was ill, possibly from eating a tainted bighorn sandwich, "Or was it that she had shot two goats and then found that they were the parents of a little kid which was left alone on the mountain."

Marguerite was hunting with Charlie one day, following a strange trail that they discovered was made by five head of cattle. A warden had kept them for meat, which was against park regulations, and had then turned them loose!

The following autumn, 1928, Lillian went hunting with Caroline again, and another friend, Mary Phrauer. Caroline shot a goat and moose, Mary got a goat also, and Lillian bagged a deer and her coveted ram.

During that summer Lillian had suggested to Caroline that she lead a hiking trip to Europe. Caroline obviously liked the idea and arranged a tour for 1929. They did a lot of hiking and climbed a few peaks also: the Ortler (3902 m) and Gross-Glöckner (3797 m) in Austria, the Cinque Torre in Italy and the Jungfrau (4158 m) in Switzerland. Then they went to Zermatt.

At Zermatt they kept hearing enticing, and contradictory, reports about the difficulty of climbing the Matterhorn — that one fellow had tried to climb it 17 times, or that it was so easy the guides could take a cow up! They determined to climb it and find out for themselves. They duly hired a guide and a porter each and arranged to go up to the Hotel Belvedere, at the base of the mountain, the next morning.

> The thought of the climb petrified me; I thought we were in no condition to attempt it. We would feel the altitude; then hour's work would exhaust us. We might get up but we couldn't possibly get down. I feared no single cliff, but oh! the dreadful succession of them! We thought the muscles of our arms would give out from pulling ourselves around. We should do a practise [sic] climb or two with our guide first. Then morning came and thanks be, it rained!

Lillian did a practice climb of the Rimpfischhorn. Everything went well and she felt fine. So she hired the same guide, Joseph Biner (she had met him briefly before, when he had spent one summer in the Rockies) and his son for the Matterhorn, and they went up to the Hotel Belevedere for a good night's sleep. Of course that was a delusion, as there was

singing and yodeling and no one turned in until nine o'clock
— a reasonable hour, except that they were to get up at midnight
for an early start!

> Nearly every big climb in the Alps is begun in the wee small hours
> of the morning. I always thought that was done because glaciers and
> snow slopes are in better condition then than in the heat of the day.
> Also avalanches are less apt to bury you alive. . . . Somehow time goes
> faster in the dark and it seems to be psychologically helpful to see
> only one step ahead. Climbing in the dark keeps you from seeing what
> you are doing and on the Matterhorn perhaps it is just as well.

She had only about an hour of sleep and the guides did
not sleep at all as there were six of them in a bed made for
three. They joined the candlelight procession up the Matterhorn.
There were two or three parties ahead of them, and an endless
number below them.

> The lantern threw a small circle of light and into that circle I climbed.
> I was so close to the first guide's heels I often got my fingers under
> his nailed boots. Occasionally I kicked the rear guide's head, but neither
> seemed to mind. At critical moments the light went out and we poised
> ourselves in mid-air till it was lighted again. As we climbed, the clouds
> grew thicker until not a star could be seen. About an hour after we
> started it began to snow. Still the guides kept up the illusion that it
> might clear. No one would turn back for fear that by some fluke one
> of the crowd might reach the summit . . . A long fixed rope dangled
> by our side and when we felt a little insecure we could grasp it and
> swing further out into space.

Finally they reached the upper hut, perched between the
rocks at the mid-way point of the climb. It was already full of
climbers and guides, but they squeezed themselves in anyway.
People sprawled in an informal manner, and they wrapped
themselves in warm blankets to await the dawn. Some people
tried to sleep while others ate and drank. People went in and
out incessantly. Two men started for the summit but returned
a few minutes later.

Lillian and Caroline had reached the hut in three hours of
steady climbing, and for the next four hours they sat there as
the snow fell heavily. Soon people began to leave the hut,
abandoning the mountain. Theirs was the last party to start
the descent. It was a gray dawn and there was now half a metre
of fresh snow on the mountain.

> [I am] cursed with the spirit but none of the other attributes of a
> mountaineer. My hands and feet must find their holds on the rock,

although my ribs know that it is really the rope that keeps them there. Over one precipice I gave up the pretence of finding foot holds and swung on the rope out into space. I didn't like it and squealed! I didn't fall an inch but I had all the sensations of helplessness, that must be the lot of those who slip. After this I used the rope more but never without warning the guide to be well anchored. In time this provoked him a little and he replied that he always had me tight. If I did not believe it, I know now that he had, by the sore places on my ribs the next day. . . . It took us five hours, and long before we were down we were soaked to the skin, and cold and shivery. . . . As we got further down the going was easier and we finally at 12:15 noon, not midnight now, walked into the Belvedere.

They turned their backs on the Matterhorn, and a few days later left Switzerland. In a melancholy mood Lillian wrote "I wonder how passionate a mountaineer am I?"

Lillian spent the next summer in Europe also. With her parents she visited London and Paris and then returned to Switzerland. Marguerite Schnellbacher joined her there. Initially the poor weather restricted the two of them to a lot of hiking and small scrambles. They had to cancel one climb but did ascend the Faulhorn and the Wetterhorn (3701 m). At the hut on the Wetterhorn they rose early and ate breakfast to "rousing Swiss yodelling songs." They also climbed the Mönch (3933 m) from the Jungfraujoch (a high pass between the Mönch and the Jungfrau accessible by railway) and Marguerite climbed the Jungfrau (4158 m) itself. Then it was back to Zermatt and another attempt on the Matterhorn. Unfortunately this time Lillian became ill and had to turn back, but Marguerite made it to the summit. They then went to England and spent some time tramping and cycling in the Lake District.

Lillian joined both of Caroline's summer packtrips in 1931. The first was to the Assiniboine area, and the second one was north of the Bow River to the Red Deer River. A porcupine assaulted their tent one night on the first trip. Caroline went outside to lift the tent pegs so they could chase it out under the side of the tent. It wouldn't go, though, so they eventually chased the animal out the door with a fishing rod. Caroline and Lillian then pursued it down the hill "dancing about shrieking in our pyjamas in the early dawn."

In between the two pack trips Lillian attended the Alpine Club of Canada's annual camp, this time at Prospector Valley in Kootenay National Park. It was her first camp, and she was keen to climb after her two summers in the Alps. From the main camp in the valley some of the group went up to Fay Hut, from which they climbed Mount Fay (3234 m) with Ed Feuz, Jr. Lillian also climbed Mount Hungabee (3493 m) with Feuz. Then there was a two-day circle trip over Wenkchemna and Wastach passes, Mitre Col, and Abbot and Opabin passes.

After the camp ended, Lillian rejoined Caroline's packtrip to the north. Later the two of them returned to the ACC clubhouse in Banff. Lillian enjoyed the camraderie of the clubhouse; climbers came and went constantly, sharing stories and plans. Lillian was an avid photographer, both stills and movies, and she loved showing her pictures in the evenings at the clubhouse to anyone who was interested. She would go downtown to shop and visit friends, and would sometimes attend concerts at the Banff Springs Hotel. The clubhouse was centrally located for climbing the mountains of the main Bow Valley; she would store gear at the clubhouse as she came and went all summer long.

When her parents came for a few weeks they always stayed at the Banff Springs Hotel, and Lillian would get a room there to be with them. Her mother was an invalid and often traveled with a nurse to take care of her. She would then move back to the clubhouse when they left.

The rest of the year Lillian returned to live with her family near Philadelphia. William Gest was head of the Philadelphia Fidelity Trust Co. Lillian was a graduate of Bryn Mawr and Vassar Colleges. When she graduated from Vassar in 1919 she had set out to get a job, but her father had dissuaded her, saying that it would deprive some man who needed that job to support a family. So Lillian turned to volunteer social work, becoming involved with the Philadelphia Children's Bureau, which sought to place children in foster homes, and the Children's Aid Society. Her interest in social work led her to obtain her M.A. in Sociology from the University of Pennsylvania, in 1931.

The year 1932 was the first in which Lillian began to climb seriously — she had discovered that she **did** have a passion for mountaineering. She hired Swiss guide Christian Häsler Jr., for most of August and September. First they climbed in Glacier National Park, B.C., traversing the three peaks of Mount Jupiter: Castor (2779 m), Pollux (2800 m) and Leda (2787 m).

Then they climbed Uto Peak (2932 m) and the northwest ridge of Mount Sir Donald (3297 m). From there it was over to Lake Louise, where they climbed a number of peaks: Mount Victoria (3464 m), Mount Odaray (3159 m) and The Mitre (2889 m).

On August 23 Lillian was joined by Caroline for a two-week walking trip. Chris guided them and Charlie Hunter helped to pack their gear. First they went to the Glacier Circle Hut in Rogers Pass, from which Lillian, Caroline and Chris climbed Häsler Peak (3390 m), named for Chris's father. Then they took the train to Field where they spent a few days hiking in the Little Yoho Valley and at Emerald Lake. Back at Field they went over Dennis and Duchesnay passes to Lake O'Hara for a few more days, then via Opabin Pass to Moraine Lake and Lake Louise. Lillian, Caroline and Chris climbed Mount Temple (3543 m) before ending the trip.

Lillian Gest and Caroline Hinman on Mount Temple, 1932.

Chris Häsler was Lillian's favorite guide, and she would hire him exclusively for the summer. He was an entertaining and interesting companion around the campfire and enjoyed talking about world events. He would choose harder routes, if the climbing ability of his clients allowed it, because he enjoyed the difficulty. Chris loved mountain goats and would follow their trails for hours, finding that theirs was often the easiest route up a mountain. Lillian and Chris became good friends over the years.

When Lillian arrived at the ACC Clubhouse in Banff in late June, 1933, renowned British climber Katie Gardiner was already there (refer to chapter on Katie, starting on page 220). They made some plans to climb together and discussed them with Chris. As usual he was interested and talked enthusiastically about all of the peaks and traverses they could do. Lillian, though, "told him not to count the chickens before they're hatched, [nor] peaks before they are climbed."

A few days later she went on a walking trip with Chris to Mount Assiniboine, probably to get into shape for the summer's climbs. As this was Chris's first time in the area, Lillian acted as his guide on the way in. When they returned, they went to the ACC camp at Paradise Valley, where Lillian tented with Katie and finalized their climbing plans.

While at the camp she traversed Haddo Peak (3070 m) and Mount Aberdeen (3151 m), and climbed Pinnacle Mountain (3067 m) twice. One chimney on Pinnacle was very smooth; Lillian "did it very badly and Chris practically pulled me up á la sack of potatoes." She also climbed Mount Temple (3543 m) and a couple of lesser peaks.

Following the ACC camp Lillian and Katie went into the Yoho with Chris and Walter Feuz. Walter was Katie's favorite guide. The group climbed Isolated Peak (2845 m) and traversed the Vice President (3066 m) and Michael Peak (2696 m) on their way to Emerald Lake.

Then, on August 9, the four of them headed off for a two week jaunt into a remote area of Yoho National Park: the Ice River in the Ottertail Range. They were outfitted by Jim Boyce and Bill Harrison. The cost was $45 per day: $25 for Boyce, $10 for Harrison and $5 each for the guides.

On August 11 they ascended the South Tower of Mount Goodsir (3562 m). Two days later they climbed Mount Ennis (3133 m). While approaching the peak through heavy timber Walter climbed a tree to scout the easiest route. On August fifteenth they climbed the North Tower of Mount Goodsir (3525 m), the third ascent of this difficult mountain. They made a first ascent on this outing, climbing Teepee Peak (now Teepee Mountain, 3118 m) on August 17. This was the first time that

Lillian had been along on a premier climb.

Walter and Chris could walk very quickly, and on the return to camp they went far ahead in an effort to speed the women up — usually to no avail. They would wait for Katie and Lillian every so often, though. On one approach Walter and Chris hurried out of sight; when the women caught up Lillian pointedly asked Walter "whether he or I was guiding Katie!" They had to turn back on one climb because Katie was very tired and slow.

Following their successful Ice River trip, Lillian went to Lake Louise for a few days. First, she climbed Popes Peak (3162 m) with Chris. Then they went up to the Abbot Pass Hut for another try at Mount Victoria. Chris attacked a marauding packrat with an ice axe and stones in an effort to dislodge it from the hut. Much to Lillian's joy they accomplished the famous south-to-north traverse with no problem.

Whyte Museum of the Canadian Rockies — Gest collection

Lillian Gest and Chris Häsler, with unidentified man, at the Abbot Pass Hut, ca.1932.

Lillian started off the summer of 1934 with a short packtrip up the Pipestone River with Caroline Hinman. Then she, with Chris Häsler and Polly Prescott (another active climber and Vassar graduate, from Ohio) travelled off to Edmonton and then Jasper for the Alpine Club camp in the Tonquin Valley. While at the main camp she climbed Alcove Mountain (2810 m), Mount Erebus (3119 m) and three of the peaks of the Ramparts: Simon (3322 m), McDonell (3270 m) and Bennington (3265 m). They then made the long walk over to a fly camp above Geikie Creek, by way of Amethyst Lakes. Their plans to climb mounts Geikie and Barbican were aborted when it rained heavily; further, Polly came down with a cold.

Then Lillian spent a week at Berg Lake with Bea McNeil and Chris. On August 9 they climbed Mount Resplendent (3426 m), and on August 11, The Helmet (3420 m). While ascending The Helmet Chris cut 267 steps. The new crampons were generally distrusted by the guides. Bea likened the summit to "an inverted plate of snow." On the descent the two women crossed snowbridges over crevasses on their hands and knees while Chris jumped them. Chris got in an argument with outfitter Roy Hargreaves when Roy said that he could make more steps with his wood-cutting axe than Chris could with his ice axe!

Back at Jasper, Lillian and Chris immediately set out for Mount Edith Cavell. They stayed at the teahouse overnight and had fine weather while climbing, but clouds obscured the view from the summit (3363 m). Lillian found the east ridge steep and interesting, but not very difficult. They descended to Verdant Pass and the Astoria River. Upon her return to Jasper, Lillian was interviewed by an *Edmonton Journal* newspaperwoman about her exploits in the area.

Then they took the train back to Banff. Before hitting the trail to Mount Assiniboine, Lillian and Chris climbed Mount Edith (2554 m) and Mount Louis (2682 m). Louis was the steepest mountain she'd ever climbed. Then they set out for their ten-day walking trip. Their dufflebags went ahead by horseback to the camp at Sunburst Lake, while they walked through a still smoldering fire along Brewster Creek. A park crew was manning water pumps, in an effort to contain it. The resulting smoke haze dimmed the mountain views during the entire trip. They camped for one night before reaching the camp.

They climbed Mount Assiniboine (3618 m) a few days later. While ascending the ridge, Lillian resolutely ignored the 1000-m drop to one side. Because of the smoke they could barely see Lake Magog at the base of the mountain. On the summit she found a letter addressed to her: greetings left by Georgia Engelhard, who had climbed Assiniboine a day or two before. They didn't use a rope on the ascent, but they did on the descent.

From Assiniboine the twosome went over Marvel Pass and camped again. They couldn't see Mount Eon, their destination, because of the great mass of Mount Gloria, but hoped it, "like prosperity, was just around the corner." After lots of traversing through ridges and gullies, they reached the base of Eon — but found they were on the wrong side for the climb. So they had to traverse along the base, frustrated over the elevation they had lost. They despaired of reaching the summit and returning to camp before dark, but they decided to attempt the climb anyway. Fortunately, they reached the summit (3310 m) quickly.

Theirs was the first ascent of Mount Eon since Dr. Stone's death (refer to page 158 for details of the accident). Lillian wrote that "the peak affords no climbing which gives joy to a climber for its own sake. It is a huge rock pile of slippery slabs and he who wishes to think of it as a gorgeous mountain, should view it only from Wonder Pass or Mt. Gloria." Returning to camp they found Georgia Engelhard had dropped by for a visit, having ridden over from her campsite. The following day Lillian and Chris climbed Mount Gloria (2908 m). They traveled back to Banff over some little-used passes and ridges.

Lillian began the 1935 season with a walking trip through Glacier National Park in Montana with Caroline Hinman. They ended their trip at WatertonLakes, where they were picked up by Marguerite Schnellbacher and Polly Prescott. Then the four of them attended the ACC Lake Magog camp at Mount Assiniboine.

Leaving Caroline behind at the main camp, the other three went on to the fly camp on the Mitchell River. Lillian was on the first ascent of Mount Watson (2970 m), while some of the other climbers went on to The Marshal. From another fly camp on Aurora Creek they ascended Mount Brussilof (3005 m). While crossing the creek on a long slim log Lillian was a little too nonchalant, with the result that she fell into the creek, going completely under. She came up unhurt, but joined the growing ranks of the "Mermaids Club," named for those who fell into streams during the ACC camp. She also lost her ice axe, and

Polly Prescott, Lillian Gest, Marguerite Schnellbacher and Caroline Hinman at Mount Assiniboine, ca. 1934.

managed the climb without it.

After the camp she and Marguerite hired Chris for a week's climbing at Fay Hut. They climbed mounts Little (3140 m), Allen (3310 m) and Quadra (3173 m) before going down to Moraine Lake. Then it was in and out of Banff and Lake Louise, climbing The Three Sisters (2936 m) near Canmore, Castle Mountain (2766 m) near Banff, Mount Victoria (3464 m) at Lake Louise and Mount Biddle (3319 m) at Lake O'Hara. From O'Hara they went up to Abbot Pass, Chris carrying firewood for the hut. Lillian had a restless night, "did not sleep well and when I did dreamed all kinds of things and all ended in sudden disaster. Chris spouted German poetry from the next room and sang lullabys," probably in an effort to help her sleep. The next day they made a successful ascent of the northwest face of Glacier Peak (3283 m). On the descent Chris felt that she was too slow and began pulling her. She tried glissading but that was one mountaineering skill she never mastered.

Lillian did not achieve much climbing during the summer of 1936 because she sprained her ankle early in the season, while descending Mount Christie (3103 m) during the ACC camp at Fryatt Valley in Jasper National Park. Instead, she spent a lot of time at the enlarged Skoki Lodge north of Lake Louise, hiking the many trails and doing some light scrambling. Toward the end of the season she was able to climb four of the peaks around Bow Lake: St. Nicholas Peak (2970 m) and mounts Olive (3130 m), Gordon (3203 m) and Rhondda (3055 m). She made one first ascent, that of Mount Weed (3080 m) with Chris and some friends.

In 1937 Lillian had her car shipped up from Philadelphia so that she could travel more easily. She and Katie hired Chris Häsler and Ed Feuz for a month of climbing. Their main objective was to climb Mount Bryce, on the southern edge of the Columbia Icefield. To get in shape for it they planned on a short trip north of Golden in the Big Bend of the Columbia River. They drove up the new road as far as they were able to[1], one getting stuck occasionally and having to be pulled out by

1. The original highway followed the Columbia River along its northward loop between Golden and Revelstoke, but was replaced by the shorter Rogers Pass route through Glacier National Park in 1961. The former highway is now drowned under the Kinbasket Lake reservoir.

a truck when pushing failed to dislodge their car. At the end of the road they met Pete Bergenhaus, whom they had hired to take them down the lake by boat. He also backpacked their supplies to the base of Mount Trident, on the west side of Kinbasket Lake. His fee was $20 a day for packing and $25 each way for the boat. With a $10 tip the cost was $170.

On July 17 they made their first attempt on Trident but discovered that they must approach the mountain from the other side. Ed and Chris had some disagreements as to the route, Ed feeling that Chris made decisions too quickly. Lillian deplored Katie's lack of interest in route-finding. A day later they ascended the mountain (3121 m). The women were tired and slow on the trip, just getting into condition.

Then it was time to make the attempt on Mount Bryce. Outfitter Jimmy Simpson packed them up to Thompson Pass, on the Great Divide near the head of the Castleguard River, where they established a base camp. From there they backpacked down Rice Brook into British Columbia. The weather was holding well, so they established a bivouac on the south slope of Bryce. But clouds appeared in the midafternoon, and by early evening it was raining. The next day they returned to their base camp to wait out the weather: "Edw. thought it would rain 3 days and I said ten at least. Unfortunately I was right." They waited out the rain at camp, and in desperation climbed a few peaks that they couldn't even see.

They made the first ascent of Queant Mountain (3120 m) in bad weather. On August 7 they climbed Mount Alexandra (3388 m) in a snowstorm; they knew they were on the summit only "because snow cornice stopped on three sides ... great disappointment and only satisfaction is that we are on top of something." Finally, on the third trip to their Bryce bivouac they succeeded in climbing the mountain (3507 m). It was the second ascent. In 1929 Feuz had been turned back on Bryce by bad weather also.

On the return trip they climbed Castleguard Mountain — Lillian's third ascent of it. Simpson was paid $600 for the four weeks, with a tip of $20 to each of the outfitters and packers, and a tip of $10 to the guides. Lillian gave Chris an extra $50 tip.

At the end of the season Lillian and Marguerite drove back to Philadelphia via the national parks in Utah. This was to be a pattern for many years — ship the car out in the spring and drive it home in the fall.

Lillian spent a number of weeks in Jasper National Park in 1939. She started off by attending the Alpine Club's annual camp at the Columbia Icefield. From a high camp on the icefield she and three other women — Christine Reid, Kathleen Chapman and Jean McDonald — were the first women to climb Mount Columbia (3747 m). Although they climbed on two separate ropes, they all went on one rope for the summit bid, guided by Ed Feuz. She also climbed Mount Athabasca (3491 m) and Mount Andromeda (3450 m). Her car was one of the few in camp and she was kept busy shuttling people to and from trailheads. Caroline Hinman was also at the camp, but she spent her time hiking in the surrounding alpine country.

After the camp six of the women — Lillian, Polly, Marguerite, Caroline, Jean and Marjorie Alton — spent six days camping at Poboktan Creek. Polly and Lillian climbed the Waterfall Peaks (2950 m) from the warden cabin, with Polly doing most of the leading. The rest of the days were spent hiking.

Lillian and Polly hired Chris for six days of exploring along the newly-opened Banff-Jasper Highway in 1940. She had her car shipped to Jasper and then drove down the highway to pick her companions up at Lake Louise. There were many fires in the upper Bow Valley that summer, some which were still smoldering along the highway. From their camp near Panther Falls they climbed a nearby mountain, which they named Christian Peak (3134 m). It was Chris's first climb since being mauled by a female grizzly bear, near Sherbrooke Lake in Yoho National Park, the previous autumn, and Lillian felt that he was as good as ever. But a strange coincidence that day must have been frightening for Chris. On the descent they were traversing at timberline, Chris in the lead, when Lillian saw him running back toward them. She immediately thought "grizzly" and wasted no time running after him. Sure enough, he had seen a mother and cub. It was unfortunate that the first time out since his accident he should run into another bear.

These events only reinforced Lillian's hatred of bears. She felt that they were "far too bold" and tried to get the parks department to kill some, and make all of them "afraid of people once more."

Lillian and the others went to the ACC Glacier Lake camp. From there Lillian climbed Peak 2 (3514 m) and Peak 3 (3511 m) of Mount Lyell, now officially named Edward Peak and Ernest Peak after two of the Feuzes[2]. She also climbed Mount Forbes (3612 m) with Phyl Munday.

Chris wasn't feeling well after the camp and returned to Golden. A week or so later, though, he guided her on Mount Burgess (2599 m) in Yoho National Park. She noticed that for the first time he was content to go slowly and not keen to start up again after rests. A few months later he died of a heart attack while shoveling snow from the roof of his house. He was 53 years old.

The death of Christian Häsler affected Lillian deeply. They were close friends and she had been his patron for many years. Although she continued to climb for another decade, she did so mostly from the Alpine Club of Canada camps. After Chris's death she seems to have lost some of her passion for mountaineering.

Lillian continued to be a strong supporter of both the Alpine Club of Canada and the American Alpine Club, (AAC) though. She started the AAC Newsletter in 1950 and edited it until 1959. She was also a councillor of that organization. She materially aided many climbing-club projects, from the Grand Tetons Climbers Ranch to the new ACC clubhouse at Canmore, and she helped with smaller projects such as the publication of Conrad Kain's autobiography *Where the Clouds Can Go.*

Lillian was a philanthropist all of her life, contributing funds to many organizations and causes.

Always a strong walker, Lillian began to spend more time hiking in the Rockies as she grew older. She was already an active member of the Appalachian Mountain Club and had helped start the Philadelphia Trail Club in 1931. She had turned to walking after becoming frustrated with golfing; hiring caddies was troublesome and she tired of carrying her own clubs.

She spent weeks staying at backcountry lodges at Mount

---

2. In 1972 the five distinct summits of Mount Lyell were named to honor the Swiss guides RudolphAemmer, Edward Feuz, Sr., Ernest and Walter Feuz, and Christian Häsler, Sr.

Assiniboine, Skoki and Lake O'Hara. She hiked and did small scrambles. She spent much of her time fishing. One day she wanted to cook some of her catch for lunch, so she scraped the butter from her sandwiches to fry the fish in. Always a flower-lover and photographer, she took up birding in the early 1950's keeping detailed lists of birds seen, when and where, and information on nesting. She wrote and mimeographed a pamplet called *The Birds at Lake O'Hara*. She found birding to be an excellent activity for "trying to stave off old age as long as possible." By this time she was in her sixties.

When she wasn't at the lodges, Lillian stayed at various hotels in Banff and Lake Louise. She kept a car in Banff and drove friends around or unselfishly loaned her car out.

Lillian became a fixture at Lake O'Hara. She was an active member of the Lake O'Hara Trails Club. She was very concerned about park policies and made her views known to the government. She was active in petitioning the parks department to keep the road to Lake O'Hara closed to private vehicles. Through her involvement with the club Lillian wrote *History of Lake O'Hara*, which she published privately in 1960. She mailed it free to friends as a Christmas gift.

That project sparked her interest in gathering the history of other areas of the Rockies and especially of the backcountry lodges, her homes away from home. In 1970 she published *History of Moraine Lake* and in 1970 History of Mount Assiniboine. The first book cost her almost $1000 for 750 copies.

At the 1974 Skyline Hikers camp at South Molar Pass, Lillian hiked in with three other elderly ladies. At the campfire she was showing how Jimmy Simpson used to jump up and down on snow bridges to test their strength and she fell on rough ground, nearly landing in the fire. She insisted that she was fine and finished her story. But in the morning she couldn't move, having injured her back. So her three companions hiked out to the trailhead, drove to Lake Louise and arranged for a helicopter rescue. It was there by noon. She recovered in the Banff hospital.

Although an avid hiker all her life, Lillian hadn't joined the Skyline Hikers until 1945, when they held a camp at Lake O'Hara. She was in regular attendance through the years. In 1977 she walked into camp at Sunset Pass. "Everybody very helpful — & push me in food line ahead of others am not used to all the attention but I am oldest in camp." Lillian was then 79. Always irrepressible, she had brought to camp some Johnny Walker whiskey in a baby bottle!

Lillian was a very organized person all of her life, and in her later years she had the foresight to make careful arrangements for the future of her vast collection of personal papers, her extensive library and her numerous photographs. The archives of the Whyte Museum of the Canadian Rockies, in Banff, Alberta, received her collection of annual diaries, photograph albums, 45 motion pictures of her trips and approximately 5500 color transparencies. Lillian's sense of the importance of this memorabilia now enables others to relive her joy of mountain discovery.

Lillian Gest died on January 5, 1986, at the age of 88. Lillian lived through many decades of changes in the Canadian Rockies, but as she always said, "The mountains have remained essentially the same."

Katie Gardiner
(1886-1974)

The 1930s was a decade of prominence for a shy, reserved British lady: Katie Gardiner. Although her home was in England, she spent most of her time alternating climbing seasons between Canada and New Zealand, with a few trips to other mountaineering areas thrown in. During this time she became perhaps the most prominent woman mountaineer in the world, and that in her forties! Katie climbed in many countries — Asia, Africa, Japan, Europe, and Australia — but her greatest expolits were in the Canadian Rockies and New Zealand's Southern Alps. In all, Katie made 33 first ascents in Canada, which was a record for women and one that has been bested by only three amateur men and five professional guides.

Katherine Maude Gardiner was born in 1886 to an old upper-middle-class Yorkshire family of coal-mine owners. She was the daughter of Frederick (1850-1919) and Alice Evans Gardiner (?-1925). Little is known about her family, but Katie had at least two brothers, one of whom predeceased her father. Frederick Gardiner was a well-known English climber. He served as vice-president of the prestigious Alpine Club of London, England from 1896 to 1898 and he was on the first ascent of Mount Elbrus (5633 m) in the Russian Caucasus, the highest point in Europe. Frederick was described as having great staying-power and a greater interest in exploration than in climbing itself, both traits for which Katie became well known.

Katie accompanied her father and brothers each season to the Alps, where Frederick encouraged his daughter's interest in climbing. They would settle in some region where their maps "did not show red lines indicating previous expeditions." Her first real climb was of the Breithorn (3762 m) when she was ten years old. Frederick was quite liberal in respect to the notion of women climbing mountains, having accompanied Lucy Walker on her climb of the Matterhorn in 1871, the first major climb by a woman.

Gardiner was also a smart investor and one of the many stocks he owned was in the Canadian Pacific Railway. When he died in 1919 Frederick left Katie a small fortune, which enabled her to live independently and to indulge in a love of exploration and travel.

Although Katie had joined her father climbing as often as she could, she was required to take care of her mother, who was an invalid. Katie attended her mother until she died in 1925.

It was while going through some family papers that Katie came across a panoramic view of Mount Cook in New Zealand. Their sublime beauty appealed to her and she decided that she must visit the Southern Alps. The following year, 1926, Katie arranged a trip to New Zealand. On the way she stopped in Cape Town, South Africa, where she climbed Table Mountain (1087 m). In Australia she climbed Mount Kosciusko (2229 m) and in Tasmania, Mount Wellington (1270 m).

During her first visit to New Zealand Katie climbed some minor peaks with guide Frank Alack. He had been assigned by the Hermitage hotel's chief guide, Vic Williams, to check out her climbing abilities. A reputation as one of the world's most notable women climbers preceded her first visit. Unfortunately, Alack found that she was not as seasoned a climber as her reputation had suggested, although he held that it was not her fault, as at no time had she encouraged the rumor. Frank was to be her guide for many years. She climbed alone with Frank on a number of first ascents of minor peaks — convention did not seem to worry her unduly. On major peaks she usually climbed with two guides, the other most frequently being Vic Williams. Her guides were also her friends and she corresponded with all of them in New Zealand and Canada. She was also very generous, providing them with the best equipment and camp supplies that money could buy.

Photographs of Katie suggest a self-conscious and retiring woman. But people who knew her well say that her reserve and formality refected her Victorian upbringing and that she was very straightforward and unprudish. She possessed a quiet sense of humor and great kindness.

In the fall of 1928 Katie headed for New Zealand again, for the six-month climbing season. On the way she made some minor ascents in India, Ceylon and Japan, and she climbed Boyan dai in Korea.

After some "warm-up" climbing she attained the summit of Mount Cook (3764 m) with guides Vic Williams and Lud

Canadian Alpine Journal

SKETCH MAP OF AREA
IN VICINITY OF MT. COOK

Mahan. An attempt on Elie de Beaumont almost ended in disaster when a serac collapsed, and the climb was abandoned. She accomplished two first ascents: Mount Teichelmann (3161 m) and Meteor Peak (2652 m), the latter which she named.

From the summit of Mount Cook Katie looked across at the dawn-rose glow on Mount Tasman (3498 m), the "stately snow queen," and in her heart she knew that someday she would climb it, too. She wanted to climb it from the west side, a route that had not been done before.

The guides didn't consider Katie a "strong climber," but in the 20s and 30s women often didn't have the opportunity to display any strength. She was considered "slow," but then she was already in her forties and fifties! Katie's main strength was in her endurance — she had staying power — and she made up in determination what she lacked in knowledge or skill. She also had the mountaineer's most valuable attribute: patience. Patience was particularly needed in New Zealand, where the weather is atrociously bad. The difficulty of climbing on the west coast of that country can be compared only to mountaineering on the west coast of Canada, where the glaciers come down to near sea level and the summits require up to 3000 m of elevation gain.

Although she was undoubtedly frustrated by the frequent poor weather in New Zealand, she also had an eye for the changes it wrought:

> There is magic in the air when the rain is over and the sun comes out on the West Coast. The rata flowers glow against the deep green foliage of the bush; a thousand delicious scents rise in the crystal clear air from tree and fern, and one by one the high peaks peep through the dispersing clouds.

In New Zealand Katie climbed primarily in the Southern Alps, basing herself in comfort at the Hermitage and the Graham Brothers' hotel at the Franz Josef Glacier. At the Hermitage one particular table with a spectacular view of Mount Cook was always reserved for her.

Following her successful climbing season in New Zealand, Katie journeyed to Canadian Rockies for the summer of 1929. She hired Swiss climbing guide Walter Feuz and outfitter George Harrison, and she spent two weeks traversing the rugged country along the continental divide south of Banff. They made five first ascents in two weeks in August: mounts Alcantara (2840 m), Brussilof (3005 m), Prince Henry (3227 m), Prince Edward (3200 m) and Cadorna (3145 m). On Mount Prince Edward they had a tricky time on a traverse, where they had to crawl along a narrow ledge overhung by another ledge above. She also climbed Mount Assiniboine (3618 m). Then followed a brief stint in the Horsethief Creek area of the Purcell Mountains.

A number of times George, Walter and Katie set up fly camps for advanced assaults on different peaks. She gave credit for her climbing success to her guide, as "I could have attempted none of the climbing without Walter's skilled help and knowledge of route finding." His and Harrison's "thoughtfulness and kindness about every detail ... made the expedition thoroughly enjoyable." Walter Feuz was Katie's favorite guide in Canada. He was the youngest of the Feuz brothers.

The following June, Katie, again accompanied by Feuz and Harrison, climbed in the French Military Group south of Banff. It was to be a season of many first ascents. Besides Harrison and Feuz the party included Hall, the cook; George's brother-in-law, Harry Smith, the wrangler; over a dozen horses, and Buster and Zip, two Airedale dogs. The cost was $155 per week.

On the way they made a first ascent of Mount Galatea (3185 m), the highest of the "Ship Mountains," so named for First World War battleships. On July 1 they made two first ascents. After climbing Mount Sarrail (3174 m) near the Kananaskis Lakes, they descended a snowfield to the Foch Glacier, which they ascended for some distance before climbing Mount Foch (3180 m).

On July 5 and 6 they climbed Warrior Mountain (2973 m), Mount Lyautey (3082 m) and Mount Cordonier (3021 m). On the second day they also attempted Mount Petain (3183 m), coming within 120 m of the summit before turning back. On the ninth of July they made the second ascent of Mount Joffre (3450 m), first climbed by Ed Feuz and J.W.A. Hickson. On this climb Harry Smith, who was the wrangler, joined them, having never climbed a snow-covered peak before. On July 12 they again attempted Mount Petain, this time accompanied by Harrison, who turned out to be a competent rock climber, and they succeeded in reaching the summit. On July 17 they made the first ascent of Mount Bogart (3144 m) to the east.

Katie was disappointed to find that theirs was not the first ascent of Mount Abruzzi (3267 m). "There was some very good climbing on our peak's summit rocks; but as they rose steeply before us, rather to our dismay we suddenly came on an empty sardine tin, and what little hope we had left was finally dashed to the ground when, after a somewhat stiff climb, we found a tumbled-down cairn with a stick near it to which some remains of a flag were nailed." They speculated as to who had been there before (the identity of the first-ascent party is still unknown.)

In August Katie attended the Alpine Club of Canada's annual camp, held at Maligne Lake in Jasper National Park. She climbed mounts Unwin (3268 m), Charlton (3217 m), Warren (3300 m), Mary Vaux (3201 m), Brazeau (3470 m), Henry MacLeod (3288 m) and also Coronet Mountain (3152 m), Valad Peak (3250 m) and Monkhead (3211 m). The Coronet Mountain climb was a first ascent.

Within a few months Katie was back in New Zealand. Between November 1930 and April 1931 she climbed 27 peaks, nine of which were first ascents: mounts Du Fresne (2251 m), Sefton (3157 m), Stephen, Elie de Beaumont (3109 m), Walter (2898 m) and also Malte Brun (3176 m), Moonlight Peak (which she named), Douglas Peak (3081 m) and Crozet Peak (2008 m). Two attempts were made on Mount Cook but they were turned back by ice near the summit both times. She also climbed and named Mount Frederick Gardiner in the névé of the Franz Josef Glacier.

Of the climb of Mount Sefton, with Peter Graham and Frank Alack as guides, Katie wrote that from the summit "one surely could not find more beautiful or varied scenery in any part of the world, with the sea, the bush and the lovely distant views of the other great peaks of the Southern Alps."

An ascent of Mount Tasman was high on Katie's list of priorities in New Zealand. Time and again over the past five years she had been defeated by poor weather and unsafe snow and ice conditions. The year 1933 was especially trying. They had already been forced to turn back three times, when on the clear morning of February 8 she set out from Almer Hut (at the head of the Franz Josef Glacier) with guides Vic Williams

Whyte Museum of the Canadian Rockies

Vic Williams and Katie Gardiner on Mount Footstool, New Zealand.

and Jack Pope and English climbing friend A.M. Binnie (a friend of her brother's). They set up two tents at a bivouac site on Pioneer Ridge and they retired for the short night, as they expected to be up at two o'clock in the morning for what promised to be a fine climb to the summit.

But during the night a bitter wind swept up, seemingly from nowhere. Katie's tent was blown away, leaving her lying on the ground, and the other tent was barely kept from the same fate. A ferocious alpine storm broke, with thunder and lightning — it was so violent that they had difficulty breathing. Realizing their peril if they stayed put, but unable to return to the hut, they slowly made their way off the ridge to a bergschrund that Vic had recognized the previous day as being useful in an emergency. At the lip of the crevasse a small snow platform had formed and here they sought shelter, scant and cramped though it was. Their shelter was at the 2400-m level; they soon named it "Camp Misery."

They had every expectation that the storm would blow itself out overnight, or at the most in a day or two. But the tempest only grew in intensity. The snow blowing into their shelter almost suffocated them and when it occasionally turned to rain they were afraid that the overhanging lip of the bergschrund might collapse. They had a little kerosene burner and one gallon of fuel, all of which was needed to melt snow for water, but were short of matches. Vic recalled that "Mr. Binnie was a pipe smoker like myself and he always used two matches to get his pipe going. So after the second day, we introduced economy measures that allowed two pipes to be lit with one match." And they had only enough food for three days, so that even on short rations by the sixth day they were almost out of food. At this point, unsure of their survival, Katie wrote a will stating that in the event that they did not live, Vic's and Jack's families would be provided for.

Luckily Jack had a bag of rolled oats which he always carried, jokingly referring to it as he "survival kit." Katie said that "it was the porridge that kept us going ... it got thinner and thinner as the days went on, but at least it was hot."

By the fifth day people at the Fox Glacier and Franz Josef Hotels had become extremely worried about the missing climbers. A party battled its way up to the Chancellor Ridge re they themselves became stormbound.

climbers were still alive, although their clothing was ely sodden and frozen, their limbs stiff and cramping. uddled in their tent day and night, singing songs and stories. Vic would play his harmonica. When they became depressed, Jack would relate some amusing climbing dent — always with a happy ending.

Just before dawn on the ninth day of their ordeal, Vic looked it on a starry sky. They hurriedly packed their gear with umbling fingers. They ate four eggs which they had kept in reserve — "the best breakfast we ever had" — and prepared to leave. But with daybreak fog rolled in and blotted out all reality. Their hopes plummeted. Luckily, a few hours later the fog lifted and they were able to slowly move down the glacier, away from what nearly became their icy tomb. Below them a row of black specks trailing off Chancellor Ridge turned out to be the rescue party coming to look for their bodies. It was led by Maori guide Joe Fluerty, who alone had remained convinced that the group was still alive. No sooner had they descended to the hut when the fog again rolled in and rain began to fall. As the weather closed in once more, they realized that they had escaped during the only respite that had occurred (the storm lasted three weeks). They were uninjured, save for a touch of frostbite on Jack's ear. Katie always credited the unselfishness and kindness of the guides as the reason that they came through the ordeal alive.

Katie tried Mount Tasman once more that season, by the Symes Route, but was unable to reach the summit. She did climb and name Mount Alack (2835 m) for her guide and friend, Frank Alack.

In the summer on 1933 Katie was back in Canada. Arriving at the ACC clubhouse in Banff was like coming home. After a few days of scrambling with Walter Feuz, the two headed to Kootenay National Park to climb Mount Foster, above Floe Lake in the Vermilion Range. Ken Jones, a young man from Golden, joined them as cook. He later became the first Canadian-born climbing guide. The bridge over the Vermilion River was washed out, so they had to take a more circuitous route up Numa Creek to reach the peak. Other than a few blazes nicked into trees, there was little evidence of the old trail that the park warden

Katie Gardiner, ca. 1932.

had advised them to take. After a long uphill trek, they arrived at Numa Pass the following day. The next day they ascended the centre peak of Mount Foster to reconnoitre the route on the main peak. Needing a rest after three strenuous days they left camp the following afternoon and bivouacked among the larch trees at timberline. They attained the summit (3204 m) without difficulty. Ken accompanied them; it was his first ascent of an unclimbed peak. From the peak they could see "range after range fading away into the blue distance."

The weather was too unsettled for more serious climbing, so they motored back to Golden via the Columbia Valley. At Edelweiss, the guides' Swiss village, Mrs. Feuz entertained Katie with some very good homemade stout. After a pleasant two weeks at the clubhouse and the ACC's Paradise Valley camp, Katie returned to the Floe Lake area with Walter and Ken. There they made the first ascent of another unclimbed, and still unnamed, peak (3120 m) at the head of Numa Creek.

In August Jim Boyce and Bill Harrison took Katie and Lillian Gest up the Ice River. Walter Feuz and Christian Häsler guided them on the north and south Goodsirs; they were the first women to climb South Goodsir (3562 m). On August 13 they ascended Hanbury Peak (2911 m). After a couple of lazy days in camp they wanted to ascend an unclimbed, unnamed peak on the northern side of the Goodsirs. Although it looked to be a good climb there seemed to be no great difficulties, so the guides laughingly suggested that the women should be the guides for the day, leading alternately. This suggestion was followed and they all ascended what they named "Teepee Peak" (now Teepee Mountain, 3118 m). They turned back on Chancellor Peak (3280 m); some difficult climbing delayed them, and they worried that they would have had to spend an unexpected night on the mountain if they had continued. (Refer to chapter on Lillian Gest, page 214, for more on their climbs together.)

After another short interlude in Golden, Katie camped near the old Glacier House hotel site in Rogers Pass with Walter and Ken. They traversed Mount Sir Donald (3297 m) and managed some other climbs before the weather forced them out. When she left Canada for New Zealand Katie carried with her many pleasant memories of "the unfailing kindness and hospitality of the Canadian mountain people." They were a balm to the lonely traveler. She had loved the "still, cloudless days" of autumn in the Canadian mountains, when "the aspens are golden with a crimson undergrowth and the powdering of fresh snow at timberline lightens the sombre green of the forest." But spring was on its way in New Zealand, and she had an unfinished task there.

Still determined to stand on the summit ridge of Mount Tasman, Katie returned to New Zealand late in 1933. She started off with scrambles up the three central volcanoes of the North Island — Ngauruhoe (2291 m), Ruapehu (2797 m) and Tongariro (1968 m) — and then headed for the Southern Alps. After her ordeal of the previous season Katie had donated funds for the construction of Pioneer Bivy, a hut on Pioneer Ridge, which was the highest building in the country at the time. Katie cut the ribbon for the formal opening of the hut. The hut became her base for attempting to climb Mount Tasman.

On two occasions they climbed Mount Lendenfeld (3216 m), but were unable to proceed past it to Tasman because of very avalanche-prone snow conditions. Finally, on December 13, they made a successful summit bid. On her ninth attempt Katie had finally achieved her dream and her two favorite guides, Frank Alack and Vic Williams, were there to share the joy of success with her. (Jack Pope had kept his vow, made in the crevasse on Tasman the previous year, that he would never climb again.) In the process she became the second woman (Freda du Faur was the first) to climb both Cook and Tasman, the king and the queen of the Southern Alps. She went on to make 20 other ascents that season, one of which was the first ascent of Mount Vic, which she named in honor of her guide and friend.

The following year the Mount Cook Tourist Company erected a hut on what was locally referred to as "Pudding Rock" and named it the Gardiner Hut, in honor of Katie and in recognition of her financial contribution. Vic Williams, and fellow guide Mick Bowie, were instrumental in transporting supplies and constructing the hut. Gardiner was also honored by the naming of "Katies Col," to the west of the Mount Cook area.

Back in Canada, Walter guided Katie again in 1935, this time into the granite country of the Bugaboos. Ken Jones was his assistant guide. Harrison had a Czechoslovakian cook, Michael Wassill, and a white collie named Max. It was a disappointing summer for her as they made no first ascents. Back in Banff she climbed Mount Louis (2682 m).

There are no records of her Canadian climbs in 1936, but Katie finished the year off in New Zealand in grand style by ascending Mount Aspiring (3025 m), a fittingly named peak, on December 31. Six weeks later she climbed Mount Tutoko (2756 m) in Fiordland district, near the tip of the South Island. This was one of the few trips reminiscent of her Canadian climbs; they traveled with 13 packhorses from Elfin Bay on Lake Wakatipu to the Lower Hollyford Valley. She also climbed, and named for her mother, Alice Peak in the same area.

Ed Feuz, Walter's older brother, started guiding Katie in 1937. Katie and Lillian Gest wanted to climb Mount Bryce (3507 m), on the edge of the Columbia Icefield. Ed, with the assistance of Chris Häsler (Lillian's favorite Swiss guide), took them on a conditioning climb in the Big Bend country of British Columbia. Katie always liked to explore new places, especially those that reminded her of her dear New Zealand. They made the first ascent of Mount Trident (3121 m).

After that warmup they drove up the partially completed Banff-Jasper highway to Bow Lake. From there Jimmy Simpson outfitted them to Thompson Pass. While waiting for better weather they climbed Mount Alexandra (3388 m) and a few other peaks. When it finally cleard, they climbed Mount Bryce in less than 12 hours — the second ascent since Sir James Outram had climbed the peak in 1912. They also climbed Watchman Peak (3009 m) and Castleguard Mountain (3090 m), and they made a first ascent of Queant Mountain (3120 m).

Katie loved the immensity of the Canadian mountains, as opposed to the contained peaks of New Zealand's Southern Alps. It was "thrilling when on the summit of a great peak out there to see range after range fading away into the dim distance and to realise that many of the mountains spread before one are as yet unclimbed."

On the way back to Lake Louise they made a first ascent of one of the Murchison Towers (3170 m) south of Saskatchewan River Crossing, which they called the "Gest Tower." Then, when Lillian left for home, Katie, Ed and Chris climbed old and new routes in the Pipestone country northeast of Lake Louise: the Three Brothers and an unnamed peak, all about 3000 m in elevation.

By the end of 1937 Katie had set her sights on Mount Robson, at 3954 m the highest peak in the Canadian Rockies. Ed Feuz told Katie that she would have to hire one of the Fuhrers at Jasper, because as a CPR guide he couldn't work in "government" territory, meaning along the Canadian National Railways line. In 1938 she made two attempts on the mountain with Hans and Heinie Fuhrer, the CNR guides at Jasper, but they were unable to get through the icefall of the southwest glacier. Almost nine years had passed since anyone had climbed Robson. She did climb Mount Resplendent (3426 m) near Robson, Mount Edith Cavell (3363 m) and Bastion Peak (2970 m) in the Tonquin Valley.

At the start of 1939 Katie let Ed Feuz plan her climbing season based on her fitness (she was 54 years old, after all) although she hoped "to get some nice peaks." She was concerned that she was "terribly out of condition" and wanted to get "hardened" a bit before doing any serious climbing. It turned out to be a busy season, with a crowning achievement, and it was to be her last one in the Rockies.

It started with a trip to the Freshfield Group north of Lake Louise. Harrison again outfitted her, and Ed Feuz and Ken Jones were her guides. From the Freshfields they went over Howse Pass, down the Blaeberry River, over Amiskwi Pass and thence to Field. They chose the Blaeberry route "partly because nobody thought we could do it" and partly because it would be a beautiful trip through new country. On this trip they climbed Mount Freshfield (3336 m), Mount Pilkington (3285 m), Prior Peak (3270 m), the White Pyramid (3275 m) and Howse Peak (3290 m). Mount Pilkington was named for her godfather, Charles Pilkington, who was a former president of the Alpine Club of London. After this trip Katie spent a few days at Lake O'Hara in Yoho National Park, where she climbed Mount Hungabee (3493 m).

Exasperated with her Robson failures, Katie kept pressuring the CPR to let her take two guides from Lake Louise. She wrote to Ed that "I've got to have you.... You handle the CPR from your end and I'll handle it from mine." Feuz asked the manager

Letter from Katie Gardiner to Lillian Gest, 1939.

of the hotel department to let him go. This would be his one chance to climb Robson, which none of the CPR Swiss guides were allowed to attempt. The manager refused, insisting that Robson was a "CNR mountain" as it was close to their railway line. Neither did they want the CNR to benefit from any publicity associated with a successful climb by such a prominent woman. Feuz, on the other hand, insisted that Gardiner was a valued customer of the CPR, traveling frequently on its steamships and railways and using its hotels. (The fact that Katie was a big CPR stockholder must have carried a lot of weight too.) And he felt that although the Fuhrers couldn't guide her up the mountain, he could — even though he hadn't seen it yet. Permission was finally granted, but Ed was told "no near misses and no advance publicity." The CPR hoped to benefit if "their" man successfully guided Katie on Robson where the CNR's couldn't. The agreement was sealed with a drink.

They attempted Robson in August. Chris Häsler was along to assist Ed. Chris accompanied Katie to the Hargreaves ranch, while Ed studied the mountain with binoculars from Robson Station, choosing their route. They spent two nights on the peak, and like climbers before and after, they were plagued by pack rats. They tried to evade the rodents by going out on a ledge in the breeze but none of them got much sleep. Although the snow was in bad shape, they followed Ed's chosen route without difficulty. When they reached the summit, on August 11, Katie pulled out a bottle of wine hidden in her pack and they toasted the old-timers — all there were over 50. "We old folk can beat the young ones any day!" said Katie. In a letter to Lillian Gest shortly afterward, Chris wrote "Robson is a very dangerous mountain and we took lots of chances and all felt a bit uneasy that day." On the way down, above the upper ice-fall, Chris twisted his knee, which slowed them down.

On the way south to Lake Louise they made ten other ascents. At Bow Lake Chris left them, and she and Ed traveled over the Wapta Icefield, on the way climbing Mount Olive (3130 m), Mount Collie (3116 m) and St. Nicholas Peak (2970 m).

Upon finding that the Second World War had broken out, Katie immediately took the train to Montreal and a boat back to England. She quietly joined the Red Cross, serving as commandant of an auxiliary convalescence unit in northwest England. After the war she lived at her home in Cheshire. Katie made one final trip to Canada to visit old friends, but she did not climb.

Except for a brief visit in 1943, it wasn't until 1948 that Katie returned to New Zealand. With Mick Bowie, who had replaced Vic Williams as chief guide at the Hermitage, she climbed two popular volcanic cones on the North Island, mounts Egmont (2518 m) and Ruapehu (2797 m). Two years later she settled in New Zealand, on Mokopeka Station at Maraetotara with Irene Chambers, another mountaineer. (She later moved to Hastings, on the east coast of the North Island.)

In that same year, at 65 years of age, she climbed the Minarets (3066 m and 3055 m, respectively). As one man wrote after meeting her at de la Beche Hut on her Minarets climb, Katie was "Still climbing long after most people have worn [out] their climbing boots in the garden!" Sometimes it seems that she is remembered in New Zealand more for the senational crevasse saga than for her climbing, which numbered over 100 ascents. She climbed more widely and had more peaks to her credit than any other person who climbed in the Southern Alps.

After moving to New Zealand, Katie continued to travel to distant places. Her last trip back to England was made in 1971.

Katie was a member of many prominent mountaineering organizations: the Alpine Club of Canada, the American Alpine Club, the Ladies' Alpine Club in England and the New Zealand Alpine Club. Early in her climbing career her ambition was to become president of the Ladies' Alpine Club, which was a prestigious position. To hold it, one had to have made a certain number of climbs, a goal that she achieved. She served as president during the war years from 1941 to 1943.

Katie Gardiner passed away at her home in Hastings, New Zealand on January 28,1974. She had continued to show a keen interest in mountains until her death. One of her favorite pieces of poetry was:

> Lord of the sovereign heights, I ask no length
> Of Honoured life, no span of gracious days,
> Yet, while I live, I pray thee grant me strength
> To follow year by year the old snow-ways.

Georgia Engelhard Cromwell (1906-1986)

As a child she was "a terrible coward" and had a paralyzing fear of heights—as a shrieking youngster she had been unable to descend a four-step stile over a fence—but Georgia Engelhard overcame this dread of high places through sheer stubbornness and willpower to become one of the more prominent women mountaineers in Canada.

Georgia was born in New York City on November 19, 1906. Her father, George Herbert Engelhard (1870-1945), was a tall, lanky lawyer. He enjoyed music, mastering both the violin and viola as an amateur. He joined with other enthusiastic musicians to play trios and quartets whenever possible. Georgia's mother, Agnes Stieglitz Engelhard (1869-1957), was the younger sister of well-known photographer Alfred Stieglitz. Agnes was diminutive in stature, and read voraciously.

Both parents enjoyed walking at Lake George, the Stieglitz family estate in upper New York State, where they spent most summers. Agnes was frequently seen hiking in a pair of her husband's scaled-down golfing pants. Her father frequently tried to wheedle Georgia into walking with him, too. It was an activity that she hated, but she eventually gave in to stop his pestering—and probably because he appealed to her pride. She adored him. In later years they really enjoyed hiking together. At age 65, George tramped 65 km with Georgia to have lunch with friends.

"Family, Westchester, 1918" by Alfred Stieglitz. Georgia Engelhard is in the front row. Her parents, Agnes and George, are second and third from the left in the back row.

The summers that Georgia spent at Lake George as a child and young adult were to have a tremendous influence on her. A precocious, wilful, witty and spirited child, she kept up an irreverent banter (she inherited a wonderful sense of humor from her father) with her uncle, Alfred Stieglitz. He taught Georgia, as well as his other nieces and nephews, to play poker. Georgia kept up a revealing correspondence with Stieglitz, particularly through her teens and early twenties. He was a sounding board for her often ribald sense of humor, her troubles and her triumphs, her maturing philosophy of life—the outpourings of her soul.

Georgia had a natural ability as a painter, a talent which Stieglitz and his second wife, Georgia O'Keeffe, nurtured. "The Kid," as she was referred to, hit it off well with O'Keeffe and was even allowed to paint beside her.

As a child Georgia attended Spence School, a very exclusive private school in New York City. She found the city stuffy and "school work hangs around my neck like a grindstone. Good Lord, how I hate it—all this hypocritical, pious, cant." She took art classes at school but they seemed to be "nothing but learning rules and making washes of bright red, enough to make even a very meek cow go crazy, not to talk about a bull." She considered art to be a process of "learning to fill spaces in an interesting way."

For three weeks in 1914 Stieglitz showed watercolors and pastels by Georgia at an exhibit at "291," his photo-secessionist gallery in New York City. He valued the art of untaught children for its fresh expression. Of six artists exhibited she was the only child. Two years later, in 1916, some of her drawings and watercolors were included in an exhibition by O'Keeffe. Her style was obviously influenced by O'Keeffe's criticism and direction. One of O'Keeffe's agents once picked up some of O'Keeffe's painting at the Lake George summer home, mistakenly packing up some of Georgia E.'s also. Several of these were deliberate copies of O'Keeffe's works and Georgia E. always wondered if some collector had bought what was supposed to be an early O'Keeffe, but was instead an "imitation by Engelhard!"

The two Georgias spent the summers boating, swimming, hiking, and in The Kid's case, horseback riding. She once lost her temper over her uncle Lee's berating of her for losing weight from too much exercise—"he makes me sick, wants one to spend one's life in a rocking chair—woman's place is in the home, etc. Really, I could have slain him!" O'Keeffe heartily agreed with her.

Many years later they "escaped" Lake George for a summer's exploration of the Gaspé Peninsula of Quebec and New Brunswick. Together they painted the grassy plateaus and golden sea-side cliffs and the picturesque buildings of the seashore. At this time Georgia E. forsook watercolors in favor of oils. On their way home, exhilarated, they tried smuggling some whiskey across the international boundary for evening nips. (The United States had prohibition at that time while Canada didn't.) Their booty was found, confiscated and they were fined. Thereafter they brewed largely unpalatable home wine, but they eventually gave that up for fear it could be poisonous.

In her late teens Georgia spent a couple of summers at camp, reveling in "the sporting life" of riding, swimming, tennis, canoeing and grass hockey. There were also artistic pursuits such as weaving and jewelry-making, at which she was not as adept at.

Georgia entered Vassar College in the autumn of 1923. All of her time was devoted to classes and studying, and she was a straight-A student. "Now I often get the urge to draw and to paint, but haven't got the time—that's why I get it I suppose. The contrariness of human nature." The following two summers she traveled overseas with her parents. In 1924 it was to Europe, where she retained "a shifting panorama" of memories from the windmills in Holland to the art galleries and the "crazy Dolomites." The next summer the family took a boat cruise "below the earth's belly," around South America. She found immense enjoyment in the weeks at sea, with the ever-changing horizons.

But Georgia was very unhappy at Vassar College.

> I'm sick of the limited life and the mental diapers up here—and I do feel the urge to paint—to create. Somehow I feel as if I were wasting myself and my vitality up here in pursuit of things for which I don't give a fig-leaf, and I'm surging with the desire to face actuality—to do something by myself. Maybe I'm foolish—maybe I'll be disappointed and disillusioned—but rather that than this horrible passivity, this demoralizing stagnation. Outside of my desire to work at art, and to really do something with it—I feel strongly the wholly artificial limited life that we live up here, away from all contact with reality, whatever that may be.

After three disgruntled years at Vassar Georgia felt that she couldn't realize her ambition of becoming a painter while attending classes, so she transferred to Teacher's College at Columbia University, where O'Keeffe had studied. There she attended art classes while obtaining a degree. She enjoyed a variety of art study courses: Advanced Painting, Art Structure, Free-Hand Drawing, Figure Construction by Life Class, Art Appreciation and Educational Psychology. She preferred to paint horses, people or landscapes, but not mountains, which she considered "too big." She found it all very stimulating and "as a symbol of my increasing grey matter, I'm sprouting my wisdom teeth."

The only down part was living with her relatives. She longed to get a job and be independent. "Being wrapped in cotton wadding for one thing, is not conducive to free and firm expression, and I feel that I cannot stand on my feet artistically until I have done so economically and socially.''

In time Georgia E.'s style began to resemble O'Keeffe's so much that she tried to change it. But she found she couldn't. This may have induced her to give up painting and concentrate on photography. Undoubtedly encouraged by Stieglitz, Georgia became an excellent photographer. She studied at the New York Institute of Photography and at the School of Modern Photography. For a while she was a darkroom assistant to a New York photographer but found that she did not have time to do her own work. She began freelancing for company newsletters and national advertising concerns. Some of her portfolios contained photos of china and funiture, but she specialized in portraits of children and animals. She also sold her photos to many magazines, including *Life, National Geographic, Holiday, Look, Harper's Bazaar,* and the *Toronto Star Weekly.* She wrote many photo articles for photographic publications, mainly about freelancing, photographing pets and about Stieglitz. While climbing she shot many landscapes and close-ups of flowers.

All her life, Georgia loved riding horses. In a letter to Uncle Al she wrote, ''I have the horse-back riding longing upon me. Oh to feel a saddle between my legs, and to go—to go like the wind on a spirited horse, and to smell the sweaty smell of the saddle and harness, and to have my hands smell of those things! I love the smell of the stables—better than flowers.'' She never owned a horse but rented one when time permitted.

In her teens she had ridden at ''Durlands,'' an indoor riding ring in New York City. And she often rode in Central Park. For several summers she had a stable job on Long Island, grooming and exercising horses and teaching children to ride. She learned to jump horses there and she worked with thoroughbreds. She also took lessons with Colonel Gary, a Russian who had established a well-known riding and jumping school, The Boots and Saddle, in New York. She also trained horses there. She rode more than once at the International Horse Show at Madison Square Gardens, and she enjoyed the Grand Ball afterwards every bit as much as she enjoyed the event itself! She was in some demand during the 1930s as a professional

Georgia Engelhard and her cousin, Hugh Straus.

"schooler" of jumpers. Her training days may have ended when a fall resulted in a broken collarbone, which was put together with the aid of a permanent platinum plate.

In later years she enjoyed riding with the hounds with a hunt club, the Golden's Bridge Hounds, in North Salem, New York. Her cousin's husband was a member of the club and she rode with him as a guest a number of times.

Very athletic and boyish, with her close-cropped sandy hair and often wearing fly-front pants, Georgia was frequently mistaken for a young man. At the Mount Royal beer parlor in Banff the bartender once furtively asked her, "Young man, are you of age?" She was also ejected from several other establishments. Even in her mid-30s people would ask her, "Sonny, your daddy taking you hiking?"

Georgia had visited the Alps and Dolomites in her teens, and although she thought them "handsome," she considered mountain climbing "a perfectly idiotic sport." Georgia's father had hiked and climbed in the Bavarian Alps as a young man and liked to climb wherever he found "respectable" mountains. He climbed Mount Washington in 1923. He took his wife on modest climbs and hikes during most of their vacations. But it wasn't until a family holiday at Washington's Mount Rainier, in 1926, that Georgia discovered the beauty and exhilaration of mountaineering. Her father convinced her to go climbing with him rather than riding the trails. Pinnacle Peak (2000 m), in the Tatoosh Range across the valley from Rainier, was a favorite "all-day" climb in the area but she and a young guide did it in half a day. She soon became "crazy" for rock-climbing.

From Mount Rainier they traveled to Lake Louise. At the Chateau they soon met the "unofficial hosts," hotel photographer Fred Armbrister and explorer Walter Wilcox. It was at Wilcox's nightly cocktail parties that they met climbers such as Val Fynn. He encouraged her, calling her his "Little Chamois." She also met Cora Best, a prominent woman mountaineer at the time. Georgia's first climb was another Pinnacle Peak (3067 m), this time the one above Moraine Lake, with Ed Feuz, Jr. They gained the summit in just three hours. Feuz said: "Waal, she just stuck her head in my rucksack and so I ran." That summer she also climbed mounts Temple (3543 m) and Whyte (2983 m), and fell in love with the region.

Georgia's mother wrote to her brother that Georgia had "a glorious time climbing glaciers and peaks of inaccessible-looking mountains. Two peaks one day with Swiss guide. Made quite a hit with them [guides] at Glacier and Rainier Parks." Her mother, though, remained ever fearful of Georgia's obsession with climbing.

The following summer she returned to the Cascades and climbed Mount Baker (3286 m). Then it was back to the Lake Louise area, to climb Mount Victoria (3464 m) from Abbot Pass. Her father went with her and Ed Feuz as far as the Abbot Pass Hut. He wrote in the hut register that he "staid [sic] below & watched them do it." Georgia also climbed Odaray Mountain (3159 m) and The Mitre (2889 m) that summer.

In the summer of 1928 Georgia joined Jack Brewster's Circle Tour, from Jasper to Lake Louise, along the present route of the Icefields Parkway. While in the Jasper area she made a first ascent of The Helmet (3420 m), an outlier of Mount Robson, with guide Heinie Fuhrer. They also made it to within 600 m of the summit of Robson before having to turn back. She also climbed Lynx Mountain (3180 m) and Mount Edith Cavell (3363 m). She finished off the season with a few climbs at Lake Louise.

"Autumn in the mountains is stupendous—snow storms making the peaks wilder than ever—golden larches against vivid blue sky and grim rock walls—and a wind that nearly blows you off the ridges when you climb." When she joined the American Alpine Club that year, at 22, she was the youngest woman to do so.

The next season was her first serious one. She came to Canada on her own and climbed extensively at Lake Louise, then at Lake O'Hara during the Alpine Club camp. She climbed nine peaks in nine days—Lefroy (3423 m), a traverse of the two Popes Peaks (3162 m), a traverse of Haddo (3070 m) and Aberdeen (3151 m), then ascents of Hungabee (3493 m), Huber (3368 m), Victoria (3464 m) and Biddle (3319 m)—which garnered her considerable publicity with the Canadian Pacific Railway. It was also the year of her first visit to the Selkirks, where she climbed Avalanche Mountain (2864 m), Uto Peak (2932 m) and Mount Sir Donald (3297 m).

On her day of departure from Lake Louise Georgia arose at four in the morning to say a private goodbye to the mountains. In two hours she was alone atop the summit of Mount St. Piran (2649 m), some 900 m above the lake.

> The lake and valley were still in deep shadow, but the surrounding peaks, all I had climbed, were bathed in golden rosy light. I was seized by an indescribable ecstasy, filled with the joy of conquest. They were all mine—my beautiful, private world of mountains. Yet, at the same time, I felt how infinitesimal I was. It was an unforgettable experience.

Georgia became known as a fast climber. The Feuzes—Ed, Jr., Ernest and Walter—were her favorite guides, although she also climbed with Chris Häsler and Rudolph Aemmer. When Ed was first booked to guide Georgia, Ernest (who had guided her already) warned him that, "You've got a fine lady, but watch out. When she starts uphill, she goes like a rocket. What she needs is a mountain goat, not a guide!" Ed described her as "tough and wiry" and said that she often had them puffing to keep up. A climbing companion once joked with Ed about borrowing a set of hobbles from the packer, or sneaking a few rocks into her pack, to slow her down. The Feuzes regarded Georgia as "difficult," mainly because she could carry as much as any man in the party and often showed up the less sturdy male climbers. The guides liked climbing with Georgia because of her natural ability and enthusiasm, and she tipped well.

In turn, Georgia was very fond of her guides, trusting them implicitly. She learned to climb by watching how the guides climbed and listening keenly to the few instructions they gave. Many were very taciturn and gruff, not given to lengthy dissertations. The fee for a guide at the time was flat $7 per day, regardless of the difficulty.

> They were short, strong, stocky men and rather monosyllabic, though both Chris and Edward had palky senses of humour. They were not great guides in that they were not artists on rock and ice and snow but very competent workmen. They had no knowledge or use for the modern techniques—the use of piton and karabiner, the art of rappelling were beyond their ken. They did use crampons on occasion, but preferred to cut steps. After World War Two when the use of Vibram soles on boots became popular, they were among the last to give up their nailed boots. But despite their conservatism they *were* great guides in that nothing delighted them more than making a first ascent or a new route. They had a terrific flair for route-finding, not only on rock and ice but also through the often dense forests that clothe the lower stretches of an ascent. They seldom went wrong.

Georgia's first really big year was in 1931 when she made 38 ascents in Yoho park and the Selkirks. She described the Little Yoho Valley as very "gorgeous" and "entrancing." She wrote to Catharine Whyte, a Banff artist, in late July of that year that "I have just finished up that section of the country as far as climbing is concerned—it has just been grand." She also fairly cleaned up the Selkirks the same season, climbing 24 peaks in three weeks there. Her artist's eye delighted in "shady forests of huge evergreens which provided rich dark frames for glistening glacier tongues that sprawl downwards into deep valleys."

Chancellor Peak was a challenge, as it had only been climbed once, thirty years previously, by James Outram and Christian Häsler, Sr. Ernest Feuz had often hunted goats in the steep gullies near its base and had repeatedly scrutinized the mountain. They wanted to climb it in one day, as opposed to Outram's two. On one difficult traverse, with few holds and no place to anchor for about 60 m, "we kept ourselves from slipping, which would have been fatal, mainly by friction holds with our feet and knees, our fingers clinging desperately to any slight knot or crack that presented itself on the smooth rock face." They were certainly relieved when they gained the arête above. Although they had to retrace their route a few times to find a better way, they were exuberant when they reached the summit.

Georgia also climbed Victoria eight times in 1931! Once she assisted Ernest at the end of the rope when Ernest had a rather inept climber along. The other seven times were for a movie, *She Climbs to Conquer,* by Bill Oliver. She was guided by Ernest, and Oliver was guided by Rudolph Aemmer. In order to obtain the footage that Oliver wanted, the team climbed for nine days. On the last day of the filming they were chased off the mountain by a violent thunderstorm. Their nailed boots and ice axes were spitting fire, and their hair stood on end.

Georgia was almost obsessed by searching out new routes and first ascents. When determining whether an ascent was the first one or not, they would look carefully for hobnail scratches on rocks, garbage or, of course, summit cairns. She was very competitve. A day off, to Georgia, might mean only a climb to a "low and unimportant" 2500-m peak!

There was likely considerable rivalry between Georgia Cromwell and Katie Gardiner, another well-known woman mountaineer of that period (see page 220). Georgia noted that Katie was quite chagrined when informed that the first ascent of Prior Peak, which Katie had just climbed, had already been made by Georgia. But perhaps Katie had the last laugh, as she had 33 first ascents in Canada, and Georgia had 32.

> Why do I like climbing? Why do you like bridge? I don't know! It's a disease and chronic, I fear. Perhaps it's the excitement, perhaps it's the beauty or the escape from conventional comforts. But it's not very hard.

The following winter Georgia "chucked" her short-term job as a sales clerk at Macy's department store in New York City; she saw no possibility of advancement there. Shortly thereafter she started a course in shorthand and typing—"it's fearful to become so utilitarian"—although she was sure that she made "a better mountaineer than stenographer." She worked only briefly for an advertising agency in that capacity, though. It was after this that she took up freelance photography in a serious way.

Her best climb of the 1933 season was the first south-to-north traverse of Mount Victoria, which had been considered impossible. In 1909 it had been done in the reverse direction

Georgia Engelhard with guide Ernest Feuz, on Mount Victoria, during the filming of She Climbs to Conquer.

A sketch drawn by Peter Whyte, signed by Georgia.

by Rudolph Aemmer, Ed Feuz and George Culver, in 24 hours. During that ascent, in the midst of a long rock ridge laced with gendarmes, was a tower which they deemed impossible to climb from the opposite direction. When Georgia's group tackled it, they noted that while the ridge was extremely exposed in many places, the "impossible pitch" proved to be quite easy. She also climbed again in the Selkirks that summer.

Georgia was on the first annual hike of the Skyline Hikers of the Rockies in 1933. The hikers were charges of Ernest Feuz and Rudolph Aemmer, in two groups. The participants were a combination of local residents and tourists. The following year Georgia was elected first vice-president of the Trail Riders of the Candian Rockies. She felt that attending the annual trail ride was "amusing once every ten years, but not at frequent intervals."

According to Georgia, her only major climb in 1934 was Mount Assiniboine (3618 m), although she also climbed a number of the Ten Peaks at Moraine Lake.

In 1935 Georgia climbed in the Alps for the first time. She climbed with Eaton "Tony" Cromwell, a mountaineer with many ascents in Europe to his credit. They did over 60 climbs and traverses, including many of the big names: Monte Rosa (4634 m), Matterhorn (4478 m), Wetterhorn (3701 m), Finsteraarhorn (4274 m), Jungfrau (4158 m) and the Mönch (3933 m). Tony was a proponent of amateur climbing, i.e. climbing without guides. After that season, whenever Georgia climbed with Tony they went guideless, "much to Ernest's disgust."

When Tony was 17 years old (he was born in 1892) he visited France's Chamonix region, where he watched mountaineers venture onto the Mer de Glace. He was so fascinated that a day later he hired a guide, and, accompanied by his over-protective mother, he joined the fraternity of mountaineers. Lacking proper equipment he slipped heavy woolen socks over his shoes; his mother's boots were lightly nailed. After one more trip he had his expensive leather boots refurbished with nails. He carried a long alpenstock and wore a green Tyrolean hat.

Shortly after beginning work for a Philadelphia bank, Tony suffered a lung infection which was incorrectly diagnosed at the time as tuberculosis. Doctors recommended that he live an outdoor life. A substantial allowance permitted him to live abroad in France and Switzerland, and there to indulge in alpinism to his heart's content. He was a prominent member of the American Alpine Club until 1939 when he resigned over

Whyte Museum of the Canadian Rockies

disagreements during the club's tragic attempt on K2 in the Himalayas. He was the deputy leader in charge of base camp.

In 1936 Tony climbed with Georgia for the first time in the Rockies (he had climbed in Canada as early as 1928). With Francis Stanley North along in the party they did many climbs at Lake Louise and Rogers Pass. "After a season in the Alps, it was indeed a pleasure to return to the Canadian Rockies, unmarred by civilization and unscarred by artificial aids, where the climber may find ample opportunity to make new routes on already ascended peaks." On tricky rock routes they would take off their boots and wear "rubber gymnasium shoes," or sneakers, for more delicate work.

Georgia and Tony were often very frustrated by the extremely rotten rock of the Rockies. While ascending Wenkchemna Peak (3173 m) at Moraine Lake Tony successfully led up a difficult chimney. But Georgia and North pulled out the last remaining holds on their ascent of it and had to rely on the rope a lot. She felt that such peaks would be much more pleasant to climb after successive climbers had cleared off much of the rubble. (Unfortunately, the rock just keeps crumbling!).

From Lake O'Hara they hiked to Field, climbing Mount Stephen (3199 m) on the way. It took them 7½ hours to reach the summit, but only three hours on the descent, as their destination, the Field beer parlor, was "extremely alluring."

In 1937 Georgia and Tony were joined by J. Monroe "Roy" Thorington, and Tony's son, Eaton Cromwell, Jr., for three weeks in the Thompson Pass and Rice Brook area on the south edge of the Columbia Icefield.[1] They were outfitted by Jimmy Simpson.

The following year Tony mentioned plans for an attempt on Mount Trident to Georgia, and he felt afterward that as a result he had to invite her. "She is a useful mountaineer anyway, and will strengthen the party." Georgia and Tony complemented each other well—both were excellent climbers, ambitious and competitive. And they both had the financial independence to indulge in their avocation to their heart's content.

---

1. When Katie Gardiner and Lillian Gest were planning their attempt on Mount Bryce in 1937 they knew that Georgia was going into the area ahead of them. Lillian wrote in her diary that if Georgia succeeded on Bryce "Katie & I will go elsewhere." As it was, Georgia's party did not climb Bryce.

In 1938 they completed the first guideless traverse of Mount Victoria, this time from north-to-south. They accomplished it in 12 hours, half the time of the original party. Upon arriving at Abbot Pass Hut they were understandably thirsty. They had some coffee left in the canteen and decided that iced coffee would taste good. While Tony chopped some ice chips outside, Georgia rummaged around in the cupboards and found what she thought was a bowl of sugar. After tasting the resulting beverage they realized it was salt! They threw the brew out and made lemonade instead, which took extra time. After drinking it they left to descend from the pass, through the narrow, avalanche-prone Death Trap, to Lake Louise. At five in the afternoon they thought they should be safe from avalanches, but when they were just above the Death Trap there was "a horrible cracking and grunting sound and tons of ice admixed with rock thundered and hurtled down" past them. If they had not been delayed at the hut they most surely would have been killed.

Despite dangers such as this, Georgia loved mountaineering — especially the challenge of doing traverses from peak to peak. She described the Victoria traverse "with its airy ridges, jagged pinnacles and sensational pitches" as the best climb in the district.

Later that summer Walter Feuz guided Georgia up the Spillimacheen River in an unsuccessful attempt to climb in the Bobbie Burns area near the Bugaboos. They ran out of time and food, but she was back with Ernest Feuz in 1939. She wanted to "get Bobbie Burns and twist his tail." First they climbed Bugaboo Spire, then they fought through deadfall and rock bluffs for a day and a half to go five kilometres from Bugaboo Creek to Bobbie Burns Creek. What had appeared from above to be lush meadows along the Creek were nothing but swamps, and they had to make camp on a sand flat along a stream. "There was sand in the water, sand in the food, in the beds, in the duffle, in the clothes, plus a fine assortment of very vicious bull-dog flies, mosquitoes and sand-gnats." This discomfort, though, was overshawdowed by her pleasure in being the first to climb in the area. On this trip, she ran Ernest Feuz and Stanley North ragged.

In 1943 they made no first ascents or new routes, mostly

because of poor weather. Tony complained that Georgia was "rather piqued by what she considers a certain lack of results." In turn, Georgia described the season as "pretty dull," because they only climbed thirty-three peaks, feeling that they should have done sixty for all the effort they put forth!

For the next four years Georgia and Tony did not come to the Rockies. During those years Georgia began to devote her full time to freelance photography. Tony was an accomplished photographer, too. She had also discovered that the American public had become "mountain conscious," and there was a good market for climbing articles and photographs. To this end Georgia and Tony visited the White Mountains in New Hampshire, the Dolomites and Pennine Alps in Europe and the national parks of the western United States. They wrote travel articles, and lectured on photography and mountain climbing to clubs, schools and colleges.

With photography as their main objective, Georgia and Tony returned to Mount Assiniboine in 1943. They spent three weeks camped at its base, so that Georgia could record a "portait" of the famous peak. They climbed surrounding peaks to get unusual shots, and endured snow and high winds to obtain just the right lighting for the pictures that she envisioned.

> Of course, on first acquaintance (1928) I took snapshots, but to make a portrait, a true portrait, takes longer acquaintanceship, longer study of the proper angles, the proper light conditions . . . Only if you love and understand mountains, only if you have lived with them, if you have observed them keenly and thrilled to their moods, can you make really effective pictures of them. Lacking this love and understanding, you might just as well leave your camera at home and save film.

To Georgia, Assiniboine was a mountain that commanded "awe and respect," and like the everchanging sea, it lured her "irresistibly."

Georgia shot a few "how-to" features, showing mountaineering techniques, on the upper Victoria Glacier and on an unnamed rock peak between mounts Fairview and Haddo. For one series she used Tony and his daughter Camilla as subjects, and Tony and young Zermatt guide Eddie Petrig for another. Ed Feuz helped them to find good locations on the glacier.

Georgia considered Ed Feuz to be the best amateur photographer that she knew. He possessed an "unerring instinct

Georgia Engelhard and Tony Cromwell at Skoki Lodge, 1946.

for action shots and a flair for making them appear candid."
Few of his photographs needed cropping as they were
wonderfully composed. "Looking at his work makes me think
that perhaps we city photographers dwell too much on technique
for effects."

Tony had become her constant companion, but he was not

yet divorced from his second wife, Katharine Dahlgren. Theirs had been a life of "luxurious idleness" according to Katharine, with the result that over the years the fortunes had dwindled significantly. They were finally divorced in 1947, in Nevada. Tony and Georgia were married immediately after, and they honeymooned in the Tetons. Tony wrote plaintively, "Now that I am so much and so often married and have so many and so large families I find it rather necessary to count the pennies." Once, in the late 1950s, when Tony and Georgia visited the United States, Katharine hit Tony with a subpoena for unpaid alimony and Georgia had to post a $10,000 bail to get them out of the country!

Part of the reason that Tony began climbing guideless may have been to save money. For a guide he wanted "some man exceptionally suitable who is willing to come for very little money."

After awhile, though, Tony began to "tire" of guideless climbing. And as guides were difficult and expensive to hire in Canada they considered returning to climb in the Alps. "Georgia has been grumbling about Canada for several seasons now, and I guess she is right. Certainly it is much easier to trot meekly along behind a first class guide, and let him do the worrying and carry the heavy load." Fifteen years later he was complaining about the cost of guides in the Alps: "Of course the Guides mostly now own modern apartments with washing machines, dishwashers, telephones, and motor cars and naturally must charge accordingly to pay for all this luxury." They also lamented the lack of European guides willing to tackle new peaks and routes, as the younger guides in the Alps seemed to prefer the established routes.

Georgia did some climbing in the United States but achieved few first ascents there. She climbed several of the "Fourteeners" of Colorado. On the West Coast she climbed Mount Baker (3286 m) in 1927. Her biggest year was 1937 when she and Tony climbed in California, Colorado, Utah and the Cascades. In the Cascades they climbed mounts Lassen (3188 m), Shasta (4317 m), St. Helens (2950 m), Hood (3425 m) and Adams (3758 m).

In 1954 Georgia had a children's book published, *Peterli and the Mountain,* which is the story of a cat that climbed the Matterhorn.

After marrying, Tony and Georgia lived in New York. But they moved to Zermatt, Switzerland in 1955, where they rented a small house—"Chalet Ultima." They loved skiing in the winter, climbing and photography in the summer. Georgia had skied only briefly, in Quebec, before moving to Zermatt. She soon loved to get on the "slats" and go touring away from the "seething mobs." Even in her sixties, to Georgia an "average day" was about 6000 vertical metres, much of which involved going up on the rope tows. Her record was 8000 vertical metres in one day, but she "could hardly navigate" afterward.

Although they made tentative plans to visit Canada a couple of times, Georgia wrote that "in a way I hesitate to come back to the scene, and to maybe have the illusions shattered by what Progress has done to the region." Although not keen to revisit Canada in the summer, she would have liked to visit in the winter for the ski touring because there would be "no emotional strings involved."

Georgia and Tony spent much of their time touring around the continent, climbing and skiing in season. One of their favorite haunts was Cortina in the Italian Dolomites. Tony was an excellent driver, but when his health began to fail Georgia decided to obtain her Swiss driver's license. She was dismayed, though, to discover that she was required to memorize hundreds of answers from an official book, many of which were only applicable to commercial driving. She also felt that the Swiss were not eager to pass an elderly foreigner, either (she was in her seventies). Thus, "When the son-of-a-bitch asked me how far from a railroad crossing I should stop if driving a truck and trailer, I just dropped my application in the waste basket and walked out!"

Georgia continued with her photography, shooting mostly color and selling it "pretty well" via an agency, Monkmeyer Press Photo Service, in New York. She missed doing her own black-and-white processing, as they had no space for a darkroom. Even some of her Canadian photos were still selling well. One of her best markets for photos, especially of the Alps, were the Japanese periodicals. She lamented that "they don't pay too much but they are consistent buyers."

In the early 1970s Georgia and Tony were coming to realize that with their climbing and skiing days drawing to a close,

Zermatt was rather isolated in terms of medical, transportation and cultural facilities. And it had become "such a slum in the mountains" due to the attitude of the local businesses, which was to exploit the tourists. They moved to Unterseen, near Interlaken, in the spring of 1973.

At 75 years of age Georgia was still walking 8 km a day, but not as steeply as she once did. After a slight accident "the sight of ice curdles my blood (fine words from the former mountain climber and skier!)." After such an active life, she didn't find old age very enticing.

Georgia died in Interlaken on September 14, 1985, and Tony died in Philadelphia on February 14, 1986.

Georgia's was a life full of triumph and exhilaration in her beloved mountains. Georgia loved quoting Ernest Feuz, who always said: "Dat Chorcha, she vants to do too much."

Agnes Harragin Truxler (1906-1988)

and

Mona Harragin Matheson (1904-1983)

Agnes Truxler pulled out a gaily-colored box and unfolded some tissue paper. She handed me the objects with pride—three brass badges that read "NATIONAL PARKS OF CANADA GUIDE." Each was emblazoned with a number and a year, from 1928 to 1930. Agnes wore the badges on the hatband of her Stetson while guiding in Jasper National Park. Agnes, and her sister Mona, were the first licensed women trail guides in Canada's national parks.[1]

---

1. Ethel Unwin, sister of Banff outfitter Sid Unwin, operated her brother's guiding business briefly while he was serving overseas during the First World War. This was before licenses were required by park authorities.

Mona Harragin Matheson and Agnes Harragin Truxler were born in Port of Spain, Trinidad on November 20, 1904, and March 4, 1906, respectively. Their parents were John Harcourt Harragin and Mary Lisle Harragin, both born in the West Indies. Mr. Harragin was in insurance and their mother was the daughter of Archdeacon Smith of the Anglican Church. Their father was a "gentleman jockey" and they inherited his love of horses.

In 1908 the family moved to Salmon Arm, British Columbia. The girls grew up there on a small farm. They both had a passion for the outdoors and animals, and for horses in particular. They both did a little work with teams on nearby farms. Knowing Agnes's love of horses, a friend suggested that she try for a job guiding in the national parks. The seed was sown.

Agnes wrote to outfitters in both Jasper and Banff national parks asking for trail jobs. The answer was the same everywhere:"We don't hire women as guides." But Fred Brewster, a pioneer outfitter in Jasper, did add that he needed two women to look after one of his tent camps. Grasping the opportunity to get a foot in the door, Agnes and Mona accepted the jobs. They arrived in Jasper in June of 1927.

The morning after their arrival, Agnes and Mona were on the trail to Maligne Lake to help prepare the newly built chalet for opening. The camp they were to run at Medicine Lake would not open for another two weeks. When they finished the last of their work for the day, they would go exploring or simply sit by the lake's edge until it was too dark to see. Agnes wrote that she "felt a surge of happiness in having chosen to find myself a niche in such surroundings."

Soon, though, they found themselves on their own at the Medicine Lake Camp. It consisted of three wooden-framed tents for sleeping quarters, and one for cooking that had an extension on the back for dining. This camp was a lunch stop for tourists going on to Maligne Lake, but occasionally a party found it necessary to stay overnight.

Over the course of the season the sisters learned many things about their guests, the hazards of camp cooking, the characters of horses and dogs and the ways of wildlife. With unquenchable enthusiasm they threw themselves into learning everything they could about horses, packing and guiding from the outfitters, guides and wardens who passed through their camp. By wrangling the horses for the guides (this usually necessitated rising about three a.m., and the men were more than happy to let Mona and Agnes do the job), the two sisters came to know the terrain around Medicine Lake like no one else.

Frequently Agnes and Mona would have to run the boat across Medicine Lake with supplies because the boatman would be hung-over from a trip to town. They'd have to take a raft from their end of the lake to the far end to retrieve the boat first.

The following season the sisters were even more determined to work as guides. In the early spring Brewster wrote the Harragins, again offering them jobs as cooks/hostesses, but also extending to them the privilege of choosing any of his camps in the park.They appreciated the vote of confidence, but after a great deal of thinking they wrote back saying that unless they could guide they would not return to Jasper. "We didn't want to do that, we wanted to get in the horse business," said Agnes. Expecting a negative reply, Agnes and Mona quickly decided that they would choose the Maligne Lake Camp if they couldn't guide. They were thus overjoyed when Brewster wrote back with an offer for them to guide on the "Circle Trip" from Jasper Park Lodge to Maligne Lake and return! Later in the season the sisters discovered that they were hired on the insistence of Mrs. Brewster, who felt that they should be given a chance. She, for one, would far rather make the journey with "one of her own kind."

After a brief confrontation with the park authorities, who were alarmed at the idea of women doing what had always been a man's job, and the payment of a one-dollar fee, Mona and Agnes were issued with their guides' licenses and badges in 1928.

The sisters shared a string of some 35 horses but worked independently, seeing each other only in passing on the trail, and occasionally in camp. The initial idea was that the women were hired just to do the guiding of guests and Brewster would provide men to do the wrangling and packing. But the packers never showed up—probably a bit of cowboy conspiracy to see if the women had the "mettle" to do it themselves. They did, which meant that their work day started in the wee hours of the morning with catching and saddling the animals. Then it

Glenbow Archives

Mona Harragin, ca. 1928.

was time to pack all of the food and equipment, which was their real test. Soon they were proficient in tying the famous "diamond hitch," a rope arrangement that kept the packs from shifting while on the trail.

At the beginning of their first season guiding, the guides and packers at the Brewster barn were a little resentful and gave Mona and Agnes bad horses to work with—often slow or poorly trained ones. Once again, when they had passed this informal test—taking matters in stride and without complaint—they were given better horses, and the men became very helpful.

A typical Circle Trip would see the guests, usually three or four, arrive at the north end of Medicine Lake from Jasper by car. They were then transported to the south end by boat. From there Agnes and Mona would take them by horseback to Maligne Lake, where a boat tour awaited them. The second night was spent at the Shovel Pass Camp, which was near timberline in the beautiful Maligne Range. The third day was a long one back to Jasper. Sometimes the guides spent the night in Jasper, but usually they "deadheaded" (returned with no paying customers) to Medicine Lake the same day. They seldom had a day off.

As Agnes and Mona suspected, once they had proved their ability to handle the job, they were also required to pack supplies (everything from food to outboard engines) into Maligne Lake from the end of the road. A few of the packhorses were quite tall, and the diminutive women had trouble lifting the heavy pack boxes high enough. Just the same, they were able to handle everything except the 90-kg outboard engines for the boats at Maligne Lake. Mona said the cook at Medicine would help her with them and "as long as he could lift them, I could get them tied on, and as long as it was tied on good, the horse would carry it." Quite a few of the horses they used also worked as teams for Fred Brewster's winter operations. Brewster had a blacksmith who would come out to Medicine Lake to shoe the

Joe Weiss

Hamming it up at the Medicine Lake Camp in 1928 are (l-r): Charlie Matheson, Gwen Pickford, Charles Golden, Agnes Harragin, Mona Harragin.

horses, but occasionally the Harragins had to tack a shoe on.

While traveling the trails, they would deliver mail to the men that were working for the parks service on the trail between Medicine and Maligne. In the evening they might play hide-and-seek or other games outside. When it got dark they simply went to bed. Sometimes they took day trips from Medicine Lake to Jacques Lake.

The sisters were very popular as guides, particularly with the tourists at Jasper Park Lodge, where most of the Circle Trips ended. With their Stetsons, monogrammed chaps and colorful neckerchiefs, they were very photogenic. Some photographers, though, wanted them to look "rough and tough" for pictures. Some of the guests thought that the sisters must have been millionaires' daughters in order to get their jobs.

At the end of the season they were sometimes invited on a "buckshee" (free or gratis) trip with outfitters and wardens. In that way they got to see a lot of the park. For the winter, Agnes and Mona would go back to Salmon Arm. Then in the spring they would work in the orchards briefly before returning to Jasper for their three-month season. In the winter of 1928-29 Agnes stayed for a while with the warden's wife at Maligne Canyon. But Mona wrote and asked Agnes to go to the West Indies with her, as she had sold a number of her paintings and was a little "flush with cash." Agnes went.

Mona gained some fame as an artist, and her watercolors of the mountains and wildlife were sold at Jasper Park Lodge. At one point she went to England to study painting in oils but returned shortly thereafter when their mother became very ill. She had been sponsored by an artist who had seen her paintings at the lodge. In later years she made tapestries from rags. Agnes was an artist also, but she preferred watercolors and pencil—painting with oils was, for her, "like playing in pudding." As a child, Agnes drew horses everywhere, including on the barn door and on hen's eggs when she had to gather them!

About two weeks into the 1930 season, rumors started circulating that Fred Brewster was suffering financially and that the staff was to be cut. One man replaced Mona and Agnes, and at lower wages. In compensation they were offered jobs at Brewster's reservations desk at Jasper Park Lodge, combined with leading day rides out from the barns. As neither woman was interested in the desk job, nor in having someone else do their saddling at the barns, they both left Brewster's employ. They also thought it might "cramp the style" of the men working there.

Within a few days of arriving back in town, the sisters were approached by Jack Otto, a former outfitter who was now running a garage. Otto offered to sell the sisters his outfit to go into business on their own. After heavy consideration they decided that would be too much of a risk, as there were already four outfitters based in Jasper, and a good part of the season was over. A few days later they were offered part-time work with Art Hughes and Stan Kitchen, one of the other outfits. They accepted.

The work with Hughes and Kitchen was mostly leading day trips to Pyramid Lake, around Jasper Park Lodge and south to Buffalo Prairie, along the Athabasca River. Mona, though, did guide a couple of long outings. One trip was to the Tonquin Valley. She handled all of the camp chores, including cooking as well as wrangling and packing. Her longest trip was almost two weeks in duration, to the south boundary of the park. She went to Brazeau Lake, then over Southesk Pass and back via the Rocky River. On that outing she had a wrangler to assist with the horses, but she still did the cooking and helped with the packing.

On October 6, 1930, Agnes married Mark Truxler, who had been a packer for Brewster and later worked for a number of outfitters. A few months later, on New Year's Eve, Mona married Charlie Matheson, a park warden.

While the sisters were operating the Medicine Lake Camp, Charlie would drop by on patrol, as did many of the other wardens and guides. While waiting for coffee to boil, these visitors would leaf through a pile of magazines in the corner, but Mona noticed that Charlie was the only one who seemed to be doing much reading—his magazine was at least held right side up! Mona had decided then that Charlie would make a good partner, even though he was 16 years her senior and obviously set in his bachelor ways. She once helped him jingle (locate and catch) his horses at four in the morning when they had pulled out on him at Jacques Lake. She walked and ran 15 km in thin running shoes to help round them up, slightly freezing her feet in the process. Charlie was sympathetic, but not easily convinced of the merits of matrimony!

Charlie Matheson was born in 1888 in Brandon, Manitoba. His family moved to Calgary when Charlie was three years old, and later they moved to Edmonton. Charlie arrived in Jasper about 1920, where he guided for Fred Brewster and packed for survey outfits, and later became a park warden.

Mona's experience with horses came in handy when she was with Charlie on backcountry patrol. She also proved herself adept at traveling on snowshoes, repairing telephone wire and doing other curious chores.

A few years after Mona and Charlie were married they were stationed at MaligneLake. It was the hot, dry summer of 1935. "We had gone up to the narrows of the lake with our boat one Sunday. About noon, here comes Harry Phillips from the camp at the north end, with two kickers [motors] on his boat, going like blazes. He told us a fire had broken out on the Horseshore Bend." The bend was on the Maligne River about 25 km from where they were at the time. They raced back to the station where Charlie picked up some tools and two horses, and galloped off down the trail. In an hour he was scouting the fire's perimeter and realized that he couldn't control it without help. He hooked his forestry field-set telephone into the phone line and called Jasper. Unfortunately 16 fires had broken out in the park that same day and all available men were already dispatched elsewhere. The Chief Warden asked Charlie to hang on by himself and he'd send him a crew the next day.

Charlie fought the fire all day and then phoned Mona late in the afternoon. He asked her to bring him the camp outfit with tents, teepee, blankets and enough food to last 20 men for three days, so he'd be ready for the firefighting crew when they arrived.

Mona had to wrangle the horses from the Opal Hills, a high alpine meadow above Maligne Lake, so it was about seven o'clock in the evening before she had them in the corral and could start packing up. She had quite a task gathering the equipment and packing the heavy teepee, the bulky crew tents, the boxes of canned goods and the fire-fighting tools. She worked into the night by lantern light and finally topped off the packs with some empty 25-pound lard pails, which would serve as cooking pots. Finally, late in the night, Mona took to the trail, Just before dawn she arrived at the fire and could feel the rush of heat coming from the ground. Charlie helped her set up the camp right away. A few hours later their fire crew arrived—all boys, the oldest being about 17. Charlie asked Mona to stay and cook since the administration had not bothered to send a camp cook.

> Now we had no cook tent, and we had no stove either. For a table, we used a pack mantle spread out on the ground. I cooked everything in those 25 pound lard pails hung over an open fire. What a job! There were three shifts of fire-fighters to be fed three times a day and only one cook. That fire burned a whole month. It went right over the top of a mountain and down into some blind hole.

When asked what she was paid for her work on the fire, Mona replied with a scoff:

> Pay! Ha! That's quite a joke. Oh, the fire-fighters got paid, of course. Charlie got his regular wages. I think $130 a month. No overtime either. They hadn't invented that yet. He had to stay on that fire twenty-hours a day, until it was dead out. ... Well, they didn't quite know what to do with me. I was the warden's wife, you see. I guess they figured it wouldn't look good, putting me on payroll. People would talk. In the end, they decided I should get something, so they gave me a cheque— for five dollars. It was about what I'd expected, and anyway, I was doing it for Charlie, not the Service. ... I remember I bought a dress with the five dollars. I called it my fire dress. It was a lovely shade of blue.

When Charlie retired from the warden service in 1937 the Mathesons bought their own outfit and founded a riding stable in Jasper. In the fall they took out hunting parties. Mona ran a free taxi to take riders from Jasper Park Lodge to their barns in town and back again. In 1940 they moved just east of the park gates and established the Circle M Guest Ranch. That first autumn they lived in a tent, moving into a cabin only at the beginning of November. They operated the ranch until 1952, when they retired to a cabin across the highway. Charlie continued to trap for a few winters. They had one son, Glenn.

Mark Truxler was born November 14, 1905 in Vernon, British Columbia. He started off by following a friend to Banff in 1923, where he put in four summers working with A. O. Wheeler's surveying parties. In the fall he guided hunting parties from Banff as far north as the Smoky River north of Jasper. He came to Jasper in 1927 and started working right away for

Fred Brewster, driving teams for the construction of the gardens at Jasper Park Lodge. He met Agnes on her first day of work, when he and Adam Joachim were taking supplies and staff to Brewster's camps at Medicine and Maligne lakes.

Social life was limited in Jasper. Residents would go to the weekly staff dances at the Jasper Park Lodge ballroom in the summer. In the winter there would be the occasional hockey game. There were also movies, rodeos, bridge, chess and visiting among neighbors. At the annual rodeo everybody bet on the races, such as the half-mile race. Agnes won a couple of horse races at the Jasper rodeo, and always regretted not having ridden the bulls.

The Truxlers moved to Entrance, near Hinton, in 1936. After working for various ranches and outfitters, Mark went to work for the parks service, initially at Miette Hot Springs and later at the east park gate. Mark retired from the park in 1970, and they moved to their small ranch just west of Hinton. The Truxlers had two children, Vernon Harragin Truxler (born 1931) and Jacqueline Mona Truxler (born 1934).

Mona passed away on June 20, 1983, predeceased by Charlie in 1976. Agnes died on August 18, 1988. They are both remembered for their good humor and spontaneity, and for the joy they brought to others through their own love of the mountains.

As to their feelings about guiding, Mona once said it best, on behalf of both sisters: "Well, you see, I've never been afraid of anything. I don't know why, but it's true. Guiding turned out to be a lot of trouble and hard work. But for me, it was worth it. Just to know I could do the job."

SOURCES

Abbreviations for commonly quoted publications are as follows:
AAJ: American Alpine Journal
CAJ: Canadian Alpine Journal
CGJ: Canadian Geographical Journal
LAC: The Yearbook of the Ladies' Alpine Club
MFP: Manitoba Free Press
NZAJ: New Zealand Alpine Journal

MARY VAUX WALCOTT

Articles by Mary Vaux Walcott:
"Across the Bow and Balfour Glaciers" in *The Daily Province Magazine*, 20 August 1910.
"American wild flowers" in *Wildflowers of America*, n.d.
"Camping in the Canadian Rockies" in *CAJ*, 1907.
"Flowers of the Canadian Rockies in *CAJ*, 1944-45.
"Observations on Glaciers in 1910" in *CAJ*, 1911.
"Observations on Glaciers" in *CAJ*, 1913.

Books by Mary Vaux Walcott:
The Glaciers of the Canadian Rockies and Selkirks. 3rd edition, 1922. (second edition in 1911 was with
      George Vaux, Jr.)
Illustrations of North American Pitcher Plants. Washington: Smithsonian Institution, 1935.
North American Wild Flowers. Washington: Smithsonian Institution, 1925.

Article sources:
"An Audubon of Botany" in *Boston Transcript*, 12 Feb. 1927.
"A Fortnight With the Canadian Alpine Club" in *CAJ*, 1910.
"Charles Doolittle Walcott 1850-1927" for National Academy of Sciences, Columbia University Press, 1967.
"Mary Vaux Walcott—In Memoriam" in *CAJ*, 1940.
"In Memoriam, Mary Vaux Walcott" in *AAJ* 1940-42.
"Mrs. C. D. Walcott Dies in Nova Scotia" in *Hawke's Bay Herald-Tribune*, 29 Aug 1940.
"Philadelphia Woman a Daring Explorer" in *Philadelphia Public Ledger*, n.d.
"Up the Bow and Down the Yoho" in *CAJ*, 1911.
"The Vaux Family's Scientific Pursuits" in *Frontiers: Annual of the Academy of Natural Sciences of
      Philadelphia*, 1981-82.
"William S. Vaux, Jr., In Memoriam" in *CAJ*, 1909.

Book sources:
Benjamin, Philip S. *The Philadelphia; Quakers in the Industrial Age, 1886-1920.* Philadelphia Temple
      University Press, 1976.
Cavell, Edward. *Legacy in Ice: The Vaux Family and the Canadian Alps.* Banff: The Whyte Foundation,
      1983.
Currier Gallery of Art, The. *The Photo-Secession.* Manchester, N. H.: The Currier Gallery of Art, 1983.
Gadd, Ben. *Handbook of the Canadian Rockies.* Jasper: Corax Press, 1986.
Hart, E. J. *Diamond Hitch—the early outfitters and guides of Banff and Jasper.* Banff: Summerthought,
      1979.
James, Edward T., ed. *Notable American Women 1607-1950.* Cambridge: Belknap Press, 1971.
Massa, William R. Jr. *Guide to the Charles D. Walcott Collection, 1851-1940.* Washington: Smithsonian
      Institution, 1984.
Panzer, Mary. *Philadelphia Naturalistic Photography 1865-1906.* New Haven, Connecticut: Yale University
      Art Gallery, 1982.
Putman, William Lowell. *The Great Glacier and Its House.* New York: American Alpine Club, 1982.
Rickett, H. W. *Wild Flowers of America.* New York: Crown Publishers Inc., 1953.
Smith, George Otis. "Charles Doolittle Walcott" reprinted from *American Journal of Science*, 1951.
Spears, Betty. "Mary, Mary, Quite Contrary". Paper presented at North American Society for Sport
      History, University of British Columbia, Vancouver. May 23-26, 1986.
Stanton, Sina M. and Julia Rouse Sharpless. *Friends Meeting of Washington.* 1 Jun 1965.
Thorington, J. Monroe. "American Alpine Club Annals" reprinted from *AAJ*, 1946.
Wade, Carson. *Human History of Yoho National Park.* Parks Canada, 1978.
Whittington, Harry B. *The Burgess Shale.* New Haven: Yale University Press, 1985.

Unpublished sources:

The Whyte Museum of the Canadian Rockies in Banff, Alberta has a collection of George Vaux papers: glacier observations and diary notes by George and Mary, unpublished notes for lectures by Mary, newspaper clippings and the Vaux family photographs. A number of oral interviews with outfitters and guides have references to the Vauxes and Walcotts.

The Smithsonian Institution Archives in Washington, D.C. houses the Charles D. Walcott Collection: personal and family correspondence, diaries, newpaper clippings, biographies, speeches, manuscripts, field notes and photographs. The archives also has the Records of the Office of the Secretary, which contains correspondence concerning the publication of *North American wild flowers*.

The Quaker Collection at Haverford College, Haverford, Pennsylvania provided a biographical sketch and other clippings about Mary. The Library of Congress in Washington, D.C. now has the records of the Society of Woman Geographers, which has a correspondence file concerning Mary.

George and Henry Vaux were most helpful with reminiscences about their aunt and about family history. George graciously allowed me to read William's diaries and other family memorabilia, and he showed me their photographic equipment. Ed Cavell allowed me access to his research files on the Vaux family.

MARY SCHAFFER WARREN

Articles by Mary Schäffer Warren:

"Among the Sources of the Saskatchewan and Athabasca Rivers" in *The Bulletin of the Geographical Society of Philadelphia,* Apr 1908.

"The Finding of Lake Maligne" in *CAJ,* 1912.

"Flora of the Saskatchewan and Athabasca River Tributaries" in *CAJ,* 1908.

"Haunts of the Wild Flowers of the Canadian Rockies" in *CAJ* 1911.

"The Valleys of the Saskatchewan With Horse and Camera" in *The Bulletin of the Geographical Society of Philadelphia,* Apr 1907.

Books by Mary Schäffer Warren:

A Hunter of Peace. Banff: Whyte Foundation, 1980. Reprint of *Old Indian Trails* with an introduction by E. J. Hart.

Old Indian Trails. New York: G. P. Putnam's Sons, 1911.

Untrodden Paths in the Canadian Rockies. Minneapolis: The Powers Mercantile Company, ca. 1910.

Unpublished articles by Mary Schäffer Warren (in the archives of the Whyte Museum of the Canadian Rockies):

"A Chapter of Accidents," n.d.

"A New Year in the Wilds," ca. 1925.

"A Ptarmigan Story," n.d.

"A Small Boy's Summer in the Canadian Rockies," 1912.

"The Beginning, the middle and the end of a hunting trip," ca. 1913.

"The Byways of Banff," ca. 1918.

"Fairy-land of the North," n.d.

"Flora of the Saskatchewan and Athabasca River Tributaries," 1908.

"My Garden," 1910.

"The Heart of a Child," n.d.

"The Monarch of the Plains," ca. 1908.

"The Story of Revelstoke," 1921.

"Teepee Life in the Northern Hills," 1924.

Untitled manuscript about survey trip to Maligne Lake, 1911.

Untitled manuscript about history of Howse, Yellowhead and Athabasca passes, 1912.

Untitled manuscript about the medical mission of Dr. Atkin and Nurse Fulcher to Ya Ha Tinda Ranch, ca. 1916.

Article sources:

"City Dweller Turns to the Great Out-of-Doors," newsclipping, n.d.

"An Early Jasper Tea Party" in *Edmonton Bulletin,* n.d.

"The Flora of Canada," newsclipping dd. 10 Oct 1905.

"Mary Scharples Schäffer . . . Rockies" in *Frontiers: Annual of the Academy of Natural Sciences of Philadelphia,* 1981-82.

"Mrs. Schäffer Tells of Rocky Mountains," newsclipping, n.d.

"Philadelphia Woman Names New Mountain" in *Edmonton Evening Journal,* 8 Aug 1911.

"Pushing Ahead of Trails" in *Canada West Monthly,* Aug 1911.

"A Quaker in Buckskin" in *Alberta Historical Review,* 1957.

"Romance in the Heart of Rockies" newsclipping, n.d.

"A Woman Mountaineer in the Tête Jaune Country" in *The World To-day,* 1910.

"To Again Visit Mountain Lake" in *Edmonton Bulletin,* 5 Jun 1911.

Book sources:
Brown, Stewardson. *Alpine Flora of the Canadian Rocky Mountains.* New York: G. P. Putnam's Sons, 1907. Illustrated by Mrs. Charles Schäffer.
Hart, E. J. *Diamond Hitch—the early outfitters and guides of Banff and Jasper.* Banff: Summerthought, 1979.
Kipling, Rudyard. *Letters of Travel, 1892-1913.* London: MacMillan & Co. Limited, 1920.
Panzer, Mary. *Philadelphia Naturalistic Photography 1865-1906.* New Haven, Connecticut: Yale University Art Gallery, 1982.
Spears, Betty. "Mary, Mary, Quite Contrary". Paper presented at North American Society for Sport History, University of British Columbia, Vancouver. May 23-26, 1986.
Wark, Mrs. Humphrey (Mary Augusta). *Canadian Born.* London: Smith, Elder & Co., 1910.

Unpublished sources:

The Whyte Museum of the Canadian Rockies has a number of collections which contain information about Mary Schäffer Warren, the most important being her papers from 1908-1939, which include a number of unpublished manuscripts. Other collections accessed were those of Humphrey Toms, Alice Fulmer, Tom Lonsdale, Raymond Zillmer and Charles Reid.
The information file on Jasper National Park at the Provincial Archives of Alberta in Edmonton, Alberta was a source of a number of newspaper clippings. The Glenbow-Alberta Institute Archives, in Calgary, Alberta had a file on Mary Schäffer, and correspondence with her was found in files on Tom Wilson.

ELIZABETH PARKER

Articles by Elizabeth Parker:
"The Alpine Club" in *MFP,* 31 Mar 1906.
"The Alpine Club of Canada" in *CAJ,* 1907.
"The Approach to Organization" in *CAJ,* 1938.
"A Backward Look at a Midsummer Holiday" in *MFP,* 30 Sept 1905.
"A Holiday Tour in the West" in *MFP,* 23 Sept 1905.
"A Holiday Trip in the West" in *MFP,* 16 Sept 1905.
"A New Field for Mountaineering" in *Scribner's,* May 1914.
"Another Rocky Mountain Book" in *MFP,* 16 Dec 1905.
"The Canadian Rockies: A Joy to Mountaineers" in *MFP,* 23 Sept 1905.
"Early Explorers of the West" in *CAJ,* 1944-45.
"Gossip About a Few Mountaineering Classics" in *CAJ,* 1912.
"The Mountaineering Club" in *MFP,* 17 Feb 1906.
"Mountaineering in Canada" in *The University Magazine,* Feb 1908.
"A Reader's Reminiscent Note" in *MFP,* 9 Nov 1922.
"The Selkirk Range" in *MFP,* 25 Nov 1905.
"Some Memories of the Mountains" in *CAJ,* 1929.
"The Upper Columbia" in *CAJ,* 1911.
Besides her book reviews in the *Manitoba Free Press* under the pseudonyms "M.T.," "A.L.O.W." and "The Bookman," Elizabeth wrote many of the reviews in the early years of the *Canadian Alpine Journal.*

Articles by Jean Parker:
"The Second: Ascent of Mt. Tupper" in *CAJ,* 1909.

Books by Elizabeth Parker:
Wheeler, Arthur O. and Elizabeth Parker. *The Selkirk Mountains: A guide for Mountain Climbers and Pilgrims.* Winnipeg: Stovel Company, 1912.

Article Sources:
"Mrs. Elizabeth Parker Dies . . . Year" in *Winnipeg Free Press,* 27 Oct 1944.
"How we climbed Cascade" in *CAJ,* 1907.
"Origin and Founding of the Alpine Club of Canada, 1906" in *CAJ,* 1938.
"To Elizabeth" in *University Magazine,* Apr 1915.

Book Sources:
Fraser, Esther. *Wheeler.* Banff: Summerthought, 1978.
Hart, E. J. *Diamond Hitch—the early outfitters and guides of Banff and Jasper.* Banff: Summerthought, 1979.
Kariel, Herb and Pat. *Alpine Huts in the Rockies, Selkirks and Purcells.* Banff: Alpine Club of Canada, 1986.

Leslie, Susan, ed. *In the Western Mountains—Early Mountaineering in British Columbia.* Victoria: Queen's Printer, 1980.
Williams, Cicely. *Women on the Rope: The Feminine Share in Mountain Adventure.* London: George Allen & Unwin Ltd., 1973.

Unpublished Sources:
Besides housing all of the back issues of the *Manitoba Free Press* (now the *Winnipeg Free Press*), the Public Archives of Manitoba, in Winnipeg, had two collections which were useful: papers of the Winnipeg Section of the Alpine Club of Canada, and the 1907-1912 minutes of the Women's Canadian Club of Winnipeg.
Elizabeth's interest in the history of Western Canada led her to correspond with outfitter Tom Wilson, some of whose correspondence is in the Glenbow-Alberta Institute Archives in Calgary.
Gina L. LaForce's master's thesis for the University of Toronto (11 July 1978), titled "The Alpine Club of Canada, 1906-1929: Modernization, Canadian Nationalism, and Anglo-Saxon Mountaineering" served to encapsulate the early history of that organization.
Miss Margaret Fleming, a long-time Alpine Club of Canada member, and one-time editor of the *CAJ*, reminisced with me about Elizabeth and Jean Parker.

MARY JOBE AKELEY

The numerous articles and books written by Mary about Africa are not listed here.

Articles by Mary Jobe Akeley:
"Camping and Climbing in the Snow Peaks" in *Field & Stream,* Aug 1912.
"Conservation of Wildlife" in Hearings Before The Select Committee on Conservation of Wildlife Resources, House of Representatives Seventy-Fifth Congress, 1938.
"The Expedition to 'Mt. Kitchie' " in *CAJ*, 1915.
"Mt. Kitchi A New Peak in the Canadian Rockies" in *Bulletin of the American Geographical Society,* 1915.
"My Quest in the Canadian Rockies" in *Harper's Magazine,* May 1915.
"A Winter Journey Through the Northern Canadian Rockies: from Mt. Robson to Mt. Sir Alexander" in *Appalachia,* Jun 1918.
"A Winter Journey to Mt. Sir Alexander and the Wapiti" in *CAJ*, 1918.
"A Woman in British Columbian Wilds" in *MFP,* Jan 1906.

Unpublished articles by Mary Jobe Akeley (in the archives of the Mystic River Historical Society, Mystic, Connecticut):
"The Quest of the 'Frozen Grail'," ca. 1910.
"Summer Camping," 1914.
"Summer Play Grounds in Cloud Land," ca. 1911.
"What a College Girl Saw in Heart of the Selkirks," ca. 1906.

Article sources:
"Brave Explorer Perishes on Duty" in *Philadelphia Record,* 10 Aug 1910.
"Canadian Peak Given Name for American Woman," Dec 1925.
"Exploration in the Rocky Mountains North of the Yellowhead Pass" in *The Geographical Journal,* Jan-Jun 1912.
"Explorations About Mount Sir Sandford, British Columbia" in *The Geographical Journal,* Feb 1911.
"Mary J. Akeley, An Explorer, Dies" in *The New York Times,* 22 Jul 1966.
"Women Blaze Trail Up Mount Sandford" in *The New York Times,* 20 Sept 1909.

Book sources:
Hart, E. J. *Diamond Hitch—the early outfitters and guides of Banff and Jasper.* Banff: Summerthought, 1979.
Olds, Elizabeth Fagg. *Women of the Four Winds.* Boston: Houghton Mifflin Company, 1985.
Palmer, Howard. *Mountaineering and Exploration in the Selkirks.* New York: G. P. Putnam's Sons, 1914.
Taylor, William C. *Tracks Across My Trail—Donald "Curly" Phillips, Guide and Outfitter.* Jasper: Jasper-Yellowhead Historical Society, 1984.

Unpublished sources:
The Library of the American Museum of Natural History, in New York City, houses a major collection of materials of Carl and Mary Akeley. Most of the collection pertains to explorations in Africa: expedition papers, notes, scrapbooks of newsclippings, published articles and books on her African explorations, Akeley's diaries, and photographs in Africa taken by both of them. However, there is some biographical information on Mary and a diary of her travels to Mount Sir Alexander in the summer of 1914.
The Mystic River Historical Society in Mystic, Connecticut houses a major collection of Mary Jobe Akeley material: handcolored glass slides, photographs, negatives, catalogues and articles about Camp Mystic, and unpublished manuscripts, lecture notes, articles, diaries (1915 and 1918), slides and photographs from the Rockies and Selkirks. Much of the material was transferred from the Thames Science Center

in New London, Connecticut. Carol Kimball has been most helpful in providing information about this collection.

The small archives at Bryn Mawr College, in Bryn Mawr, Pennsylvania provided some biographical and educational information about Mary Jobe Akeley.

CAROLINE HINMAN

Articles by Caroline Hinman:
"Camping in the Canadian Rockies" in *The Civic Pilot,* n.d.
"A Packtrain Trip North From Jasper, Alberta" in *CAJ,* 1923.

Article sources:
"Bags a Grizzly" in *The 1906 Hamper,* 13 Jun 1925.
"Caroline B. Hinman 1884-1966, obituary" in *CAJ,* 1967.
"Caroline Hinman Named President" in *The Skyline Trail,* Nov 1950.
"Caroline Hinman . . . Dies at 83" in *The Summit Herald,* 21 Jul 1966.
"The Four Day Trip" in *Rod and Gun in Canada,* Jan 1914.
"Miss Caroline Hinman . . . To The Canadian Northwest" in *Summit Press,* 13 Mar 1941.
"One Month on the Trails—with Caroline Hinman" in *Trail Riders Bulletin,* 1 Jul 1943.
"On Horseback and Camel-Hump" in *The Woman Citizen,* n.d.

Book sources:
Gest, Lillian. *History of Mount Assiniboine.* 1979.
Hart, E. J. *Diamond Hitch—the early outfitters and guides of Banff and Jasper.* Banff: Summerthought, 1979.
Smith College. *Official Circular 1902-03.*
Taylor, William C. *Tracks Across My Trail—Donald "Curly" Phillips, Guide and Outfitter.* Jasper: Jasper-Yellowhead Historical Society, 1984.

Unpublished sources:
The Caroline Hinman collection at the Whyte Museum of the Canadian Rockies contains photographs, movies, brochures, newsclippings and some correspondence. Their Lillian Gest collection contains diaries written on Hinman trips, an untitled manuscript about trips together, correspondence and photographs. On two oral history tapes, outfitters make references to Caroline Hinman.

The Smith College Archives in Northampton, Massachusetts provided me with Caroline's educational background, some correspondence and scrapbook newsclippings.

Caroline's niece and nephew, Eunice Rodman Packer and William L. Rodman were most encouraging and helpful with biographical information.

GERTRUDE BENHAM

Articles by Gertrude Benham:
"The Ascent of Mt. Assiniboine" in *CAJ,* 1907.
"The Canadian Rockies" in *The Alpine Journal,* 1904-05.
"Lefroy and Victoria: First Ascents of the Season" in *Banff Crag and Canyon,* 16 Jul 1904.

Article sources:
"A New Ascent of Mount Fay, Canadian Rockies" in *Appalachia,* 1905-08.
"The Fuhrerbuchs of Hans and Christian Kauffman" in *AAJ,* 1943-45.

Book sources:
Dowling, Phil. *The Mountaineers—Famous Climbers in Canada.* Edmonton: Hurtig Publishers, 1979.
Griffiths, Alison and Wingenbach, Gerry. *Mountain Climbing Guides in Canada: The Early Years.* Parks Canada, 1977.
Kauffman, Andrew J. and William L. Putnam. *The Guiding Spirit.* Revelstoke: Footprint Publishing, 1986.

Putnam, William Lowell. *The Great Glacier and Its House.* New York: American Alpine Club, 1982.
Tiltman, Marjorie Hessell. *Women in Modern Adventure.* London: Harrap, 1935.

Unpublished sources:
Maura Benham, of England, was most helpful in providing biographical information about her cousin, and extracts from a "Family Records Book" compiled by William Gurney Benham, which includes newsclippings about Gertrude's world travels.
There are only minor references to Gertrude Benham in the Whyte Museum of the Canadian Rockies.

HENRIETTA TUZO WILSON

Articles by Henrietta Tuzo Wilson:
"Memories of the Mountains" in *Canadian Geographical Journal,* Jul 1930.

Article sources:
"The Fuhrerbuch of Edward Feuz, Sr." in *AAJ,* 1948-50.
"Henrietta Loetitia Wilson" in *CAJ,* 1956.

Book sources:
Cavell, Edward. *Legacy in Ice: The Vaux Family and the Canadian Alps.* Banff: The Whyte Foundation, 1983.
Dictionary of Canadian Biography. Vol. VIII.
1948 Canadian Who's Who.

Unpublished sources:
The Provincial Archives of British Columbia, in Victoria, has files on Henrietta Loetitia Wilson and Dr. Henry Atkinson Tuzo. The J. Monroe Thorington Collection in the Whyte Museum of the Canadian Rockies (original copies are in Princeton University in Princeton, New Jersey) contains correspondence with Henrietta. The Whyte archives also has a file on John Tuzo Wilson.
Henrietta's son, John Tuzo Wilson, was most generous in allowing me access to his mother's diaries, photographs and other memorabilia.

ELIZABETH LARNED MacCARTHY

Articles by Elizabeth MacCarthy:
"Over the Wilson and Duchesnay Passes" in *CAJ,* 1910.

Articles by Albert H. MacCarthy:
"First Ascents of Mt. Farnham and Mt. Farnham Tower (1914)" in *CAJ,* 1914-15.
"The Howser and Bugaboo Spires, Purcell Range" in *CAJ,* 1917.

Article sources:
"Albert H. MacCarthy . . . Local Businessman," newsclipping, n.d.
"Detailed Account of What Really Happened" in *The Purdue Alumnus,* 1922.
"Explorations About Mount Sir Sandford, British Columbia" in *The Geographical Journal,* Feb 1911.
"Mrs. MacCarthy Died . . . Home" in *Evening Capital,* 12 Feb 1944.
"Women Blaze Trail Up Mount Sandford" in *The New York Times,* 20 Sept 1909.

Book sources:
By-Laws and Register of The American Alpine Club. 1940.
Dowling, Phil. *The Mountaineers—Famous Climbers in Canada.* Edmonton: Hurtig Publishers, 1979.
Garden, J. F. *The Bugaboos—An Alpine History.* Revelstoke: Footprint Publishing, 1987.
Kain, Conrad. *Where the Clouds Can Go.* New York: American Alpine Club, 1979.
Kauffman, Andrew J. and William L. Putnam. *The Guiding Spirit.* Revelstoke: Footprint Publishing, 1986.
Kruszyna, Robert and William L. Putnam. *Climber's Guide to the Interior Ranges of British Columbia—South.* New York: American Alpine Club, 1977.
Palmer, Howard. *Mountaineering and Exploration in the Selkirks.* New York: G. P. Putnam's Sons, 1914.

Unpublished sources:
The Alpine Club of Canada and other collections at the Whyte Museum have minor references to the MacCarthys.
The archives of the United States Naval Academy in Annapolis, Maryland provided biographical information on Albert MacCarthy and a few newsclippings. A detailed article about Dr. Stone's death was obtained from the Purdue University Library in West Lafayette, Indiana.

PHYLLIS JAMES MUNDAY

Articles by Phyllis Munday:
"First Ascent of Mt. Robson by Lady Members" in *CAJ,* 1924.
"Mount Reliance: A Letter from Canada" in *LAC,* 1948.
"To Waddington With Hillary" in *CAJ,* 1956.

Unpublished articles by Phyllis Munday:
"B.C. Woman First on Mt. Robson," ca. 1924.
"Nature for its Own Sake," 1967.
"Take Care of Your Feet," n.d.

Articles by W.A.D. (Don) Munday:
"Adventurous Exploring in British Columbia" in *Scarlet and Gold,* Ninth Annual, n.d.
"Among Bella Coola Mountains, 1938" in *CAJ,* 1938.
"The Apex of the Coast Range" in *CAJ,* 1926-27.
"Bella Coola Mountains" in *CAJ,* 1937.

"Beyond Bute Inlet" in *CAJ*, 1941.
"Canada's Newest Mountains" in *CGJ*, Dec 1932.
"The Cariboo Range . . ." in *CAJ*, 1940.
"A Coast Range Pioneer" in *CAJ*, 1949.
"Early Explorations in the Coast Mountains" in *CAJ*, 1941.
"Exploration in the Coast Range" in *CAJ*, 1926-27.
"Exploration in the Coast Range of British Columbia" in *The Geographical Review*, Apr 1928.
"Exploring Western Icefields" in *CGJ*, Oct 1936.
"The First Ascent of Mt. Queen Bess" in *The Vancouver Sun*, 22 Aug 1942 and 29 Aug 1942.
"Glaciers of Mt. Waddington Region" in *CAJ*, 1934-35.
"In the Heart of the Coast Range" in *CGJ*, Jan 1944.
"High Peaks of the Coast Range" in *CAJ*, 1933.
"Historical Sketch of Mt. Waddington Region" in *CAJ*, 1929.
"The Hunlen Falls and Turner Lake . . ." in *The Geographical Journal*, 1939.
"Mt. Queen Bess" in *CAJ*, 1942-43.
"Mt. Reliance" in *CAJ*, 1947.
"Mt. Saugstad" in *CAJ*, 1939.
"Mt. Waddington" in *CAJ*, 1928.
"Mt. Waddington, 1934" in *CAJ*, 1934.
"Mrs. Munday Trapped by . . ." in *The Vancouver Sun*, 12 Jul 1939.
"The Rainbow Mountains . . ." in *CGJ*, Jan 1939.
"Ski-Climbs in the Coast Range in *CAJ*, 1930.
"Skiing in Garibaldi Park" in *CAJ*, 1944-45.
"Skiing on the Forbidden Plateau" in *CAJ*, 1937.
"That Terrible Snow-peaked Range" in *CAJ*, 1948.
"West of the Kliniklini River" in *CAJ*, 1934-35.
"Western Mountain Flowers" in *CGJ*, May 1944.
    Don Munday was a prolific newspaper and magazine writer and the above is only a partial list of his material.

Books by W.A.D. (Don) Munday:
The Unknown Mountain. London: Hodder and Stoughton, 1948.
The Unknown Mountain, reprint. Seattle: The Mountaineers, 1975.
Mt. Garibaldi Park—Vancouver's Alpine Playground. Vancouver, 1922.

Books by Phyllis and Don Munday:
Wild Flowers of British Columbia. Vancouver: Home Oil Distributors Ltd., ca. 1958.

Article sources:
"B.C.'s Alpine 'Dean' is Dead" in *Calgary Herald*, 13 Jun 1950.
"Reflecting" in *Vancouver Magazine*, Aug 1978.
"Mountaineers in the twenties" in *Discovery*, Jan 1988.
"A Mountain 'Found' " in *Yorkshire Evening Post*, 17 Sept 1938.
"The 1934 Attempts on Mt. Waddington" in *AAJ*, 1935.
"Phyllis Munday: Pioneer Mountaineer" in *Mountain News*, Jul/Aug 1984.
"To find their mountain" in *BC Outdoors*, May 1980.
"Triple-threat Career Woman" in *B.C. Magazine*, 23 Feb 1957.
"Walter Alfred Don Munday" in *CAJ*, 1951.
    Articles about Phyllis and Don Munday appeared regularly in the various Vancouver and Victoria newspapers for many decades, and are too numerous to list here.

Book sources:
Akrigg, G.P.V. and Helen B. *British Columbia Place Names*. Victoria: Sono Nis Press, 1986.
British Columbia Mountaineering Club. *The Mountaineer: Fiftieth Anniversary 1907-1957*.
Culbert, Dick. *A Climber's Guide to the Coastal Ranges of British Columbia, 2nd Edition*. Banff: Alpine Club of Canada, 1969.
Dowling, Phil. *The Mountaineers—Famous Climbers in Canada*. Edmonton: Hurtig Publishers, 1979.
Duffy, Dennis J. *Camera West: British Columbia on Film 1941-1965*. Victoria: Provincial Archives of British Columbia, 1986.
Kauffman, Andrew J. and William L. Putnam. *The Guiding Spirit*. Revelstoke: Footprint Publishing, 1986.
Leslie, Susan, ed. *In the Western Mountains—Early Mountaineering in British Columbia*. Victoria: Queen's Printer, 1980

Unpublished sources:
    The Provincial Archives of British Columbia, in Victoria, has a tremendous amount of information on Phyllis and Don Munday: diaries, notebooks, manuscripts, photographs, oral history tapes,

newsclippings, and so on. The Royal British Columbia Museum, also in Victoria, has some artifacts from their climbing days. The library at the University of Victoria has most of the British Columbia newspapers on microfilm. The City of Vancouver Archives has a fine collection of newsclippings about the Mundays.

The Whyte Museum has microfilm copies of Don Munday's diaries, an oral history tape with Phyllis and other miscellaneous references, including some in the Alpine Club of Canada collection.

Edith Wickham, Phyl's daughter, was most encouraging and helpful in reminiscing about her parents. Jean Bannerman, of Vancouver, allowed access to the archives of the Girl Guides of British Columbia, and showed me a videotape of a television interview with Phyllis. Margaret Fleming, of Winnipeg remembered Phyllis from the Alpine Club of Canada camps in the 1930s.

LILLIAN GEST

Articles by Lillian Gest:
"Above Panther Falls" in *CAJ,* 1940.
"Birds at Lake O'Hara," n.d.
"Caroline B. Hinman 1884-1966, obituary" in *CAJ,* 1967.
"Second Ascent of Mount Bryce" in *AAJ,* 1937-39.
"Summer Movies in Color" in *CAJ,* 1938.
"Katie Gardiner Obituary" in *CAJ,* 1974.

Books by Lillian Gest:
History of Lake O'Hara. Philadelphia, 1961.
History of Moraine Lake. Philadelphia, 1970.
History of Mount Assiniboine. Banff, 1979.

Article sources:
"Lillian Gest Collection" in *The Cairn,* summer 1986.
"Lillian Gest" in *AAJ,* 1987.

Book sources:
Goldstrom, Marian, ed. *Fifty Years of Trails and Tales.* Calgary: Skyline Hikers of the Canadian Rockies, 1982.

Unpublished sources:
Lillain Gest's vast collection of material was bequeathed to the Whyte Museum in Banff. It contains yearly diaries, an untitled manuscript, correspondence about her books, correspondence and newsletters from the American and Canadian alpine clubs, photo albums, some 4500 slides and 45 movie films. It was a tremendous wealth of information. There are also minor references in other collections in the archives.

KATIE GARDINER

Articles by Katie Gardiner:
"An Ascent of Mt. Sefton from the West Coast" in *NZAJ,* 1931.
"Ascents South of Banff, 1929" in *CAJ,* 1929.
"Climbs in the Rockies and Selkirks During the Summer of 1933" in *CAJ,* 1934.
"The Mountains of Canada and New Zealand" in *LAC,* 1932.
"Mount Robson and Other Climbs" in *LAC,* 1940.
"A Pack Train Trip to the French Military Group" in *CAJ,* 1930.
"Tasman From the West" in *NZAJ,* 1934.
"Two Climbs" in *LAC,* 1935.

Article sources:
"Eight days awaiting a nod from death" in *The New Zealand Woman's Weekly,* 1 Jun 1970.
"Eight Days in a Crevasse," Feb 1933.
"The end of a guiding dynasty—Walter Feuz passes" in *Banff Crag & Canyon,* 31 Oct 1984.
"Frank Alack always the explorer" in *The Timaru Herald,* 6 Aug 1985.
"Fox Glacier Drama Recalled" in *New Zealand Weekly News,* 19 Jan 1970.
"Gardiner Hut—Upper Hooker Valley" in *NZAJ,* 1935.
"Katie Gardiner" in *New Zealand Alpine Club Bulletin,* 1974.
"Katie Gardiner (1886-1974)—a memoir" in *NZAJ,* 1978.
"Katie Gardiner in Memoriam" in *LAC,* 1975.
"Katie Gardiner Obituary" in *CAJ,* 1974.
"Mountaineer Katie Gardiner" in *Hawke's Bay Herald-Tribune,* 29 Jan 1974.
"Porridge Saved . . . in 1933," newsclipping, ca. 1983.
"Second Ascent of Mount Bryce" in *CAJ,* 1937-39.

Book sources:
Alack, Frank. *Guide Aspiring.* Auckland: Oswald-Sealy Ltd.
Dowling, Phil. *The Mountaineers—Famous Climbers in Canada.* Edmonton: Hurtig Publishers, 1979.
Kauffman, Andrew J. and William L. Putnam. *The Guiding Spirit.* Revelstoke: Footprint Publishing, 1986.
Wilson, Jim. *Aorangi: the Story of Mount Cook.* Christchurch: Whitcombe & Tombs, 1968.

Unpublished sources:
Many people in New Zealand have been most helpful in answering my questions and searching out published articles for me: Pip Lynch, who is working on a book about women mountaineers in New Zealand; Junee Ashurst, who, with her husband "Hap," was a guide at Mount Cook; and Frank Alack, who was Katie's guide and friend.

Some newsclippings were obtained from the Hocken Library, University of Otago, Dunedin, New Zealand. The archivist also put me on the right track with other addresses. The Alexander Turnbull Library, of the National Library of New Zealand in Wellington put me on the right line for published sources of information, as well as finding some newsclippings for me.

GEORGIA ENGELHARD CROMWELL

Articles by Georgia Engelhard Cromwell:
"Lake Louise Days: a letter from Georgia Engelhard Cromwell" in *Lake Louise: A Diamond in the Wilderness,* 1982.
"Mountain Man . . . The Photographs of Edward Feuz, Jr.," n.d.
"New Routes on Familiar Canadian Peaks" in *AAJ,* 1933-36.
"Portrait of a Giant," n.d.
"Switzerland's Enchanted Val d'Herins" in *National Geographic Magazine,* Jun 1955.
This list does not include a number of articles on photography written for the magazine *American Photography.*

Books by Georgia Engelhard Cromwell:
Peterli and the Mountain. Philadelphia: J. B. Lippincott Company, 1954.

Article sources:
"American Alpine Club Annals," *AAJ,* 1946.
"The Challenge of High Places" in *The Christian Science Monitor,* 30 Jun 1937.
"First Lady of Mountain Photography" in *Art Photography,* Aug 1951.
"Georgia Engelhard Finds Peaks . . .," newsclipping, n.d.
"Sunset Social Empire," newsclipping, 12 Oct 1947.

Book sources:
Doty, Robert. *Photo-Secession Stieglitz and the Fine-Art Movement in Photography.* New York: Dover, 1978.
Fisher, Joel Ellis. *Bibliography of American Mountain Ascents.* New York: American Alpine Club, 1946.
Jameson, Sheilagh. *W. J. Oliver: Life Through a Master's Lens.* Calgary: Glenbow-Alberta Foundation, 1984.
Kauffman, Andrew J. and William L. Putnam. *The Guiding Spirit.* Revelstoke: Footprint Publishing, 1986.
Lowe, Sue Davidson. *Stieglitz: A Memoir/Biography.* New York: Farrar Straus Giroux, 1983.
Norman, Dorothy. *Alfred Stieglitz: An American Seer.* New York: Aperture, 1973.
Vassar Alumnae Magazine. Dec 1953.

Unpublished sources:
Georgia's stepson, Eaton "Pete" Cromwell, Jr., was most generous with his reminiscences about Georgia and his father, and very encouraging with my project. He was also instrumental in putting me in touch with other individuals. Two of her cousins, Sue Davidson Lowe and Flora Straus, also provided information about Georgia's childhood.

Gertie Marrs shared with me her memories of a long friendship with Georgia. She also allowed me to peruse the photograph albums, guidebook and clippings of her father, Edward Feuz, Jr.

The Stieglitz Archive in the Beinecke Rare Book and Manuscript Library at Yale University, Connecticut contains correspondence between Georgia Engelhard and Alfred Stieglitz. Newsclippings and educational information was obtained from the Alumnae Association of Vassar College, Poughkeepsie, New York.

AGNES TRUXLER and MONA MATHESON

Article sources:
"Sportsman remembers early years" in *Jasper Booster,* 19 July 1972.

Book sources:
Marty, Sid. *Men for the Mountains.* Toronto: McClelland & Stewart Ltd., 1978.

Unpublished sources:
I had the pleasure of interviewing Agnes Truxler a number of times about her and Mona's guiding careers, before she died in August of 1988. The Jasper-Yellowhead Historical Society, in Jasper, Alberta has a file on Agnes Truxler and Mona Matheson.

The Whyte Museum archives has an oral history tape with Mark and Agnes Truxler. The Glenbow Institute Archives has material on Charlie and Mona Matheson.

SELECTED BIBLIOGRAPHY

Women in the mountains:

Cavell, Edward. *Legacy in Ice: The Vaux Family and the Canadian Alps.* Banff: The Whyte Foundation, 1983.

Dixon, Ann. *Silent Partners: Wives of National Park Wardens.* Pincher Creek: Dixon and Dixon Publishers, 1985.

Hart, E. J. *A Hunter of Peace.* Banff: The Whyte Foundation, 1980. (With reprint of Mary Schäffer's *Old Indian Trails.*)

Munday, Don. *The Unknown Mountain,* reprint. Lake Louise: Coyote Books, 1993.

Oltman, Ruth. *Lizzie Rummel—Baroness of the Canadian Rockies.* Exshaw: Ribbon Creek Publishing Co., 1983.

Taylor, William C. *Tracks Across My Trail—Donald "Curly" Phillips, Guide and Outfitter.* Jasper: Jasper-Yellowhead Historical Society, 1984.

General history:

Fraser, Esther. *The Canadian Rockies—Early Travels and Explorations.* Edmonton: Hurtig Publishers, 1969.

Hart, E. J. *Diamond Hitch—the early outfitters and guides of Banff and Jasper.* Banff: Summerthought, 1979.

The Selling of Canada: the CPR and the Beginnings of Canadian Tourism. Banff Altitude Publishing, 1983.

MacGregor, J. G. *Overland by the Yellowhead.* Saskatoon: Western Producer Prairie Books, 1974.

Marty, Sid. *A Grand and Fabulous Notion: The First Century of Canada's Parks.* Toronto: NC Press Limited, 1984.

Putnam, William Lowell. *The Great Glacier and Its House.* New York: American Alpine Club, 1982.

Sandford, R.W. *The Canadian Alps — The History of Mountaineering in Canada, Volume I.* Banff: Altitude Publishing, 1990.

Whyte, Jon. *Lake Louise—A Diamond in the Wilderness.* Banff: Altitude Publishing, 1982.

Mountaineering history:

Dowling, Phil. *The Mountaineers—Famous Climbers in Canada.* Edmonton: Hurtig Publishers, 1979.

Garden, J. F. *The Bugaboos—An Alpine History.* Revelstoke: Footprint Publishing, 1987.

Kariel, Herb and Pat. *Alpine Huts in the Rockies, Selkirks and Purcells.* Banff: Alpine Club of Canada, 1986.

Kauffman, Andrew J. and William L. Putnam. *The Guiding Spirit.* Revelstoke: Footprint Publishing, 1986.

Leslie, Susan, ed. *In the Western Mountains—Early Mountaineering in British Columbia.* Victoria: Queen's Printer, 1980.

Fraser, Esther. *Wheeler.* Banff: Summerthought, 1978.

Mountaineering guides (there have been various editions, all of which contain some details on first ascents):

The Rocky Mountains of Canada—North.
The Rocky Mountains of Canada—South.
Climber's Guide to the Interior Ranges of British Columbia—North.
Climber's Guide to the Interior Ranges of British Columbia—South.
A Climber's Guide to the Coastal Ranges of British Columbia.

INDEX

ABOUT THE AUTHOR

Cyndi Smith was born and raised on a cattle ranch along the shore of the Red Deer River, in the heart of the Alberta badlands. She spent her childhood roaming the coulees and cutbanks, searching for fossils and wildlife.

Captivated by the outdoors, Cyndi studied biological sciences at the Northern Alberta Institute of Technology, in Edmonton, graduating in 1978. Then followed two seasons working as a fisheries guardian near Bella Coola, on the west coast of British Columbia.

But the Canadian Rockies have been a magnet to Cyndi since 1974, when she first moved to Jasper National Park. Since 1980 she has worked for the Canadian Parks Service, first as a park naturalist, then as a patrolwoman and now as a park warden. Cyndi spent two memorable summers patrolling the backcountry areas of Jasper park on horseback and on foot. In 1989 Cyndi worked in Kluane National Park in the Yukon, enjoying the opportunity to explore that spectacular region of Canada. She currently works as a backcountry warden out of the Lake Louise area in Banff National Park.

Cyndi started writing in 1979 and her work has been published in various magazines and newspapers. While working as an historic specialist she wrote a pamphlet about the history of Jasper National Park, entitled *People, Places and Events.* In 1985 she authored *Jasper Park Lodge: in the Heart of the Canadian Rockies,* which is a history of the Canadian Pacific resort hotel (formerly owned by Canadian National) in Jasper.

As a park naturalist Cyndi introduced many children to the outdoors, and she has written two coloring and activity books for children: the *Rocky Mountains Coloring Book* and *Dinosaurs of the Alberta Badlands.*

An avid skier, backpacker, sea kayaker and mountaineer, Cyndi takes every opportunity to travel off the beaten track in Canada's wilderness areas.